ROUTLEDGE LIBRARY EDITIONS: THE GERMAN ECONOMY

Volume 7

T0300067

ECONOMIC POLICY-MAKING BY LOCAL AUTHORITIES IN BRITAIN AND WESTERN GERMANY

ECONOMIC POLICY-MAKING BY LOCAL AUTHORITIES IN BRITAIN AND WESTERN GERMANY

NEVIL JOHNSON AND ALLAN COCHRANE

Routledge
Taylor & Francis Group

LONDON AND NEW YORK

First published in 1981 by George Allen & Unwin Ltd

This edition first published in 2018
by Routledge
2 Park Square, Milton Park, Abingdon, Oxon OX14 4RN

and by Routledge
711 Third Avenue, New York, NY 10017

Routledge is an imprint of the Taylor & Francis Group, an informa business

British Library Cataloguing in Publication Data
A catalogue record for this book is available from the British Library

ISBN: 978-1-138-29360-1 (Set)
ISBN: 978-1-315-18656-6 (Set) (ebk)
ISBN: 978-0-415-78807-6 (Volume 7) (hbk)
ISBN: 978-0-415-78814-4 (Volume 7) (pbk)
ISBN: 978-1-315-22558-6 (Volume 7) (ebk)

Publisher's Note
The publisher has gone to great lengths to ensure the quality of this reprint but
points out that some imperfections in the original copies may be apparent.

Disclaimer
The publisher has made every effort to trace copyright holders and would welcome
correspondence from those they have been unable to trace.

ECONOMIC POLICY-MAKING BY LOCAL AUTHORITIES IN BRITAIN AND WESTERN GERMANY

NEVIL JOHNSON

ALLAN COCHRANE

London
GEORGE ALLEN & UNWIN
Boston   Sydney

First published in 1981

GEORGE ALLEN & UNWIN LTD
40 Museum Street, London WC1A 1LU

© Nevil Johnson and Allan Cochrane, 1981

British Library Cataloguing in Publication Data

Johnson, Nevil
   Economic policy-making by local authorities in Britain
   and Western Germany.
   1. Local government – Great Britain
   2. Local government – Germany (West)
   3. Great Britain – Economic policy – 1945 –
   4. Germany (West) – Economic policy – 1945 –
   I. Title   II. Cochrane, Allan
   352.1′22′0943   JS3111

ISBN 0-04-352097-9

Set in 10 on 11 point Times by Red Lion Setters, London
and printed and bound in Great Britain by
William Clowes (Beccles) Limited, Beccles and London.

PREFACE

This work is based upon a research project carried out jointly in Britain and Western Germany by the authors and a corresponding team under the direction of Professor Renate Mayntz of the Institute for Applied Social Research in the University of Cologne. Research started towards the end of 1977 and was completed by October 1979. It was carried out with two principal objectives in mind. The first was to identify and describe those activities undertaken by local authorities and regarded by them as serving primarily economic purposes. The second was to examine the political and administrative conditions at the local level under which these activities are undertaken and to set these within the wider national governmental context. On the basis of evidence relating to these factors comparisons were then made between the two countries. These comparisons do not, of course, relate only to the particular activities of an economic nature carried out by local government in the two countries. They bear also on wider structural questions, notably on the extent to which the differences in institutional arrangements and legal powers have any significant effects on the range and kind of economic activity open to local authorities, and on contrasts and similarities in the ways in which local authorities fit into the wider pattern of government in the two countries.

The structure of the study presented here has been strongly influenced by the layout and contents of the research reports on which it has been based. The research project relied heavily on case studies carried out by an Anglo-German team, one of whose members worked on local authorities in England, whilst another did very similar work in North Rhine-Westphalia. The eventual outcome was three reports: the first described in detail the economic activities of a group of local authorities in England and set out the results of the case studies undertaken; the second presented similar findings in respect of the German experience; the third, which was a collaborative endeavour in which the whole team was involved, provided a comparative evaluation in both English and German of the results of the research.*

Reflecting the original research reports this study opens with a chapter devoted to some of the problems associated with the attribution

* Reports to the Anglo-German Foundation for the Study of Industrial Society, 1979: *Economic Policy-Making by Local Authorities in Britain and the Federal Republic of Germany*.
Part I: A Report of the English Case Studies.
Part II: Bericht über die deutschen Fallstudien.
Part III: Comparative Conclusions (also available in a German version).
Copies on application to the Anglo-German Foundation for the Study of Industrial Society.

of an economic policy role to local authorities. It looks at the reasons why, despite these problems, there is some justification for looking at the economic functions of local authorities, and discusses the questions chosen to structure the empirical research on which this study is based. The next three chapters, the first of which is chiefly contextual, deal with the economic activities of English local authorities, and in particular with the seven local authority cases which were examined in some detail. The chapter following (5) turns to the German experience of the same matters. It presents the evidence much more briefly, however, than do the preceding chapters on local economic activity in England. This is because it represents a condensation or summary of the original German account of how the selected authorities in North Rhine-Westphalia deal with their economic functions. It was felt that a certain disproportion in the amount of descriptive material relating to the two countries was justified on two grounds. One is that some further information and comments on the German experience are incorporated into the comparative analysis. The other is that as the English case studies did yield a substantial amount of information about activities on which little has previously been written, it seemed desirable to include as much as possible of this in the present study. But it has to be admitted that the price paid for this is an overall bias in favour of explaining how English local authorities engage in economic activity. The account of what German local authorities do is then followed by two chapters in which we turn to evaluation and comparison. This calls for a juxtaposition of the experience of local authorities in the two countries and an attempt to highlight those features of it which appear to account best for similarities and differences. Inevitably the comparative conclusions involve a certain amount of recapitulation of what has gone before, but it is hoped that this has been kept to the minimum needed to render the comparisons comprehensible and to provide a factual basis for them.

We are deeply indebted to the Anglo-German Foundation for the Study of Industrial Society who financed the research for this publication as part of its programme of study of social and economic policy issues. We are particularly grateful to the Foundation's officers for their constant support and interest. We would like to thank too our German collaborators, Professor Renate Mayntz, Dr Kerstin Kiessler and Miss Gerda Zill. We derived great benefit from the close co-operation which was established with them in the course of the research programme. To all the staff and members of local authorities as well as of other governmental agencies we owe a debt of gratitude for information and advice willingly given. For the manner in which all the evidence given to them has been used as well as for the accuracy of the final results the authors alone are responsible. Finally we wish to record our gratitude to Mrs Lyn Yates of Nuffield College, Oxford, for her tireless secretarial support.

NEVIL JOHNSON
ALLAN COCHRANE
June 1980

CONTENTS

PREFACE TO THE RE-ISSUE OF 2017

In many respects Nevil Johnson and I made an odd couple. He was some-one deeply rooted in a conservative philosophical tradition for whom Hegel was bed-time reading (and he was early to adopt Margaret Thatcher as one of his own); I had a radical background, an activist in left-wing organisa-tions and with recent experience of working for the Birmingham Community Development Project. He was a Professorial Fellow at Nuffield College and I was research officer on a project led by him. But he never treated me as his inferior – our discussions were always open, we worked together in developing the research strategy and, in developing the arguments presented in this book, we followed where the fieldwork evidence led. I am not sure that he learned much from me, but he taught me to appreciate some of the complexities of political philosophy as well as the significance of wider constitutional debates. Politically we remained very far apart.

There are, I think, two aspects of this book which make it of continuing relevance. The first relates to its comparative focus; the second to its concern with local economic policy.

The work on which the book draws was funded by the (now long gone) Anglo-German Foundation for the Study of Industrial Society (remarkably enough, in those days it was somehow still acceptable to use the prefix 'Anglo' to mean UK). At the time (the late 1970s), the British problem was widely spoken of, with a particular focus on industrial relations and low productivity, and it was assumed that West Germany's industrial miracle would provide the lessons required to counter the symptoms of decline.

And that was the more or less unspoken but clearly understood starting point for our project, too. With the help of our partners at the University of Cologne (Renata Mayntz and Gerda Zill) we would show how much better German local government was at fostering economic growth and supporting local business. In practice, however, the research outcomes were much more ambivalent, as we traced the detailed practices of council officers and politi-cians. If the starting point was the contrast between constitutionally guaran-teed local self-government in the German case and the more explicitly unitary model that characterised the UK's institutional settlement, the research itself required a more nuanced Interpretation. In terms of comparative method, it confirmed the need for openness and reflexivity in practice – listening to what was said rather than imposing a predetermined template; in thinking about the distinctive experiences of the UK and West Germany it highlighted the possibility of dialogue across difference.

Perhaps in the context of Britain's impending exit from the EU and Germany's role at the heart of the European project, the need for continuing engagement is even clearer than before.

But the second reason why it seems to me that the book has a strong contemporary resonance relates to its focus on economic policy making by local governments. Although others had written about similar issues, the economic role of local authorities, particularly in Britain, was not generally understood to be a significant one. In that sense the focus of our argument was highly prescient. In a sense (although I suspect Nevil was less excited by this than I was) some of what we identified prefigured the initiatives pursued by the new urban left authorities in the 1980s – South Yorkshire (one of our case studies) was already widely identified as a 'people's republic' and Sheffield went on to have its own dedicated Employment Department, building on and questioning the approaches set out in the chapters of the book.

The moment of the new urban left turned out to be brief but the rise of the economic as a focus of local political concern has been more long-lasting. Today an interest in urban competitiveness is a fundamental aspect of the localist endeavour, particularly in big cities across the world. In England such an understanding has justified the introduction of mayors (on models familiar from and different to those common in Germany) to run city regions, delivering infrastructural investment to underpin private endeavour and support business development. But (as the book suggests) the supposed relationship between economic success and local well-being is one that frames policy development in small towns as well as city regions.

The experience explored in the chapters that follow confirms that economic questions and development initiatives were already important concerns for local government some time ago, but it also highlights the political shift that was only beginning at the time we wrote. If it seemed slightly eccentric to focus on these issues in the late 1970s, today their significance is taken for granted. If the local government was once a basic pillar of the welfare state, today its role has been reinterpreted to fit with a policy environment that is defined through competitiveness rather than social solidarity.

Allan Cochrane, Professor Emeritus of Urban Studies, The Open University
October 2016

Chapter 1

THE LOCAL AUTHORITY AS AN ECONOMIC AGENT: POSSIBILITIES AND LIMITS

SPECIAL FEATURES OF ECONOMIC POLICY-MAKING IN
LOCAL GOVERNMENT

This study deals with those activities of local authorities in England and
the Federal Republic of Germany which are explicitly directed to the
strengthening of the local economy. Through an inquiry into a variety
of measures undertaken by local authorities with the aim of influencing
the local economic environment, it attempts to establish whether and to
what extent local authorities can be said to engage in economic policy-
making.

In Britain it would until recently have been unusual to consider local
authorities as bodies with economic functions, still less as bodies with
an economic policy.[1] At first sight this is in fairly sharp contrast to the
West German perception of this matter. In the Federal Republic it is
quite usual to talk of economic policy (*Wirtschaftspolitik*) as a function
of local government and this is often reflected by the presence within
the organisation of local authorities of an office or department for
economic policy or affairs. But in practice economic policy has generally meant economic development and promotion (*Wirtschaftsförderung*) which in turn means a variety of specific measures to encourage
industrial and commercial development. Such a situation has been
found to resemble in many respects that often now prevailing in British
local authorities. In the Federal Republic as in Britain the question
whether a collection of measures adds up to a policy, or the regular
pursuit of specific activities to policy-making, still remains to be
answered, notwithstanding the fact that different organisational labels
and different perceptions of the role of local authorities may initially
suggest divergent answers.

Despite a certain unfamiliarity in the idea of an economic role for
local authorities, there is no doubt that local authorities in Britain have
for some time and in varying degrees been engaged in what must loosely
be described as economic activities. Such action has been undertaken
with the express intention of influencing in various ways the level of
industrial activity and employment in the local authority areas. Some —
perhaps many — local authorities would now go so far as to claim that
they do have an economic policy and that they can set the particular

activities they describe as economic into a framework of economic objectives. This points directly to one of the issues to be considered here. After setting out just what kind of activities are seen as coming under the heading 'economic', it will be necessary to consider to what extent they really do provide a justification for acknowledging that local authorities may actually have an economic policy.

These questions have been tackled by collecting evidence from a range of cases: seven local authorities in England and five in the Federal Republic. The choice of authorities as cases for analysis presented a number of methodological problems. How these were resolved and how the local authorities were selected in England is set out in the Appendix at the end of this book. In the design of the case study investigations it was decided that there was likely to be little advantage in attempting to establish whether local authorities were regarding all or the greater part of their activities from an economic perspective. Similarly, for reasons touched on further below, no attempt was made to construct a more or less formalised model of the local economy into which the empirical inquiry would have then been fitted. The best approach appeared to be to establish what particular activities were held by local authorities themselves to be the most straightforward forms of economic intervention available to them, and then to see how far such activities might be held to constitute a sector of economic policy-making. This meant that attention was concentrated chiefly on action intended to have some impact, even if small, on local employment opportunities and on the level of local industrial activity. What was known about the West German experience of local economic policy-making already pointed to this interpretation of economic activity by local authorities and it turned out in practice to correspond remarkably closely to the English local authorities' perception of what kind of economic action was feasible for them too. It was seen predominantly as action intended in the first place to encourage or facilitate industrial development and the maintenance or creation of employment opportunities. Such action includes, for example, the provision of land, premises or financial support. Equally, it may take the form of infrastructural improvements thought to be necessary to attract industrial and commercial development or to maintain a particular pattern of employment opportunities.

Clearly, economic action of this kind by local authorities differs markedly from many other things they do. In Britain it is of fairly recent origin, hardly detectable at all before about 1960.[2] As a field of activity it has taken shape against the background of a powerful belief that economic policy is essentially within the responsibility of central government and that local contributions to it, even if practicable, can hardly avoid coming into conflict with national economic priorities. Equally important is the fact that local authorities have been seen chiefly as providers of services in the fields of social welfare and protection. Each service depends on statutory provisions and generally requires specialised techniques and organisation. As a result local authorities developed over the years a highly compartmentalised organisation marked by separate departments with their distinctive service orientations. In such a framework not only was there no official place for economic functions, but it was also hard even to develop informally an area of activity which by its nature would require the co-operation of several separate departments. Certainly, the intra-local authority organisational developments of the past decade or so have tended to reduce this particular obstacle to the assumption of economic responsibilities by local authorities. But this has not altered the fundamental fact that local authorities in England do not have a clearly defined set of economic functions derived from statutes. Given the absence of a general competence to act for the benefit of their areas analogous to that possessed by German local authorities[3], this means that the economic role of English local authorities has had to be built up on the basis of a variety of rather limited and specific powers and to some extent construed from other functions, notably land use planning, which have long been discharged by local government. Whilst the absence of clearly defined statutory duties may to some extent inhibit initiatives by local authorities, it is also a fact of some importance that in such a situation there is likely to be relatively little scope for control or intervention from the outside and in particular by central government. This suggests the possibility that economic activity may be something which is very much within the area of discretion enjoyed by local authorities. Similarly, how they organise such activities and define their economic role may be very much a matter for experiment and decision by individual authorities.

A major problem affecting the study of economic action by local authorities lies in the fact that it is hard to define a local economy in such a way as to make it a useful category which can be applied in the policy-making context. There is a literature on local labour markets and on several other partial aspects of economic relationships and behaviour within regional and sub-regional or local contexts. But clearly there are nearly always powerful empirical objections to the drawing of sharp distinctions between one local economic area and another. The patterns of work and settlement do not conform to local administrative boundaries; natural resources are distributed without regard to such boundaries; transport systems have grown up with only a limited correspondence to local authority areas, a fact which is further reflected in the presence of commuting patterns revealing on many occasions a sharp separation between areas of work and residence; and above all, local authority areas are subject to so many inter-area transfers and transactions that it becomes virtually impossible to define those elements in a given local economic area which originate within it and are controllable there, whether by public or private action. In other words, the economic structure of nearly every local authority area is thoroughly porous. This is especially true of the districts of England, but the comment applies too to the counties, despite their greater territorial size and population.

The difficulties inherent in defining the local economy do not, however, prevent local authorities from recognising economic problems and needs, nor from taking action intended to have an impact on such problems. National economic trends can be identified within local authority areas, notably the level of unemployment and rates of growth or decline in particular branches of industrial activity. Thus local authorities cannot avoid being aware of the overall employment situation in their areas and of the ways in which structural changes in industry and commerce may be affecting future employment prospects. Moreover, in the course of discharging their planning functions local authorities at both the county and district levels have to reach conclusions on desirable patterns of land use in the future, having regard not only to local needs but also where appropriate to regional and national priorities. Within such a framework local authorities are to an increasing degree impelled to pay explicit attention to the economic aspects of their planning policies and decisions.

Just as the territorial limits of a local economy can rarely be defined, so there are serious obstacles in the way of constructing a model of the local economy expressed in terms of transactions within the area of local jurisdiction. In principle such a model would enable all local authority activities to be comprehensively subsumed under input and output categories. No attempt has been made here to construct such a model for analytic purposes. This was in part because the concern here has not been with applied economics nor with impact analysis and it is in such connections that an input–output model of the local economy might in principle have been most relevant. But without doubt neglect of such a possibility was also due to the fact that local authorities themselves do not appear to consider such economic model-building to be either feasible or useful. This was confirmed in the course of the research on which this study is based: we found no examples of a local authority working with anything like such a model, whether related to the production and exchange of goods and services in its area or to the economic significance of its own range of activities. Since the chief interest in this research has been how the authorities actually conceive of economic action, how they carry it out and in what policy contexts they justify it, there appeared to be no case for trying to apply to their activities conceptual categories remote from those they adopt themselves.

EXTERNAL INFLUENCES ON LOCAL ACTION

The scope for local authority intervention in the economic environment obviously depends substantially on the powers and resources available, matters to be considered in detail in later chapters. But when outlining the general direction of this study it is important to stress that in the field of economic development the local authority is highly dependent both on the actors in the local economic area and on the external governmental structure in which it finds itself. Let us first make a few remarks about the actors in the local economy.

Clearly in any local authority area very many decisions affecting economic activity and prospects are made by private agents – usually firms and businesses – or by public bodies independent of the local authority. Such decisions may often require local authority endorsement or support, but nearly always the local authority is reacting to action contemplated or taken by external agents rather than taking an initiative itself. So far as prompting decisions by these agents goes, the local authority may be able to offer inducements, but is rarely in possession of more substantial leverage. In addition it has to be remembered that inevitably the local authority is to some extent exposed to competition from other local authorities in its dealings with private firms: they may be able to change the location of their activities if a given local authority adheres too rigidly to its particular requirements.

A further point of some importance is that the structure of industry in Britain and the Federal Republic has revealed for many years now a trend towards concentration of control. Consequently major developments are likely to be determined by people with little or no direct links with a particular local authority area. Since it is well known that locally variable costs such as the level of rates payable in Britain have not so far been a decisive factor in determining the location of major investment projects by larger firms, the local authority is likely to be poorly placed to exert much influence on such decisions. Lobbying and persuasion will often be attempted and a local authority may well claim to offer residential and infrastructural advantages. But in the case of the larger enterprises it is very doubtful whether the preferences of local authorities and what they offer to do can have more than marginal significance. Nevertheless, it is the larger firms which may be able to make the biggest impact on locally available employment opportunities, at least in the short term, and if the scope for influencing their decisions is small, this presents local authorities with a problem.

It is no doubt an awareness of the relatively high degree of autonomy enjoyed by the larger firms that goes a long way towards explaining why, as this study indicates, local authorities have put a lot of emphasis on measures to encourage development by small firms. It is, of course, also well known that the overall economic recession of recent years, the employment-reducing effects of rationalisation in many sectors of industry and the growing criticism of the disabilities imposed by public policy on small and new enterprises have combined to boost support for the encouragement of small businesses, a reaction even stronger in Britain than in the Federal Republic. This is then seen to be an area naturally suited to local authority support and intervention. Smaller firms are more likely to seek information and advice from the local authorities, some of their needs, for example, for sites or loans, can be met fairly easily by local authorities, and it is probable that the small and medium-sized firm can more often be brought within the ambit of the redevelopment needs of those local authority areas with a heritage of inner urban dereliction.

In considering possible economic strategies a local authority must, however, have regard not only to the economic conditions and prospects of its area and to the independence of private economic agents in it, but also to its own position within a network of governmental relations, in Britain reaching up to ministers in the central government. Economic policy in general and industrial policy as a particular aspect of economic policy have in Britain fallen chiefly within the responsibility of the central government. National legislation has conferred on ministers the power to make loans and grants in support of industrial development, it is the Department of Industry which takes the lead in applying the regional financial incentives intended to favour areas with persistently high unemployment and structural deficiencies, and it is central government which takes decisions in relation to the major elements in macro-economic management. This implies, of course, that the central government determines the overall target level of expenditure by local authorities within the framework of its public expenditure planning. In addition, local authorities are subject to a wide range of specific ministerial powers which in principle at least confer on the central government substantial rights of intervention in relation to the provision of many services.

At first sight, therefore, local authorities appear to operate within a hierarchy of powers leaving them very dependent on ministers and their officials. But it may be that the preponderant influence of the central government needs to be substantially qualified. After all, the quality and range of local services do still depend very much on local decisions; in the distribution of resources between services local authorities have, subject to the mandatory nature of many of their activities, a fair amount of discretion; and in the development of new initiatives in many services it is the executive agents at the local level who count rather than the writers of circulars at the centre. These qualifications to the familiar picture of central government predominance apply generally to the broad range of locally provided services. But, as will be indicated in more detail in the course of this study, they apply particularly to economic support measures. In part this is because, as already mentioned, there is no extensive statutory framework determining what economic activities British local authorities may undertake. It is thus very much an area for development and experiment.

It is evident, therefore, that there are two contrasting aspects of the economic role of local authorities. On the one hand it is clear that economic powers are limited in scope and whatever economic measures local authorities take have to be set within external conditions determined extensively by central government policies. On the other hand, however, whether local authorities do in fact seek to use the powers available to them for encouraging economic development seems to be very much within their own discretion. Local authorities encounter many problems operating within a complex structure of powers. But in the economic field it is necessary to establish whether they regularly find formal impediments or prohibitions in their way. If not, then there is likely to be room for initiative by the local authority, even though the results of such initiative may remain modest in scale.

THE CASE STUDIES

It is now necessary to make a few remarks about the case studies on which the account of the economic activities of local authorities provided here rests. In particular something has to be said about the principal questions used to structure this research.

The broad intention was, of course, to collect evidence about local authority economic activity, to consider this as a policy area and to examine the political and administrative conditions under which local authorities do engage in a range of economic activities. But the investigation of particular authorities had to be guided by rather more specific questions if it was to yield useful results and these questions had to reflect the need to pass from evidence about local perceptions of particular economic activities to a critical appreciation of the complex context, internally and externally, in which the local authority operates.

The first structuring question, or more accurately group of questions, referred to the kind of understanding local authorities have of their economic role. The primary concern here was to establish how local authorities understand and justify such economic measures as they take. This relates both to the manner in which they evaluate particular measures as well as to the extent to which they regard those activities carried out for economic purposes as being part of a sector of local economic policy.

There are plainly several possibilities in respect of a local authority's evaluation of its economic role. It may at one extreme refuse to accept that it has one at all; or it may accept such a role but define it broadly or narrowly; and it may interpret its role in voluntaristic or reactive terms, or in some combination of the two. If the local authority takes a firmly voluntaristic line, it will see itself as capable of initiation and of responding in a positive manner to surrounding conditions. Alternatively, the reactive view can be held to predominate when the economic role is seen chiefly in terms of accommodation to circumstances, including whatever priorities may be laid down by higher levels of government.

Typically, of course, one would expect to find some mixture of these elements. Local authorities may attempt, for example, to take the initiative by constructing industrial estates, they may look to local industry for a lead in determining infrastructure improvement priorities, whilst they may be anxious to respond to central government priorities by establishing schemes to assist unemployed school-leavers. The balance between these elements is very likely to vary from one authority to another and will certainly change over time.

The development of an economic role depends, however, on appropriate organisational arrangements for carrying out activities seen as constituting that role. The second set of questions focused on these matters. Such arrangements may vary considerably from one authority to another, both at the level of administrative organisation and at the level of the council and its committees. Since economic support activities do not yet constitute a well-established functional area in British local government at least, it is not surprising that the responsibility for such action was found to be attached to a variety of organisational units within the local authority structure, and that it is defined in different ways.

Whilst interest was concentrated on activities and how they are organised, it was also necessary to consider how far they are seen as constituting a policy sector. Does the policy come first, followed by the activities, or the policy emerge later as a justification for the activities? These issues were tackled by working outwards from a detailed survey of the forms of economic activity actually undertaken by selected local authorities in both countries. In England these matters have not received much attention up to now, no doubt in part because of uncertainty about what local authorities might properly do in this field.

When working from this clarification of activities to an examination of how and to what extent these are justified in terms of goals set and policy guidelines laid down for them, the impact of organisational and structural variables becomes apparent. These include factors which are quite specifically concerned with the organisation of the local authority such as the effects of allocating responsibility for economic activity to one type of committee or to one particular department as compared with another, the significance of seeing economic functions within a scheme of corporate management or planning, and the effects of relating economic activities primarily to one major functional area such as planning as compared with another such as estates management.

Then there are more generally applicable structural conditions expressed in the distinctions of role as between councillors and officers which influence the definition of policy goals. The impact of these conditions is, of course, affected by particular organisational arrangements; some will seek to facilitate a direct political influence on policy determination, others will allow the contribution of the political leadership to be mediated by varying opportunities for administrative initiatives.

The translation of goals into activities and the identification of activities as a continuing policy concern are likely to be marked by a variety of conflicts of interest. These may occur between different parts of the local authority administration, even within a single large department, between political parties or groups or between committees and sub-committees of a council. Needless to say, external factors may strongly influence such conflicts of interest. The effective realisation of economic measures will depend in part on how such conflicts are resolved: are there, for example, recognised methods of achieving political compromise? Does the chief officer have a major part to play in resolving conflict? Is there a balance amongst departments that has to be respected and which points towards particular solutions favourable to one department or another? Such aspects of the process whereby impediments to the carrying out of a programme of activities are overcome and the activities themselves are adapted to broadly stated policy goals will be seen to have a major influence on the economic role which local authorities claim to be developing.

Reference has already been made to the relatively high degree of dependence on external circumstances experienced by the local authority in attempting to take economic action. This points to the third group of questions pursued in this research: what kind of limitations or restrictions affect the local authority's economic activity as a result of its position in a complex administrative system and within a largely autonomous economic environment? Clearly it is impracticable to pursue all possible sources of dependence and, therefore, of restrictions on the local authority's freedom of action. But three main types of restriction can usefully be distinguished. First, there are restrictions imposed formally or informally by other levels of government. These must include restrictions inherent in the legal powers available and in the procedures often laid down in statute for the carrying out of many local authority functions. But in addition attention has to be paid to the impact at the local level of national government policies, for example regional policy or industrial policy. Such policies, it would be claimed, are guided by broad national considerations of social benefit and cannot be expected to be open to much direct influence by local government.

To the extent that the central government (or in the Federal Republic the state more widely interpreted) has an interest in monitoring or directly supervising local authority action, this will often constitute a restrictive influence on what the local authority is able to do. Nevertheless, it has to be remembered that direct state intervention or stimulus may also be regarded as an opportunity for local initiative, as, for example, in Britain in the case of the various programmes for the inner urban areas.

Secondly, important restrictions and constraints stem from internal local authority administrative and political organisation and from the relations between different levels of the local government system. Some of these problems arise also under the preceding set of questions relating to the manner in which the local authority puts its conception of an economic role into practice. More broadly it is necessary to consider what are the effects on possibilities for action of this need to reconcile divergent claims within the internal structure of the local authorities themselves.

Thirdly, there are the restrictions stemming from the relatively high autonomy of the actors in the local economic area. The local authority is generally in the position of someone making an appeal: it hopes for a response but cannot guarantee one. The difficulty of forecasting the results of a range of economic promotion measures is likely to induce caution on the part of local authorities, even when the policy commitment to economic support measures is strong.

It may not be possible accurately to weigh the effects of one set of restrictions or limitations against those of another. Nevertheless, it is hoped that the findings of this study provide some guidance in assessing the relative importance to be attached to the more formal internal and external constraints affecting local authorities acting in the economic field as compared with those imposed by the general economic environment.

In the presentation of the evidence gathered on how local authorities in Britain and the Federal Republic are attempting to encourage industrial development and the creation of employment opportunities in their areas the emphasis in the descriptive sections of this study is rather more on the English cases than on the German. Nevertheless, a substantial part of the work reflects our concern with comparison between the two countries. This affects activities – what local authorities actually do in this policy sector, administrative and political organisation for such activities; and the constraints internal and external under which they operate. As will be seen subsequently, both contrasts and similarities can be identified in all these directions. But equally important is the fact that there are structural determinants at work in the economy at large which combine with the existing distribution of roles and responsibilities between the different levels of the governmental system to produce a relatively circumscribed definition and understanding of what kind of economic measures a local authority in either country can actually undertake and, therefore, of the kind of economic policy-making role to which it can reasonably aspire. Through an examination of activities in the economic field and of the conditions under which they are carried out it will become apparent that the substantive content of local economic action in the two countries does not differ all that much. The points of departure in time have been different, and the institutional structure with its allocation of powers presents marked contrasts. But within such differing conditions there may be surprising similarities in the actual contribution of local authorities to the development of the economy and the handling of specific local economic problems. This study tries to show that this is so and to throw some light on why in this policy field institutional differences in the broad sense of that term have only a limited impact on the scope for action.

NOTES

1   A recent survey suggests that 64 per cent of authorities with Industrial Development Officers first appointed them between 1971 and 1978, and 41 per cent did so between 1975 and 1978: N. Falk, *Local Authorities and Industrial Development: Results of a Survey* (London: Urbed, 1978).
2   In the interwar period some local authorities took quite extensive economic measures. Sixty-nine county boroughs and 285 municipal boroughs and urban districts in England and Wales were involved in development organisations and the Commissioner for the Special Areas criticised the view that 'the future of the Areas must be left to the Government' and stressed 'the necessity for self-help' by local authorities: *First Report of the Commissioner for the Special Areas 1934–35*, quoted in M. M. Camina, *Local Authorities and the Attraction of Industry*, Progress in Planning, Vol. 3, pt 2 (Oxford: Pergamon, 1974), p. 88.
3   West German local authorities have general authority to act for the benefit of their areas; in Britain such a right exists only to the very modest extent of being allowed to spend up to the product of a 2p rate for purposes of general benefit and not otherwise provided for by statute.

Chapter 2

THE FORMAL FRAMEWORK FOR LOCAL ECONOMIC ACTION: POWERS, FUNCTIONS AND FINANCE IN BRITAIN

With only minor qualifications English local authorities carry out their functions in virtue of specific statutory powers conferred on them by Parliament. Unlike German local authorities they have no general competence to act for the benefit of the populations within their jurisdiction. Nevertheless, it should be stressed that the dependence of English local authorities on specific powers does not mean that their discretion in matters of policy-making is always narrowly confined within the limits of statute or subject to the overriding control of central government. Some of the powers of local authorities are expressed in very broad terms (as in parts of the Local Government Act 1972) and can therefore be applied flexibly. Many of the statutes dealing with specific functions and services (for example, the Town and Country Planning Acts and the Housing Acts) leave room for much interpretation of what action is permissible under them and for adaptation to new situations. Moreover, the interpretation of local authority powers and responsibilities has to be seen in relation to the fact that many (and probably most) local authorities now regard themselves as generally responsible for taking an overall view of the situation and needs of their areas.[1] This means that whatever the formal position as to specific powers may be, there is a tendency to try, initially at least, to deal with problems through an adaptive use of existing powers and this is usually regarded as a proper course for authorities to follow.

When considering what powers local authorities in Britain might use for a variety of economic purposes it is helpful to set the possibilities within an historical context which draws attention both to the evolution of particular powers and to the prevailing view in local government of its main concerns.

Before 1945 British local authorities had in virtue of their public utility holdings a direct concern with important forms of economic activity. But such responsibilities were for the most part taken away from them as a result of the nationalisation of gas and electricity shortly after 1945, and much more recently in 1973 most of the remaining local responsibility for water supply also passed to regional organisations having their own statutory powers. Nevertheless, despite the loss of such responsibilities involving the production and sale of services and the enforced retreat from important sectors of social service provision, notably in the field of health services, new functions have regularly been conferred on local authorities in the course of the past thirty years, the range of many familiar tasks has widened and the overall volume of local expenditure has steadily risen. From 24 per cent of total public spending in 1963 the local authority share rose to 29 per cent in 1973 and stood at about 27 per cent in 1978.[2]

By far the greater part of this expenditure is devoted to services which can be regarded as traditional for local government, that is to say, services which have been aimed at social support and protection in its different forms, including education, the service which claims about half of local government spending from the general rate fund. This emphasis in the type of services provided has been important in shaping the way local authorities, their members and officers see themselves, and the way in which councillors are seen by both central government and local electors. Councils are in effect often seen as the means by which many nationally agreed services of social support are locally administered. There is scope for significant variation between authorities in service provision and the distribution and levels of spending to cater for local needs, but the basic activities and tasks remain the same. Even though local authorities have responsibilities of a somewhat different nature in the land use planning field, on the whole planning has also until recently been seen primarily in terms of protecting and improving the social and built environment rather than as a pattern of activity which should be directed also towards the economic development and growth of local areas.

This historical bias in the understanding of local authority functions provides at least part of the explanation for the fact that local authorities still have no general economic functions and responsibilities clearly distinguished in the statute book, although they do have a number of rather narrow and specific powers to be considered below. Nevertheless, there are many signs that under the impact of more difficult economic conditions many local authorities have begun to reassess their priorities and now recognise the need for what might be called a constructive use of their existing powers for economic purposes. In particular this has involved growing acceptance of a broader view of the planning function and a more flexible application of the planning legislation.[3] In the case of planning powers the position was changed quite substantially by the Town and Country Planning Acts of 1968 and 1971 under which planning departments in local government did indeed gain a wider responsibility. County structure plans were introduced to encourage strategic planning which needs to take broad economic and demographic factors into account, while local and district plans (on which the direct development control process is based) are to translate structure plan policies into more specific measures suited to local conditions. Thus it can be said that the planning responsibility of local authorities does now embrace a more explicit requirement than previously to consider the economic implications of the decisions they take both in the planning field and under related service provision responsibilities. Local authorities can claim to have a legitimate, even if uncertainly defined, concern with the economic development of their areas. Recognition of such an economic role found expression in the Department of the Environment's circular 71/77 which encouraged them to contribute to the central government's industrial strategy by themselves formulating policies to promote economic development. It might be held too that the Inner Urban Areas Act of 1978 underlined recognition of a local authority involvement in important aspects of economic policy-making.

THE USE OF PLANNING POWERS FOR ECONOMIC DEVELOPMENT PURPOSES

It is now necessary to consider in rather more detail how and to what extent planning powers can be used for economic ends by local authorities. It is, however, important to stress straight away that planning is an ambiguous term both in respect of how far it reaches as a function entrusted to local authorities and on account of the fact that it leads directly to the problem of how responsibilities are shared between central and local government. And it is not just a question of the sharing of planning responsibilities: there is also the question of whether the central government might claim to have such extensive and exclusive economic policy responsibilities as to exclude local authorities from that field, despite their inclination to use planning powers now for economic purposes.

Since 1947 land use planning (or town and country planning as it was usually called) has been an important responsibility in which both national and local government share. Throughout this time a division between economic planning and land use planning was also maintained. The former has been more or less the sole responsibility of central government, whilst the latter has been left to a large extent with local government, subject to a variety of possibilities for central supervision. Since the mid 1960s it has increasingly been accepted that there is a need for more explicit connections between the two types of planning, but what these connections are, or should be, has remained uncertain. The Royal Commission on Local Government in England stated: 'if central government is inextricably involved in local planning, so is local government in central planning. It seems often to be assumed that economic planning is a matter for central government, while land planning is, initially at any rate, for local government. But the two are indivisible. Some facets of economic planning are, of course, outside the sphere of local government, but planning authorities must concern themselves with economic prospects in their areas. Indeed, these are central to all a local authority's decisions on priorities.'[4]

There has been a marked contrast between the relatively formal structure of local land use planning and the more fluid system of economic planning and intervention established by the central government. The method by which a development plan is to be completed is outlined in statute and circular, but the means by which such components of national economic policy as an 'industrial strategy' or a 'regional policy' are formulated are far less explicitly stated.

The 1960s were years of increasing uncertainty for town planners in Britain. It was clear that the traditional forms and methods of town planning were becoming inadequate in a situation in which economic growth became harder to sustain and land use planners were anxious to raise their eyes from the detailed work of development control. Within the planning profession arguments were increasingly being raised about the need for planning to concentrate on strategic issues and to take an interest in broad economic and social developments which might affect or be affected by the actions of the planners.[5] At the same time central government began to change its approach as the Ministry of Housing and Local Government's own land use planners became concerned that they were spending too much time on the detailed and unnecessary perusal of local authority plans and planning applications at the expense of exerting any significant influence on the overall pattern of development.

The debates of the 1960s resulted in the Town and Country Planning Acts of 1968 and 1971 which were intended to lay the basis for a flexible system of medium-term physical planning and to provide the means by which central government could oversee and influence the planning policies of local authorities without the need for direct intervention on minor issues. Under the 1971 Act it became the duty of the county council to prepare a structure plan for its area and submit it to the Secretary of State for the Environment for his approval. From this structure plan stems (or is intended to stem) the whole organisation of development control and land use within the county. The plan is to be a broad statement of the local authority's policy and general proposals regarding development and other land use in its area and their relationship to neighbouring counties over a fifteen year period and subject to regular review. It should also identify areas where action is needed and for which local plans are to be prepared later. The form of these plans represented a major break from the traditional planning documents with their maps and specified sites and zones — instead they were to be written statements with diagrams and justified by supporting evidence, including the results of a detailed economic and social survey of the area. For the first time the planners acquired a statutory responsibility to consider the economic problems of their areas.

Structure plans are, however, essentially strategic documents covering large areas. Executive action still depends on local plans which are usually prepared by the district councils. Action plans and special topic plans (for example, on minerals) may also be drawn up. Such plans must be consistent with the policies of the structure plan. When the district draws up a local plan it has to be certified by the county council as in conformity with the structure plan before it can become fully operative. Such local plans are closer in form to the planning documents of the past, including maps, diagrams and illustrations, as well as a written statement. Uses for specified areas of land are identified and this indicates to industry where the local authorities want development to take place. The plans also forecast where services and infrastructure will be needed, but do not usually lay down restrictions on size, shape or design – that is left to the detailed consideration of planning applications. It is unusual for the Department of the Environment to intervene at the local plan stage if the structure plan has already been approved and the county is simply using it as the yardstick against which to test the local plan.

Development control is operated within the framework of the development plan (that is, structure plan plus local plans) and is primarily the responsibility of the district council. All planning applications (from prospective developers) have to go to the district and need to be referred to the county only in rare cases (where they deal with 'county matters' such as mineral development or the disposal of mineral waste, or where the district intends to give planning permission and the application conflicts with the policies of the structure plan). The county has no control over refusals by the district, even if the structure plan encourages development which the district is not prepared to countenance. The way in which responsibility for executive planning action is divided between the two tiers of local government does, of course, mean that most of the powers of control as well as much of the scope for taking initiatives rest with the district level.

The British land use planning system builds up from the local authorities and is now hinged on the structure plan. There is no attempt to prepare a national development plan or even detailed regional plans identifying areas of growth and centres for development, except as an incidental side-effect of the work of the Department of Industry. The only elements of a national planning system which can be identified derive from the fact that structure plans themselves have to fit into regional strategies (where they exist) agreed by central government and formulated until 1979 through a system of regional Economic Planning Councils, and must have due regard to any statements of national policy (for example, the Industrial Strategy,

Regional Policy, New Towns Policy, major circulars, and so on).[6] Whether there is any reality behind this appearance is a matter taken up again in later chapters. There is, however, bound to be a significant degree of tension within such a decentralised system in which the central authority has no clearly defined directive role in land use planning, even though it retains important powers over structure plans and in some cases intervenes over specific issues of development control, whilst at the same time it disposes of a wide range of powers affecting the industrial and economic context in which local authorities have to carry out their land use planning. What is more, within the local government system the county planners have a major strategic planning role, but can exert little control over the development which actually takes place. As a result there is also likely to be tension between them and the districts.

Whilst the methods of land use planning have changed in ways which encourage more attention to be paid to economic considerations and prospects, there are inherent limitations to the positive use of planning powers to promote economic development. Planning powers can indeed be most readily used to restrict economic development of all kinds rather than to start it off. The refusal of a planning application will generally stop action, although an appeal to the secretary of state is still possible. A policy of restraint may, of course, be a perfectly reason-able economic policy to pursue, and at a county level it would even be consistent to encourage restraint in one area while hoping for growth and development in another. But in practice few of the local authorities interested in economic policy-making would now want to restrict them-selves to such negative uses of planning powers.

It is relatively easy to see why local authorities find it hard to use their planning powers in a positive manner. Certainly structure plans and local plans can be used to make it clear that new development is welcome and that there will be few restrictions, particularly in certain specified areas of a county or district. Similarly, the planners can give priority to industrial planning applications, can help potential develop-ers through the complex process of making such applications and can be more sympathetic to planning applications for industrial develop-ment and from small firms. Nevertheless, the success of these policies depends on an initiative from others. Even at the local level the main powers of the planners are permissive and reactive rather than interven-tionist or directive.

LAND AND DEVELOPMENT

Suitable land is a basic requirement for industrial development. Under various Acts local authorities have powers to acquire and develop land. Under the Local Authorities (Land) Act 1963 (which began life as a

Private Member's Bill) they first received the power to acquire and develop land for the benefit and improvement of their area or residents. Many local authorities (particularly the former county boroughs) already owned a great deal of land under other powers (including housing powers) which could not be returned to its original use and many had inherited land from their predecessor authorities and had large corporate estates.

Land can also be purchased and developed under the planning Acts 'in the interests of proper planning of the area'. Thus local authorities are able to provide land and premises for employers, particularly smaller businesses, and are able to help find alternative sites for firms dislodged from inner city areas or clearance areas. Powers to build industrial estates also exist under the Housing Act 1957, a striking example of the way in which a power plainly concerned with economic activity has been tacked on to a body of legislation directed to quite different functions.

The Community Land Act 1975 (the repeal of which was announced after the change of government in May 1979) complicated matters for local authorities, although in principle it need not have made action in the economic sphere any more difficult. It did not withdraw existing powers, but did require development land to pass through a Land Account and made it impossible to dispose of land freehold. Although the Act made extra finance available for land purchase, the Community Land Scheme was primarily intended as a method of sharing the profits of land transactions between local authorities and central government rather than as a means of encouraging local authority development.

Local authorities are able to offer only limited material incentives to employers and developers. The legislation is clear that in most cases local authorities must charge a commercial rate for any land or buildings they supply, but that rate has to be defined by the council and it is common commercial practice to allow limited rent-free periods and other financial incentives. The requirement to charge the market rate does not exist for short-term leases (up to seven years) nor for rented property and such properties may include refurbished older premises and modern small units.

Local authorities are able to advance money under the Local Authorities (Land) Act to a person who wishes to develop a building on land leased or sold by the local authority. The loan may amount to a maximum of 75 per cent of the value of the developed land and has to be repaid at a fixed rate within thirty years. Until recently, the interest rates were slightly lower than commercial ones, but are now often a little higher. The Inner Urban Areas Act 1978 extended the right of designated local authorities to lend to developers on any land within the broadly defined inner city areas and the limit in these areas has been raised to 90 per cent.

PROMOTION AND THE PROVISION OF INFRASTRUCTURE

There is no serious obstacle in the way of local authorities engaging in promotional work. They have the power to advertise their areas to attract commercial and other development, and may also encourage visitors for recreation, conferences, trade fairs and exhibitions. Councils can produce reports on their areas for distribution or sale and they may also encourage local firms to join their promotional campaigns (often at nominal cost) to help sales, particularly exports, and to attract orders.

The counties are responsible for the construction of non-trunk roads and the maintenance of roads within their areas and their priorities, particularly in road building, can influence markedly the location of industry. Counties also have a responsibility for the overall planning of public transport and metropolitan counties (through their Passenger Transport Executives) have the responsibility of operating a public transport system. Policies under these heads may influence the labour supply by altering travel to work patterns, journey to work times and the costs of travel. Alterations to car parking policy (part of which is a county and part a district responsibility) might be expected to influence the economic state of shopping areas, particularly in the cities.

Housing is an aspect of the local infrastructure too which may be important in affecting economic development. District councils can offer 'key worker' housing to incoming industry which needs to bring in skilled or managerial labour. Variations in the mix of housing provided, such as the encouragement of executive housing, might also be offered in order to make a district more attractive to firms contemplating investment.

The significance of education functions is more indirect. Although education authorities can alter school syllabuses to fit better the requirements of industry, there is no sign that they do this. The most relevant educational powers are probably those to provide training facilities at colleges of further education and polytechnics which can be directed to the needs of local industry. The careers service, too, which is charged with the task of helping school-leavers and young people to find employment provides a means by which local authorities may attempt to influence the local economy.

GENERAL AND PRIVATE ACT POWERS

Then there are powers both very general and highly specific which local authorities may invoke for economic purposes. Section 137 of the Local Government Act 1972 allows the spending of the product of a 2p rate on any matter felt by the council to be to the advantage of the local area and its residents. Under this clause it is possible to subsidise rents, rates and other costs and even to buy shares in publicly quoted companies. Indeed it appears from recent experience that s. 137 would allow spending on any activity not otherwise expressly forbidden. Section 111 of the same Act also appears to confer significant powers by stating that 'a local authority shall have the power to do anything (whether or not involving the expenditure, borrowing or lending of money or the acquisition or disposal of any property or rights) which is calculated to facilitate or is conducive or incidental to, the discharge of any of their functions'. But in practice this has usually been interpreted restrictively by local authorities and their legal advisers.

Individual local authorities are able to promote private bills in Parliament with the intention of acquiring additional powers specific to their own needs. In the 1930s the government supported some private Acts to encourage local authorities to take economic action and some (in particular those for Liverpool CB in 1936 and Jarrow MB in 1939) gave them significant extra powers. Such Acts are now being rationalised as a consequence of territorial reorganisation. Since 1974 one of the most important examples of revised local Acts has been the Tyne and Wear Act 1976. Under it the county council and its metropolitan districts gained the right (at least until 1984) to lend to developers even on land owned by others, to make grants to firms to cover the cost of machinery, and to help cover rent, rates and the costs of service installation by statutory undertakers. A local authority can also make loans to enable persons to buy or lease land in its area.[7] The Department of the Environment does not favour the continued extension of local authority powers through private Acts, but it appears that most metropolitan county councils are trying, some more successfully than others, to follow the example of Tyne and Wear Metropolitan County Council.

In a similar fashion local authorities may have private Act powers for specific developments, for example to run docks or an airport, or a development like the National Exhibition Centre in Birmingham. These Acts help the bodies which have been set up to have a formally separate existence from the local authorities involved whilst remaining under their overall control. Such bodies can often borrow money, invest in other concerns and carry out development which the local authority cannot do. Even without the promotion of private Acts local authorities can co-operate with others (usually developers) in joint organisations whose powers are no longer so restricted and may, for example, raise finance without recourse to the council's locally determined sector allocation. Another way of achieving the same end is to carry out a lease/lease back agreement with a developer.[8]

Passenger Transport Executives are examples of bodies with special powers, having been first set up independently of local authorities under the Transport Act 1968. They can invest and buy shares in companies whose work is relevant to their overall transport responsibilities – the definition of which can be stretched fairly wide. In take-overs which have already occurred some Executives now own or have shares in garages selling petrol to the public and one even has shares in a travel agency.

The legal powers of local authorities are neither as confusing nor as rigid as the traditional account of them sometimes still voiced by local authority legal officers might make it appear. The preceding paragraphs have tried to make this clear for the sector of economic activity. Despite the formal need for a specific statutory basis for action by local authorities, much of what they do falls in the grey areas where there is no explicit statutory duty laid on the local authority, but where it is reasonable to construe various powers as allowing an authority to incur additional expenditure without serious risk of legal challenge. It is now common, for example, for local authorities to employ industrial development or industrial liaison officers, but there has been no need for a desperate search through legal textbooks or old statutes to find a justification for this. Even in those areas of spending where there seems to be tight restrictions there is usually scope for flexibility, like that used in estimating commercial or market rates for premises, particularly where there is only a small private market. The picture is further complicated by the division of authorities into metropolitan and non-metropolitan councils and the fact that the division of responsibility between metropolitan county councils and their districts is not the same as the division in non-metropolitan counties.[9]

THE DIVISION OF LOCAL AUTHORITY POWERS AND THE EFFECTS OF INTERNAL ORGANISATION

What powers can be used and how depends in part on the manner in which they are distributed between different types of local authority as well as on the internal allocation of responsibilities within local authorities.

The precise distribution of functions between different types of local authority is now regulated principally by the Local Government Act 1972. Although the principles governing this distribution are not explicitly stated in this legislation, in effect local government responsibilities are divided into two main categories – those regarded as broadly strategic in character, and those concerned chiefly with the direct provision of services, many of them cost intensive. Most of the strategic functions have been entrusted to the county level of local government, whilst many of those functions involving extensive service provisions have been assigned either to non-metropolitan counties or to the metropolitan districts. A major exception here is housing which is everywhere a district function.

The current distribution of major functions in England and Wales outside London can be summarised as follows:

(a) *Metropolitan counties*. Strategic land use planning (that is, structure plans); traffic management, transport and county roads; police; fire services; consumer protection; refuse disposal; small holdings.

(b) *Counties* (non-metropolitan). As for metropolitan counties but also education, social services and libraries.

(c) *Districts* (non-metropolitan). Local planning regulation (including most development control); housing; roads (very limited) and car parks; building regulations; environmental health, refuse collection; cemeteries and crematoria.[10]

(d) *Metropolitan districts*. As for districts, but in addition education, social services and libraries.

This division of functions and responsibilities leaves a number of questions open and underlines the degree of overlap between the tiers in relation to powers bearing on economic development. It is not clear, for example, exactly how the distribution of planning functions is intended to operate and how strategic considerations can be made to influence detailed local planning. In some areas no division of responsibility is specified. This is true of the sector now under investigation – both counties and districts can justifiably claim that a concern with economic promotion and development stems from their planning functions. In addition each tier is entitled to use both such general powers to assist industry as they have under current legislation and, where applicable, any local powers which they have inherited or acquired for similar purposes. Thus overall it can be said that most of the powers relevant to economic activities are held concurrently and may be exercised competitively.

Nevertheless, the two tiers are plainly under some pressure to ensure that they do not get into serious conflict with each other. The two levels have to work in parallel and to recognise the scope for initiative which each possesses. Despite the continuing influence of an image of upper and lower tiers (an image that tends to encourage antagonism), it is a major characteristic of local government relationships that the lower tier of the system is very rarely in a subordinate position *vis-à-vis* the upper. The latter has hardly any scope for issuing directives to the lower tier. Thus a separation of institutions and a mixing of powers create powerful incentives at both levels to seek a reasonable accommodation of conflicting interests and priorities.

How powers are used and for what ends does, however, depend on far more than the terms of the statute book. In particular it is affected by the way in which a local authority is organised and the approach it develops towards its own policy-making functions. To set this point into context it is necessary to comment briefly on the changes which most local authorities have been making in their internal organisation during recent years and what view of policy-making and the use of powers these changes reflect.

Since the late 1960s many authorities have attempted to strengthen overall policy control and most councils now have a policy and resources committee or equivalent, the purpose of which is to secure co-ordination of policy-making and to encourage a coherent distribution of resources amongst committees. Policy and resources committees are generally made up of leading councillors from the major parties on the council and tend to include most service committee chairmen. Alongside the policy and resources committee there is on most councils also an inner group or executive drawn from the majority party alone which tries to provide the main policy impetus both in the policy committee itself and in the council as a whole through the majority party. Party group organisation is now vitally important in most authorities, even those which have in the past been dominated by non-party groups.

Discussions of local government administrative methods in the 1960s and early 1970s concentrated a great deal on the desirability of improving the methods of management. In particular it was argued that each authority should be viewed as a unit or corporate entity for which an overall corporate plan could be prepared. It was widely held that the internal structure should be organised and rationalised accordingly. Several official reports[11] encouraged local authorities to move in this direction and local authorities themselves often commissioned management consultants to help overhaul their organisation. Some, like Coventry and Stockport, became pace-setters and their example was followed elsewhere. Local government reorganisation in 1974 was intended to facilitate such internal organisational and management developments by creating bodies of a sufficient size to cope adequately with the needs of their areas.[12]

Just as most local authorities have now set up policy and resources committes of varying importance to bring together the major policy-making functions of the different council committees, so on the administrative side it has become increasingly common to set up management teams made up of chief officers and headed by a chief executive. These bodies are intended to co-ordinate the work of the various departments and sometimes to help prepare a corporate plan for the authority. It is the chief executive's responsibility to oversee this and in some cases to initiate action to be taken by other departments. The effectiveness of management teams and chief executives varies greatly, however, from authority to authority. In some cases the chief executive has a predominantly advisory role with very little executive responsibility, in others he is basically a chairman of the leading officers concerned with mediating between them and with the co-ordination of their work, and sometimes he is the council's main initiator of action and able to act as a leader *vis-à-vis* other chief officers.

The patterns of organisational development in recent years do, however, remain varied both in relation to the functional divisions in councils and their committee structures. The local administrative services are still usually organised on a specialised basis – education, social services, finance, planning, and so on – and each major service is normally run as a separate department of the council. Most departments report to one committee only and most committees are concerned chiefly with the work of 'their' department. Thus, despite marked reductions in the number of specialised departments and committees, local government is still characterised by a fairly high degree of functional compartmentalisation. Moreover, the centralisation of policy-making remains difficult despite the strengthening of chief executives, the use of management teams, the introduction of policy committees and the move towards various forms of corporate planning. In both the formulation of policies and their execution the co-ordination of separate parts of the local administration remains a crucial requirement. Such organisational conditions obviously present difficulties for the successful development of a new function, and especially one like economic development which depends upon contributions from several parts of the local administration.

THE FINANCIAL FRAMEWORK

Like nearly all the activities of local authorities economic development and promotion measures have to be financed out of the general budget, and this means that they have to compete for resources with other services, most of which are much more firmly established in the pattern of local spending. As far as the sources of revenue go, it is well known that local authorities depend on three sources – income from rates levied on property, government grants and a range of fees and charges. But the fact that the first and third of these sources of revenue are broadly within the control of local authorities does not mean that securing finance for a new activity is simply a matter for the local authority to settle by raising the yield of those taxes and charges which it controls. The scale of central government grants has enormously increased, and there is, of course, a complex pattern of interdependence between what the Exchequer contributes to local revenues and what the local authorities themselves raise.

Changes in the sources of local government revenue are set out in Table 2.1. The importance of Exchequer grants to local authorities is greater than the figures in Table 2.1 suggest because the total amounts now to over 60 per cent of spending which would otherwise fall to be met from the rates. Most of the income categorised as 'other' is already committed – for example, to the housing revenue account in the case of council house rents and to the commercial operation of public transport

Table 2.1   *Local government revenue in England and Wales:*
percentage share of main sources

	1949/50 %	1973/4 %	1977/8 %
Government grants	34·0	39·6	46·4
Rates	34·0	24·6	23·8
Other[a]	32·0	35·8	29·9

[a] Other includes fees, charges, sales, superannuation and special funds.

Sources: Department of the Environment and Welsh Office, *Local Government Financial Statistics, England & Wales*, 1973/4 and 1977/8 (London: HMSO, 1975 and 1979).

in the case of bus fares. In principle it might be expected that such high levels of Exchequer grant would give to the government departments a great deal of detailed control over local authority activities, but in fact the methods used for the calculation and distribution of funds have not so far worked in that direction.

In assessing the major grant to be paid, the Rate Support Grant, the central government is heavily influenced by the Treasury's view of the correct balance of public expenditure in relation to other demands on the economy and of what the public sector borrowing requirement target should be. These considerations apply both to the calculation of relevant expenditure in relation to which RSG is paid[13] and to the decision on the proportion of such expenditure to be met from the aggregate Exchequer grant. If the sum for relevant expenditure is underestimated by the Treasury, as the local authority associations often claim, and this is accompanied by cash limits on grant increase orders from the Department of the Environment, or if the proportion met from government grant is cut, then clearly this can be expected to have an effect on all local authorities and their activities. The impact of this should be spread evenly unless the distribution of grant between authorities is also altered.

The Rate Support Grant now accounts for about 87 per cent of the aggregate Exchequer grant, and is the residual left after various specific and supplementary grants[14] are subtracted from that total. The RSG's distribution is intended to help equalise rate levels between local authorities and to provide additional funds to those councils with the greatest spending needs. It is divided into three elements – needs, resources and domestic – of which the needs element is the most important, accounting for some 60 per cent of RSG (see Table 2.2).

The RSG is paid as a block grant and once it enters a local authority's accounts it can be spent on any of its activities. The Department of the Environment circular which accompanies the RSG settlement has no

Table 2.2   *The division of RSG into its three elements, 1976/7*

	£m.	% of total RSG
Needs	3,565	60·2
Resources	1,716	29·0
Domestic	640	10·8
	5,921	100·0

Source: N. Hepworth, *The Finance of Local Government*, 4th edn (London: Allen & Unwin, 1978), p. 62.

standing as a legal instruction, being rather an informal estimate of what central government hopes will happen, based on past performance and consultation with local authority associations. It is likely, therefore, to be considered carefully by most authorities, and may even be used in internal arguments about resource allocation, but it is not binding.

It can be seen that the level of Exchequer grant does depend substantially on overall levels of spending by local authorities. In determining their expenditure local authorities have so far been fully autonomous in setting their own rate levels, that is, what they themselves decide to contribute. The rate system with its large lump-sum annual payments has been much criticised inside and outside local government,[15] and the idea of a local income tax has often been canvassed. Nevertheless, the rates remain the most important source of local government revenue outside the control of central government. In the present atmosphere of concern about the levels of local government spending there is reason to suppose that central government is content to leave councils the right to levy an unpopular tax in the hope that it will discourage them from increasing their expenditure.[16] Certainly it remains reluctant to contemplate new sources of local revenue. Even the recent legislation on local authority lotteries (Lotteries and Amusements Act 1976) lays down restrictive rules for raising funds and has not been as useful as some authorities had initially hoped.

Conditions governing capital expenditure differ from those affecting current or revenue spending. All local authorities (except parishes) may borrow to cover their capital expenditure, although other methods (for example, financing from revenue) are also possible as is shown in Table 2.3. In recent years about 20 per cent of local authority expenditure has been in the form of capital spending and only five years ago the proportion was higher, at over 30 per cent.

Local authority capital spending is more closely monitored by central government than is current expenditure. The bulk of the former is on key sector schemes (nearly 81 per cent of local authority borrowing)[17]

Table 2.3   *Methods of financing capital expenditure, 1973/4*

Method of finance	*% of capital expenditure*
Government grants	5
Revenue	10
Sale of capital assets	10
Loans	75
(Public Works Loans Board)	(40)

Source: Report of the Committee of Enquiry into Local Government Finance (Layfield), Cmnd. 6453 (London: HMSO, 1976)

and borrowing to undertake such schemes requires loan sanction from central government. Central government is interested not only in how much borrowing is undertaken, but also in how the loans are spent.

The key sector of local authority capital spending covers the larger capital schemes for those areas in which ministers have responsibilities. It includes schemes in housing and community land (Department of the Environment), education (Department of Education and Science), the police (Home Office), personal social services (Department of Health and Social Security), transportation (Department of Transport). Some schemes are examined separately and loan sanction is granted only if the projects are in line with central government policy. In such areas the scope for local authority initiative is limited, although a council still has the important responsibility of submitting schemes for approval.

Increasingly, however, central government has changed its method of assessing key sector capital spending, both to obviate the need for excessively detailed control, and to encourage local authorities to present their capital requirements as part of an integrated rolling programme rather than in the form of separate justifications for individual schemes. This is intended to enable local authorities and, above all, central government to form a clear picture of policies as well as offering an effective means of budgetary and policy control. This method of allocating capital finance is already used for housing (Housing Investment Programmes) and transport (Transport Policies and Programmes) and is to be extended to capital spending in personal social services. A similar process operated for the Community Land Scheme. This approach probably allows more independence to local authorities in so far as central government is slighly more concerned about overall figures than with particular schemes and once the programme has been approved the local authority can proceed within the agreed limits. Nevertheless, central government amendments to submitted plans remain quite extensive and councils continue to complain that they are subject to excessive detailed control.

In addition to these major capital schemes, the Department of the

Environment annually specifies a maximum figure for locally determined schemes within which local authorities may borrow in order to
finance whatever capital schemes they wish, subject only to the condition that what is proposed must be within their statutory powers. This
sum is divided amongst the local authorities on an agreed basis through
the local authority associations. The sum allocated to the locally determined sector in England and Wales has been significantly reduced over
recent years to £48m. in 1979/80. It was nearly twice as high in real
terms in 1973/4. Capital grants from central government are also available for particular schemes (for example, for land reclamation or under
the Urban Programme) but these represent only a very small part of
local authority capital finance.

Local authority capital spending (like current expenditure) has been
strongly influenced by government attempts to control public expenditure and the public sector borrowing requirement. In the annual public
expenditure survey, the Treasury makes a projection of future local
government capital spending. As already noted it is able to control key
sector spending directly but cannot control other forms of capital
spending so easily. A projection is therefore made of non-key sector
capital spending from which is subtracted the spending expected to be
financed other than by loans (including, for example, lease/lease back
arrangements, and the use of capital funds) and the residual becomes
the Department of the Environment's allocation for locally determined
schemes. In previous years Treasury projections have not accurately
reflected the wishes of the local authorities and they have actively
looked for other sources of finance. This has itself affected the out-turn
of local government capital spending, but instead of revising projections of future spending the central government has simply provided a
diminishing residual amount for locally determined schemes. The
amount for such schemes thus appears to be exposed to the risk of
disappearance.

THE CENTRAL GOVERNMENT AND LOCAL ECONOMIC
INITIATIVES: A FLEXIBLE FRAMEWORK?

There can be no doubt about the dominance of the central government
in relation to public economic policy-making in general. Nor can it be
disputed that central government is the main source of finance for
public measures of intervention in the economy and support for industrial investment. But in relation to the kind of encouragement which
local authorities can give to industrial development the central government has few direct responsibilities and its supervisory or control
powers are limited. Moreover, it has in recent years been the declared
policy of the central government to reduce the degree of detailed
control over the activity of councils, provided they act within their

powers and where relevant within the framework of plans agreed with the appropriate departments of central government.

Admittedly the process of withdrawing from detailed supervision has not gone ahead smoothly and consistently. There have been sudden reversals of policy on particular matters which have been held to be of national or regional importance. The Department of the Environment has continued to monitor many of the activities of local authorities and to apply pressure by letter or circular, behind which there is often the implicit threat of more directive intervention. Under much legislation central government retains substantial residual powers (for example, over the calling in of planning applications) and, if political circumstances were held to require it, there is little doubt that such powers could be applied more vigorously or extended, as is indicated by the present Conservative government's proposals to penalise authorities which increase rates to levels above those acceptable to central government. Similarly central government retains a significant interest in capital spending and its control over some plans, such as Housing Investment Programmes or Transportation Policies and Programmes, has important effects on council activity. Nevertheless, the trend in recent years has been towards overall financial controls combined with extensive use of advice by circular. This latter device often leaves much room for discretionary interpretation by local councils.

What the central government has chiefly done in respect of industrial investment has been to provide a framework of financial incentives, the provision of which has also been directed in part to influencing the distribution of growth as between regions. It is within these general conditions laid down by the centre that local authorities have had to develop their own initiatives.

Policies in support of industrial development have been pursued in recent years primarily through the Department of Industry and to a more limited extent through related agencies such as the National Enterprise Board set up in 1975. The work of the Department of Industry does not involve it in supervising or directing the activities of local authorities, but its intervention is of great significance in setting the framework within which individual local authorities have to operate. Its main tasks have been: first, to implement what may be designated formally or informally as the government's industrial strategy. This work includes the provision of assistance to industries and firms under s. 8 of the Industry Act 1972, the purpose of which is to encourage modernisation and rationalisation. The Department exercises general oversight of the National Enterprise Board which has up to now been expected to work in the same direction. Secondly, the Department has been the principal agent in implementing the government's regional policy, although in this other departments such as Employment, Transport and the Department of the Environment have a stake also. This work includes the provision of financial assistance to firms likely to provide additional employment in specified assisted areas under s. 7 of the Industry Act and the distribution of regional development (capital) grants to those who carry out new investment in the same areas. The Department of Industry is also responsible for an advance factory programme in the assisted areas through the issue of industrial development certificates. No industrial development of over 50,000 sq. ft [18] may now take place outside the Development Areas without such a certificate, and without one no developer can proceed to make a planning application to the local planning authority. [19]

To sum up, the position regarding powers and resources for economic development activities is complex and often ambiguous. Some specific powers to encourage industrial development and the creation of employment exist, but to a large extent local authorities must proceed by adaptive interpretation of their existing powers originally conferred for other purposes. However, there have been important changes in the structure of planning legislation and there is no doubt that these have contributed both to the legitimisation of an economic role for local authorities as well as to the establishment of an approach to planning much more favourable to identification of the economic objectives which sound planning should serve. At the same time organisational and management developments within local authorities appear to have removed many of the obstacles to the emergence of an economic role inherent in the high degree of fragmentation and specialisation which characterised local government internal organisation until the later 1960s.

The general pattern of resource allocation has rendered local authorities highly dependent on central government, and it is clear that when all the pressure is in the direction of restraining public expenditure in general and local spending in particular, this is bound to impose limits on the extent to which local authorities can improve existing services or take steps to establish such new activities as are required for the support of industrial and commercial development. Nevertheless, the financial system does leave substantial discretion to local authorities at the margins in the distribution of their expenditure and this alone makes it easier to accommodate a new function which does not necessarily call for a large slice of expenditure. Whilst it is almost certainly true that the British system of local finance contains no significant incentives to encourage local authorities to embark on economic development programmes, it is also a fact that the system as it presently operates places no insuperable barriers in the way of local authorities which do decide to adopt such programmes.

Finally, there is no doubt that the central government is a major factor in relation both to finance and powers. But its impact on the scale of available financial resources is far more direct than its influence on the manner in which powers are actually used. Whilst important supervisory powers are still exercised by the central government, there has for some years now been a tendency on the part of the central departments to disengage themselves from detailed control of many local government activities. The Department of the Environment in particular has encouraged this trend, although such a policy has not prevented it from continuing to issue a large amount of informal advice to local authorities. In relation to the promotion of economic development by local authorities it is, however, the framework of industrial and regional policy maintained by the central government which has had a more direct bearing on their prospects of success than any action by those departments which actually share in some way in the responsibility for the provision of major local government services.

NOTES

1 This is endorsed in the Bains Report which states that 'Local government is not in our view limited to the narrow provision of a series of services to the local community . . . It has within its purview the overall economic, cultural and physical well-being of that community.' *The New Local Authorities: Management and Structure* (London: HMSO, 1972), p. 6.

2 *The Government's Expenditure Plans 1979–80 to 1972–83*, Cmnd 7439 (London: HMSO, 1979), Table 14.

3 Local authority spending on assistance to industry is included by central government under the heading of local environmental services in its estimates of public spending and more specifically is identified as part of the 'activities carried out under town and country planning powers': ibid., p. 107.

4 *Report of the Royal Commission on Local Government in England* (Redcliffe-Maud), Cmnd 4040 (London: HMSO, 1969), para. 51.

5 See, for example, *The Future of Development Plans: A Report by the Planning Advisory Group* (London: HMSO, 1965), and, more recently, D. Eversley, *The Planner in Society* (London: Faber, 1973).

6 It must be remembered, however, that such policy commitments as are cited here often have a transitory quality apart from sometimes being vaguely stated. The Industrial Strategy, for example, was essentially a summary of the aims of Mr Callaghan's government in relation to industrial development.

7 Tyne and Wear Act 1976, Parts III and IV. The County of South Glamorgan Act 1976 contains similar provisions.

8 For example, leasing a site to a developer at a peppercorn rent on the understanding that certain buildings are erected and then leasing the completed buildings from him. In effect this is a way of borrowing from insurance companies and banks, which often fund the developments, without needing loan sanction. Local authorities usually agree to purchase the buildings at an agreed point or over an agreed period.

9 A further complication arises in the special case of Greater London, the structure of which is closest to that of the metropolitan counties and districts, but also differs in some important respects.

10 Changes in the allocation of functions between the two tiers of the system have recently been mooted, such changes to be brought about by a process of 'organic change'. The principal proposal was that some of the more important functions might be transferred from the counties to the larger districts (in non-metropolitan areas). See *Organic Change in Local Government* Cmnd 7451 (London: HMSO,

1979). Since the change of government in May 1979 such developments have become less likely, except in the planning field where the potential for scrutiny by counties of local plans and development control has already been restricted.

11 For example: *Report of the Committee on the Staffing of Local Government* (Mallaby) (London: HMSO, 1967); *Committee on the Management of Local Government, Report* (Maud) (London: HMSO, 1967); *The Local Authorities*, op. cit.

12 There is an extensive literature on organisational development in local government during the 1970s. See, for example, J. Dearlove, *The Reorganisation of British Local Government* (Cambridge: CUP, 1979); R. Greenwood and J. D. Stewart, *Corporate Planning in Local Government* (London: Knight, 1974); R. Hambleton, *Policy Planning and Local Government* (London: Hutchinson, 1978).

13 The projection of total rate-borne expenditure for the following year.

14 Principally for the police and transport.

15 See *Report of the Committee of Enquiry into Local Government Finance* (Layfield), Cmnd 6453 (London: HMSO, 1976), for a fuller discussion of this.

16 The new Secretary of State for the Environment announced in late 1979 that he was considering how best to discourage local authorities from raising their rates to excessive levels. Legislation to this end involving major changes in the methods of assessing and paying Exchequer grant was introduced in early 1980.

17 Key sector borrowing accounted for 80·9 per cent of capital spending in 1977/8: *The Government's Expenditure Plans 1979–80 to 1982–3*, op. cit., pp. 214–15.

18 Before August 1979 the limit was 15,000 sq. ft (12,500 sq. ft in the south east).

19 Many Development Areas have been downgraded since 1 August 1979, and some have been declared Special Development Areas. Many existing Intermediate Areas are to lose that status over a three year period. The level of regional development grants is to remain the same in Special Development Areas but has been reduced in the Development Areas. No such grants are to be available in the remaining Intermediate Areas, but industrial development certificates will no longer be required. Aid under ss. 7 and 8 of the Industry Act is also to be restricted and most of the special industrial schemes under s. 8 have been withdrawn. The basic structure has not been changed, but it is hoped that the proportion of Britain's employment population living in assisted areas will be reduced from 40 per cent to 25 per cent over the next three years.

Chapter 3

POLICIES AND ACTIVITIES

This chapter is very largely descriptive. In it an attempt is made to present a picture of what economic activities are undertaken and by what means in the seven English local authorities examined, and to show what understanding of economic policy-making opportunities is held by the councils concerned and their administrations. Inevitably, when trying to summarise what happens in several authorities the account becomes complex and detailed. Yet even so substantial simplification has been necessary and a lot of the evidence acquired from each of the case studies has had to be omitted. We begin with a short socio-economic profile of each of the authorities studied. For an account of the terms on which the authorities were selected, the reader is referred to the Appendix at the end of this work.

THE ENGLISH CASES: AN OUTLINE OF THEIR SITUATION AND PROBLEMS

South Yorkshire Metropolitan County Council
The administrative county of South Yorkshire had a distinctive economic and social structure which marks it off from the rest of Yorkshire and Humberside region. It covers an area of 1,550 sq. km and has a population of 1·3m. divided amongst the four district councils of Barnsley, Rotherham, Sheffield and Doncaster. Sheffield is by far the largest district in the county (with a population of 0·56m.), but it is not economically quite so dominant as are some of the largest districts in other metropolitan counties.

The county's major industries are special steels, heavy engineering and coalmining. Less than half the workforce is employed in the service sector, this contrasting sharply with the national figures. The broad picture also disguises important differences between the districts. Sheffield and Rotherham have fewer miners than the county average and Sheffield's steel industry is more concentrated in specialist production than that of Rotherham. Barnsley and Doncaster have a higher than average dependence on coalmining and share the Dearne Valley, where coalmining has traditionally been dominant, with Rotherham.

As a centre of traditional heavy industry, South Yorkshire has a concentration of skilled male manual workers and miners. This means that average wages for male manual workers are higher than the national average, but non-manual workers and women workers tend to be less well paid than in other regions and the female activity rate is lower than the national average. Dependence on declining industries for basic employment also means that South Yorkshire's unemployment levels have consistently been above the national average and concentrated in the districts with the greatest dependence on coalmining and basic steel production. Since its creation South Yorkshire as a whole has been an Intermediate Area under the government's regional policy, but most parts of the county, including Sheffield, are to lose this status by 1982. Mexborough Travel to Work Area and Rotherham Employment Office Area have been up-graded to Development Areas.

City of Sheffield (Metropolitan District Council)
Before 1974 Sheffield was a county borough and despite the alteration of its boundaries as a result of the reorganisation its population was not significantly increased nor was its economic structure altered. Traditionally, despite improvements in the road and rail links to the city which give it easy access all over the country, Sheffield has been a self-contained town rather than a major regional centre like Leeds. One author comments: 'The general impression remains, therefore, of a city which is homogeneous in its population, relatively static in its composition and comparatively unaffected by the outside influences that affect a major centre of commerce or communications.'[1] The city was also described several times in interview as 'the largest village in England'. Nevertheless, Sheffield now constitutes an important source of employment for commuters from beyond its boundaries, and there has been significant private housing development in North East Derbyshire to cater for commuter demand.

Sheffield's employment structure is dominated by industries connected with metal manufacture, metal working and associated engineering. It has not fully established itself as an office and service centre, but the situation has begun to change and between 1971 and 1975 the proportion of Sheffield's workforce in the service sector rose from 42·8 to 48·3 per cent (still below the national figure of 56·3 per cent).[2]

There are serious fears locally that Sheffield's current prosperity, with unemployment below the national average, is insecure. Employment in the city's famous cutlery industry has fallen by half since 1959,[3] although some of this fall has been offset by the transfer of production to high quality metal-ware and hand tools. In the years 1961–71, 25,000 jobs were lost in Sheffield's manufacturing industry[4] and South Yorkshire's structure plan estimates that there will be a further decline of 15·8 per cent over the next ten years.[5] Sheffield's economic security has been based on the strength of specialist engineering firms and the production of special steels even in its British Steel Corporation plants. Many of its steel firms are privately owned and middle-sized, and there is an extensive network of small sub-contractors undertaking work for the larger firms. Despite this traditional strength the city may be vulnerable as a result of the general contraction of employment in manufacturing industry and the international problems of the steel industry.

South Yorkshire and Sheffield: Selected Statistics

Table 3.1   *Industrial structure: percentage of workforce employed in various sectors, 1975*

Industry	South Yorkshire	Sheffield	Great Britain
Primary	10·6	2·3	3·4
Metal Mfg	9·8	13·6	2·3
Metal goods n.e.s.	9·1	14·6	2·6
Vehicles and eng.	7·4	7·1	13·1
Remaining Mfg	11·8	8·5	16·6
Total Mfg	38·1	43·8	34·6
Construction	5·6	5·6	5·8
Services	45·6	48·3	56·3

Source: South Yorkshire Statistics (South Yorkshire County Council, 1976).

Table 3.2   *Percentage of workforce unemployed, 1966–75 and 1979*

	Average unemployment rates, 1966–75	Unemployment rate, February 1979
South Yorkshire	3·4	6·3
South Yorkshire excluding Sheffield	4·4	—
Sheffield	2·4	4·8
Great Britain	2·8	5·9

Source: An Economic and Social Survey, Vol. 1 (South Yorkshire County Council, 1975), and the *Department of Employment Gazette*.

Nottinghamshire County Council

Nottinghamshire has a population of nearly 1m. and covers an area of 2,164 sq. km and Nottingham is the most populous of its eight districts – the others are Bassetlaw, Mansfield, Newark, Ashfield, Gedling, Broxtowe and Rushcliffe.

The county can be divided (as it is in the structure plan)[6] into three distinct economic systems. The first, Greater Nottingham and its hinterland, contains 60 per cent of the county's population and is dependent on employment in the Nottingham conurbation. Traditionally this has been a prosperous area with a wide range of manufacturing employment and a high female activity rate, particularly in textile manufacture. Until the late 1960s its population was growing, but recently there has been a drop in population and the economic base seems to have become slightly less secure. There has been a dramatic decline in female employment in manufacturing both as a result of national pressures and because some firms have moved to neighbouring areas (the traditional mining areas) where there is a surplus of cheaper female labour. Greater Nottingham still has a wide range of middle-sized manufacturing concerns supported by a significant and expanding service sector, but unemployment is now rising for male workers, particularly in the City of Nottingham. Whilst the increase in service employment has compensated for the decline of manufacturing employment the overall loss of jobs in the system (also taking employment changes in mining, agriculture, construction and other areas into account) amounted to nearly 3,000 between 1966 and 1974.

The second area, the mining system, contains 30 per cent of the county's population and 36 per cent of its male employment is in mining. In the 1960s there was a significant decline in mining employment and more pit closures were predicted for the 1970s. Large parts of Nottinghamshire's coalfields were declared Intermediate Areas[7] to help counteract this decline, but the scale of closures has been less than expected. The concentration in mining still presents problems because male employment fell between 1966 and 1974 and is expected to continue to fall. But in recent years this has been offset by the local growth of manufacturing (against the national trend) and service employment. In the years 1966–74 the total number of jobs available in the mining system rose slightly while there was a fall in the county as a whole so that the mining system (if the structure plan's estimates for the run-down of mining employment can be accepted and major pit closures can be excluded) is no longer quite as vulnerable as in the past.

Thirdly, the rural system contains just over 9 per cent of the county's population spread over small settlements and the two small towns of Castleford and Newark. Ten per cent of its male employment is in agriculture and there is a continued slow decline in agricultural employment, but the system's main problems stem from a decline in manufacturing employment in the two towns. Between 1966 and 1974 nearly half Nottinghamshire's employment decline took place in this system. Matters have improved since 1974, but the rural system still has unemployment levels above those of the county as a whole, particularly for women.

City of Nottingham (District Council)

Nottingham is not only the centre of a wider and dependent economic system in the south of Nottinghamshire, but also provides employment for commuters from a significant area of Leicestershire and Derbyshire.

Nottingham includes the older parts of the conurbation and has few greenfield sites for new development since its suburbs come within the jurisdiction of other district councils and its population of 287,000 (1974) is only about 57 per cent of the conurbation's total.

Nottingham is usually seen as a prosperous city with a balanced economic structure and an important role as a regional, commercial, shopping and cultural centre. Its manufacturing firms have been a source of strength because they have typically been of medium size and it is not dominated by any one firm or any one industry, for example employers include manufacturers of pharmaceuticals, bicycles, cigarettes and cigars, furniture, stage lighting, textiles and clothing.

In recent years, however, its manufacturing base has shown signs of weakness. Over the past ten years manufacturing jobs have been lost at four times the rate in Great Britain as a whole and service employment has grown at less than half the national rate. The decline has hit female employment (concentrated in textiles and clothing) and small firms in the inner city particularly hard. The structure plan states: 'It is likely that most of the loss of manufacturing jobs from the conurbation between 1966 and 1973 was from the inner area', and this has been confirmed by other studies.[8] Nottingham's unemployment is now as high as the national average and is higher still in some parts of the city. It is higher than in the East Midlands as a whole, and higher too than in Nottinghamshire's erstwhile assisted areas.

Nottinghamshire and Nottingham: Selected Statistics

Table 3.3   *Percentage employment by industrial sector and sex, 1974*

	Nottingham[a]			GNHS[b]			Notts.			Great Britain		
	M	F	T	M	F	T	M	F	T	M	F	T
Agriculture }	3	0	2	1	0	1	2	1	2	3	1	2
Mining }				6	1	4	15	1	10	2	0	1
Manufacturing	35	30	33	37	33	35	34	36	34	37	26	33
Construction }				10	1	6	10	1	6	11	1	7
Services }	62	70	65	46	64	53	39	60	47	46	71	56
Other }				0	1	0	0	1	1	1	1	1

[a] 1975 figures
[b] Greater Nottingham and Hinterland System
Sources: 'Nottingham . . . known for the company it keeps!' (City of Nottingham, n.d.), and *Nottinghamshire Structure Plan, Report of Survey* (Nottinghamshire County Council, n.d.), p. 57.

Table 3.4   *Percentage of workforce unemployed, 1977 and 1979*

	April 1977	*February 1979*
Nottingham	5·8	5·3
Nottingham Employment Exchange Area[a]	5·5	—
Bulwell and Basford Employment Exchange Area[a]	6·9	—
Workshop Intermediate Area	4·8	—
Erewash Intermediate Area	4·3	—
Nottinghamshire	4·9	5·3
East Midlands	4·9	5·2
Great Britain	5·8	5·9

[a] Nottingham EEA and Bulwell and Basford EEA together make up Nottingham. Bulwell and Basford covers both a peripheral council estate and a part of the city's inner area. They do not, of course, constitute Journey to Work Areas so that the figure should be treated with great caution.

Sources: 'The Inner City' (City of Nottingham, 1975), and *Department of Employment Gazette.*

Cambridgeshire County Council

Cambridgeshire is the most western county of East Anglia, bordering on the East Midlands and the South East region. It is a medium-sized county, covering an area of 3,410 sq. km with a population of 560,000 (1976) and a mixture of urban and rural development spread over its six districts (Cambridge, East Cambridgeshire, Fenland, Huntingdon, Peterborough and South Cambridgeshire). Although it contains two cities with populations over 100,000 (Peterborough and Cambridge), over one-third of its urban population lives in towns with populations of between 5,000 and 20,000.

Cambridgeshire has been one of the fastest growing counties since the war in terms of population and East Anglia is the fastest growing region. This growth has been the result both of voluntary migration and deliberate policy through the town development schemes at St Neots and Huntingdon and the new town development at Peterborough. Although some of the migration has been of commuters working in North Hertfordshire and London, the growth in employment in the county also rose by 15 per cent between 1963 and 1973.[9] Despite this overall picture of growth two districts, East Cambridgeshire and, still more, Fenland, have faced problems of stagnation. Whilst the population of all the districts rose between 1971 and 1976, in Fenland this was only possible on the basis of large-scale out-commuting for employment.

Except in the districts of Peterborough and Cambridge, Cambridgeshire has a level of agricultural employment well above the national average. The land is very good for arable farming and is particularly good in the Fens where there is also significant horticultural development. The decline in agricultural employment has been particularly notable: the numbers employed fell by more than a half between 1954 and 1974 to less than 13,000.[10] This reflects significantly increased productivity rather than a declining industry and has been accompanied by a county-wide shift to employment in manufacturing and professional and administrative services.

The county has a wide range of manufacturing industry, with different types prominent in different areas, including high technology-based firms in and around Cambridge. While manufacturing has decreased as a source of employment nationally, it has significantly increased in Cambridgeshire and service employment has risen by far more than the national average, with much of this concentrated in Cambridge and South Cambridgeshire.

The county's unemployment rate has been consistently below the national average and only Fenland has had serious unemployment problems. But levels in Peterborough are now close to the national average and there is concern that the situation in Huntingdon may deteriorate as the children of those who moved under the town development scheme enter the labour market.

City of Peterborough (District Council)

Peterborough is now the most populous of Cambridgeshire's districts (118,900 – 1976) and its population is likely to rise significantly because its urban area is designated for new town expansion. The city experienced fast population growth in the 1950s and 1960s, but since 1968 (when the new town was designated) the rate of increase has been still faster, despite the decline in the national rate.

Although Peterborough has good access to north–south and east–west road and rail routes, the links with Cambridge (the county's administrative centre) are not so good. It is more closely linked in economic terms to the East and West Midlands and the east coast ports. It is still a market centre for agriculture (for example, staging the East of England Show), but the importance of this has declined and the proportion of agricultural employment is below the national average.

In the mid-nineteenth century Peterborough became an important rail centre and first moved away from its role as a market town. In the early 1960s it became clear that there was going to be a significant drop in rail employment and there was a danger of long-term decline for the city. Despite the fall in its employment, British Rail is still one of the ten largest employers in Peterborough and Peterborough is still heavily dependent on a limited range of firms and industries (concentrated in the manufacturing sector). Four engineering firms account for 25 per cent of the city's employment and 62 per cent of manufacturing employment.[11] Peterborough's employment base has broadened since the early 1960s. Most of the employment growth has been in the service sector.

Nevertheless, in recent years unemployment has begun to rise in line with national trends. This reflects the city's concentration of employment in manufacturing industry and the special problems it faces as an expanding town seeking to attract new industry and employment in a period of recession.

Fenland District Council

Fenland is in the north east of Cambridgeshire, close to the Wash. It covers an area of 546 sq. km and with a population of 66,000 (1976) has a significantly lower population density than the rest of the county. It consists of four main urban settlements (Wisbech, March, Whittlesey and Chatteris) with small rural settlements between them and is not dominated by any single town. Wisbech and March are the largest of these and there has traditionally been rivalry between them.

Table 3.5   *Population of Fenland's main towns, 1976*

	Population	Population as % of district population
Wisbech	17,200	25·8
March	14,900	22·4
Whittlesey	11,200	16·8
Chatteris	6,000	9·0
	49,300	74·0

Source: 'Industry in Fenland' (Fenland District Council, 1978).

The isolation of Fenland is emphasised by its poor contact with the national road and rail system. Only one trunk road passes through the district, at its northern tip in Wisbech, and although March is still a major British Rail marshalling yard, it is important for through traffic from the Haven ports to the north rather than traffic generated in Fenland. The port at Wisbech provides a useful outlet for some local trade and the import of agricultural goods like fertilisers, but it is likely to remain small.

Fenland is an important agricultural area. The increasing efficiency of agriculture has, however, brought a dramatic decline in agricultural employment, coupled with high levels of seasonal employment in fruit-picking in the horticultural areas. In 1975 the proportion of Fenland's employees in agriculture was nearly ten times that for England and Wales and a large part of the district's manufacturing employment is in agriculture-related industry such as canning, sugar-processing and the production of fertilisers. Although there was an increase in manufacturing and administrative employment between 1961 and 1971, this was far outweighed by the decline in agricultural and other employment (mainly British Rail in March). In the years since 1971 this process has continued.

These conditions have had a number of important consequences for Fenland: its population has until recently been growing more slowly than the national average and its average age is rising; it has an unbalanced labour force with a large preponderance of manual employees and a very small professional sector; there is a very high rate of out-commuting for employment and there is the low female activity rate common in rural areas. Nevertheless, when new manufacturing industry has come to Fenland it has tended to use more female labour so that between 1971 and 1976 female employment increased by over a third in Wisbech and March and between the same years male employment fell by 22 per cent in March and 6 per cent in Wisbech.

Cambridgeshire, Peterborough and Fenland: Selected Statistics

Table 3.6 *Employment structure: percentage of workforce employed in various sectors, 1975*

	Agriculture	Manufacturing and minerals	Administrative and professional	Other
Fenland	16·5	24·7	19·6	39·2
Peterborough	1·4	39·7	19·5	39·4
Cambridgeshire	6·0	28·8	27·8	37·5
England and Wales	1·7	34·8	27·8	35·7

Source: Cambridgeshire Facts and Figures (Cambridgeshire County Council, 1976).

Table 3.7 *Percentage of workforce unemployed, 1974–6 and 1979*

Employment Exchange Area	Approximate equivalent district	June 1974	June 1975	June 1976	February 1979
March/Wisbech	Fenland	2·6	4·8	8·0	—
Peterborough	Peterborough	1·7	2·9	5·7	5·9
Cambridgeshire	—	—	—	4·5	4·6
Great Britain	—	2·3	3·7	5·6	5·9

Sources: Cambridgeshire Facts and Figures, op. cit., and *Department of Employment Gazette.*

LOCAL AUTHORITY GOALS

It is natural to treat goals as logically prior to the policies and activities which are developed for their achievement. According to this view activities have the status of means appropriate to the realisation of such objectives as have been established. But in reality there is often a far less clear relationship between what an organisation seeks to achieve and the specific policies and methods of implementation which it adopts. Stated goals may be of such a general nature that it can be claimed on behalf of a very wide range of policies and activities that they contribute to their fulfilment. Equally any particular statement of goals may in fact emerge from and serve as a justification for policies developed in response to very specific needs or demands and have little direct connection with broad functional objectives. The question posed here, and underlying our study of the seven cases, is whether local authorities set economic goals to which some of their policies and activities are plainly instrumental, or whether the goals they claim to have generally emerge from the aggregate of their activities.

The attempt to answer this question is made difficult by the fact that quite different levels of goal definition are often mixed together in local authority documents and decisions. These levels can best be divided as follows:

(a)   broad objectives and aspirations affecting the whole range of the authority's work;
(b)   operationalisable aims and policies with goals appropriate to functional sectors;
(c)   particular activities and instruments expressing specific objectives in action.

The uncertainties stemming from this tendency to mix up goals of differing degrees of generality are likely to be greater in a field like economic development, in part because it cuts across a wide spectrum of local programmes and in part because it is a relatively new sector of local authority activity and is not rooted in well-defined statutory commitments or operational procedures.

All of the local authorities concerned in this study expressed a commitment to economic policy-making, at least in the sense that their officers and councillors saw themselves as committed to the pursuit of broad aims under the first of the above headings. Needless to say, the connections between such general goals and specific policies are not always easy to establish. All of the authorities, for example, wanted adequate levels of local employment for their residents, an aim which could be interpreted differently by different councils. Cambridgeshire was concerned only that enough employment should be available for its existing population and for natural increases, although there is likely to be a continued high level of immigration to the county from other parts of the country. Peterborough, on the other hand, wanted a sufficient increase in employment opportunities to cater for new arrivals encouraged to move there by the Development Corporation, whilst South Yorkshire and Fenland hoped that employment would be attracted to counteract the predicted fall in population likely to be accelerated by loss of jobs in existing industries.

Several of the authorities were concerned that employment should grow in areas with particularly severe economic problems. This view was most clearly argued by South Yorkshire County Council which identified Job Priority Areas and Environmental Priority Areas in its structure plan and called for development in each, but above all where the areas coincided. Cambridgeshire's structure plan takes a discriminatory approach by actually attempting to restrict development in the south and to a lesser extent in the west of the county, whilst encouraging development in its north eastern parts. Nottingham and Sheffield are both now committed to countering economic decline in their inner areas. The Nottinghamshire/Derbyshire sub-regional study[12] together with early drafts of Nottinghamshire's structure plan and the county's initial economic development policies were directed towards the Mansfield/Ashfield area and the surrounding mining settlements. But more recent policy statements have argued that employment growth is needed throughout the county and that no emphasis should be placed on particular areas.

All of the cases except Cambridgeshire aimed for a diversification of their industrial structures, and particularly for an increase in office, professional and administrative employment. In Fenland the emphasis was on the need to increase non-agricultural employment, and small-scale manufacturing industry was favoured; in South Yorkshire, Sheffield and Nottingham the need for new service employment was strongly emphasised. Both Sheffield and South Yorkshire identified specific industries as priorities for their promotional and publicity campaigns.

All of the local authorities were concerned about the future levels of population in their areas and several had developed specific population goals. South Yorkshire and Fenland were particularly concerned to stem out-migration, and whilst Cambridgeshire was prepared to accept necessary growth, it wanted to avoid excessive strain in its southern part. Peterborough, consistent with the master plan prepared by the Development Corporation and revised by the Secretary of State for the Department of the Environment, aimed for a population of 160,000 in its urban area by the mid-1980s (that is, a growth of about 60 per cent) and would have preferred to have adhered to the master plan's original target of 180,000. Both Cambridgeshire and Fenland were concerned to reduce the levels of out-commuting for employment by their residents.

The efficient management of council-owned land is a goal which can have important implications for local firms seeking land and premises.

The need to develop and dispose of existing council-owned land was particularly important in Sheffield which owns a great deal of land unsuitable for housing and recreational development accumulated as a result of past redevelopment policies. Similar pressures exist, on a smaller scale, in Peterborough and Nottingham.

The formulation of broad economic goals was easiest to observe at county council level, chiefly because such goals are encouraged by the structure plans. At district level it was generally more difficult to find occasions for such explicit statements and they were often contained in proposals for specific action or in the reports of relevant departments or officers. The development of policies from stated goals can be illustrated by reference to the case of South Yorkshire. South Yorkshire's structure plan outlined the basic goals in some detail in its chapter on employment,[13] including details of necessary employment growth in sub-county areas, and from these the officers prepared more detailed proposals for action, both in planning department documents[14] and in the Corporate and Financial Plans for the economic development programme area.[15] The methods of policy development in the other authorities have been more pragmatic, but not necessarily any less effective. In Nottingham a brief set of proposals was prepared through the corporate structure and presented by the Chief Executive as the basis for economic action. In addition an impetus was expected to develop from the work of the Industrial and Commercial Development Officer. In Fenland the main commitment has been to appoint an Industrial Development Officer responsible for initiating policies in conjunction with the Chief Planning Officer. Cambridgeshire's structure plan stated broad economic goals, but the development of more detailed policies was clearly expected to be the result of an accumulation of decisions on specific issues. Nottinghamshire's policies have been the result both of overall strategic concerns and of the work of its Economic Development Division whose reports have provided the basis for policy discussions. Sheffield's 'Objectives',[16] which outlined both medium-term and more immediate policy aims for a wide range of council functions, provided essentially a description of how the current situation had taken shape.

To sum up this account of the variations in approach to the definition of goals, it appears that economic goals are in fact expressed chiefly as a general justification for specific measures rather than in the form of precisely stated regulative guidelines on the basis of which policies are then worked out. It should be underlined too that these economic goals often merge into a general concern for the well-being of the local authority's area to which other policies, for example those falling under land use planning, are seen as making a major contribution. Referring back to the question posed earlier it can be seen that there is a certain degree of artificiality in attempting to work from goals to activities, despite the influence of the appreciable shift towards corporate planning which has taken place and which means that it has become common for local authorities to claim that the activities of their separate departments are integrated within a wider framework of authority objectives. It remains true that in general broad policy objectives proceed from or support particular activities rather than determine very decisively what is to be done. Thus it becomes necessary to look in more detail at the range of activities undertaken and methods of encouraging economic development actually used. On this basis it becomes possible to see how more narrowly stated sectoral aims and policies can be fitted into the broader statements of purpose in which local authorities express their views of overall policy goals.

ECONOMIC ACTIVITIES

Local authority economic activities can be put into seven main categories, the importance of which varies significantly.

The provision of land and premises
The ability to provide suitable land and premises to industry is one of the few direct incentives councils can provide. The presentation of a full package of serviced land and, for smaller firms, advance factories may persuade a potential developer or new employer in a marginal situation. Similar arguments hold for retail developments and local authority assistance has been crucial to the development of a number of shopping complexes, for example in Nottingham. The importance of land as an instrument of economic policy is well understood and all of the authorities clearly committed to economic development work were also committed to intervention through the management of land and premises. Only Cambridgeshire was not involved in the provision of land for industrial development. This was due to various factors: opposition to the use of the Community Land Act, a commitment to the restriction of spending levels, and reluctance to formulate a policy involving a measure of public intervention into an already efficient economy held to be operating, in general, to the county's advantage.[17]

The larger districts, particularly Sheffield, are most active in the provision of land for industrial development whilst the county councils generally still need to build up land-holdings. Sheffield has large holdings of industrial land – two-thirds of the city's industrial land is shared between the British Steel Corporation, the Duke of Norfolk's estate and the city council. These holdings have accumulated over generations into a substantial corporate estate and the authority is able to offer serviced land of its own not only for industrial estate development, which is important, but also for larger commercial developments. Even if it is unable itself to supply the necessary land to a potential developer its agreement with the other major landowners usually ensures that suitable sites can be made available. Nottingham, too, has extensive landholdings and in 1978 a survey of industrial land available showed that 57 per cent of available land was city-owned.[18] But Nottingham's role is more restricted than Sheffield's because the tightness of the city's boundaries excludes the possibility of greenfield development and the industrial land freed in the course of urban redevelopment has not been so extensive.

Nottinghamshire and South Yorkshire own far less land and their estates functions are, therefore, more limited. Both, however, have been active in trying to accumulate land for future development, usually in the form of industrial estates. South Yorkshire County Council which inherited only a small amount of land from previous councils was one of the most active users of the Community Land Act and by 1978 owned 60 hectares of industrial land.[19] Its plans are for continued expansion. Before 1974 Nottinghamshire followed a deliberate policy of accumulating a land bank in the Mansfield/Ashfield area, but as council policies moved against the idea of the Mansfield/Alfreton growth zone, so the land bank policy was dropped. The Community Land Act 1975 also made it impossible to follow the policy since the Act required a relatively quick return on land purchases. The county council's largest industrial estates are in the Ashfield district and when completed will cover about 49 hectares.

The smaller district councils have been involved on a far more limited scale in land acquisition. In Peterborough the council has offered some small plots of its own land for industrial development and the bulk of Fenland's industrial land remains the stock of 30 acres bequeathed by Wisbech Municipal Borough. Although Fenland district also has a ninety-five-year lease on some developed land in March it appears to have been slow in supplying land outside Wisbech to COSIRA, the Council for Small Industries in Rural Areas, for its proposed developments.

All of these authorities are also engaged in varying degrees in the provision of advance factories. Whilst Sheffield's main emphasis is on the provision of serviced land rather than unit factories and its officers see no reason to become heavily involved in factory-building already being carried out effectively by private developers, the city has a policy of constructing units at the lower end of the market and this programme of unit factory construction is expected to increase under the inner city programme. Advance factory construction is central to the policies of Nottingham, Nottinghamshire, South Yorkshire and Fenland councils. Nottingham already owns twenty-seven advance factory units and Nottinghamshire has been involved in their provision since before reorganisation. The county now commonly leases land from one of its districts for a peppercorn rent, constructs a factory unit, leases it and shares the proceeds with the district concerned.[20] South Yorkshire has not only used the Community Land Act extensively to purchase land, but also to develop advance factories. The county's estates are intended to consist largely of advance factories and, unusually for a local authority, it has envisaged the provision of 'nursery' office units on one site.

It is now widely accepted that the private market is not always able to provide adequate premises for smaller firms, chiefly because it is not sufficiently profitable to do so, in part because of planning and other controls. Many small firms are used to cheap, older (often inefficient) premises and cannot afford to pay fully commercial rents. Most of the advance factories provided by local authorities are between 600 and 2,500 sq. ft, although some authorities also provide slightly larger or smaller premises. The upper limit is the level at which private developers are likely to provide premises, whilst some of the smaller units are for one or two man firms. In many cases the units can be combined to provide space for larger firms or to allow growth by smaller businesses. In Peterborough the leasing of rather larger units (up to 8,000 sq. ft) has proved difficult because wider marketing is needed than can adequately be organised by the city. In contrast the smaller units can be easily marketed locally. South Yorkshire on the other hand is committed to a national marketing campaign and its larger units are held to be useful in forwarding this.

There has been some suggestion that local authority provision of premises may be reaching saturation point, but the evidence is inconclusive. None of the local authorities in this study was having any difficulty in disposing of small premises, most of which could be leased well before completion. In Nottinghamshire premises are often disposed of as soon as the plans have been completed. Despite the growth in advance factory construction by councils the amounts involved remain small. Sheffield's programme of construction (30,000 sq. ft per year)[21] is currently the largest amongst the cases studied, although South Yorkshire was planning a far more extensive development of up to 117,000 sq. ft of new factory space for 1979/80.[22]

Even on council-owned estates and in their advance factories, the cost of premises remains high for many small firms. Attempts by authorities to cut costs and, therefore, rents, have included compromises on planning policies and external design on some new inner city estates and an element of rent subsidy. Even so, new premises of any sort are bound to be costly compared to the very low rents in inner city areas (some small firms in 1978 in Nottingham paid £3 per week compared to £20 per week market rents for, admittedly, superior new premises which were then the only alternatives). Several authorities have, therefore, attempted to convert older premises into smaller units. For example, Nottinghamshire County converted several obsolete schools into small workshops, whilst Nottingham City offered a small number of 'house-shells' in inner city clearance areas for industrial use, leaving the new occupants to provide all but the basic services. Nottingham also undertook the conversion of an old canal warehouse for both council and commercial use and South Yorkshire has plans to refurbish a large factory in Thorne. Nevertheless, such premises cannot be as good as new units and after conversion it has sometimes been difficult to let them.

Promotion and publicity

Promotional campaigns are an important part of local authority economic activity, even if they are concerned only with the marketing of sites for development. The amount of resources devoted to them and the form of the campaigns vary significantly between authorities. Sheffield's promotional activity is the most ambitious and provides a useful illustration of the extent to which a local authority can develop in this direction and against which other local authorities can be viewed.

The city's work on industrial promotion is organised through the Industrial Development Officer and the council's publicity department. The budget for industrial development, excluding staff and administrative costs and capital spending, was over £36,000 in 1977/8 and this does not take the significant contributions from the publicity department into account. The publicity material produced ranges from literature extolling the virtues of Sheffield as a place of residence to details of particular developments and packages describing sites and premises available in the city. Much of the broad publicity, including the tourist publicity, is aimed at overcoming Sheffield's reputation as a grimy industrial city, so that it becomes attractive for more modern industrial and office development. When offices move away from London it is often as important to persuade existing staff as senior management. This concern permeates the material directed at potential developers and new employers too. A quarterly publication, 'Development Sheffield', produced for that audience contains regular reference to the city's potential as an office and commercial centre and its advantages over the congested south east both for firms and their employees. It and other literature emphasise that Sheffield is based on skilled and specialist industries with a versatile labour force and a good industrial relations record. Brochures and leaflets have been produced to help local firms expand their sales abroad and the emphasis on specialist firms is also intended to improve the city's image amongst potential investors. In addition to the production of its own publicity literature, the city carries out advertising campaigns in the property press and in specialist magazines such as *Trade & Industry*.

The active search for new investment and new orders for local firms involves a heavy commitment by Sheffield to two kinds of exhibition work. Touring exhibitions with audio-visual aids as well as printed material have been organised in the south east of England. These have been mainly intended to attract inward investment, although some of the special exhibitions in London (including one at the Design Centre) have been based on the recurrent theme of the high quality of Sheffield's metal goods. Similar touring exhibitions have been organised in Europe, concentrating on parts of Western Germany, and the council sponsored a delegation to the west coast of the USA. As well as attempting to attract inward investment, one of the purposes of the latter was to attract new orders and to learn what skills were needed to sell goods in the American market. A brochure 'Business Opportunities in Sheffield' was prepared as part of this campaign and the trip was followed by seminars on the American market for firms in Sheffield. Visits to the city for German businessmen have been organised in the past in order to introduce them to representatives of local firms, to encourage orders for locally produced goods and to promote investment in the city.

Sheffield takes part in trade and industrial exhibitions in Britain and Europe. Again its participation has the dual purpose of attracting industry and helping existing local firms. At exhibitions of industries which are not represented in Sheffield the emphasis will, of course, be on the attraction of new firms, but the council also makes it possible for local firms to attend large exhibitions by providing a stand and professional and advertising expertise where appropriate. This assistance has been particularly important at foreign exhibitions – in 1973, for example, a stand was organised at the Gothenburg World Trade Fair and seventy companies were represented, selling £1¼m. worth of their goods. More recently, in 1978, Sheffield's stand at Interidex (a world exhibition of industrial development) was shared with ten concerns (mainly firms interested in property development).

Sheffield's promotional activity is not indiscriminate. The Industrial Development Office has identified a number of industries which it would like to see develop further and it is towards these that publicity campaigns are directed. These industries are mainly complementary to rather than competitive with existing industry, partly in order to avoid increased pressure on wages due to extra demand for the same type of labour. On the other hand the degree of discrimination implied in this promotional activity should not be exaggerated. In practice the authority would probably accept most new development even if falling outside its stated preferences.

Of the other authorities South Yorkshire has the most consistent promotional input, following Sheffield's pattern, but with more limited resources. It, too, produces publicity literature, both general and advertising its own developments, and attends exhibitions in Britain and abroad. It does not, however, have its own touring exhibitions. Nor does it prepare a register of available industrial and commercial property, chiefly because such information is obtainable at district level, and the county sees one of its main tasks as the attraction of inquiries which may be passed on. Like Sheffield, South Yorkshire has identified those industries and companies which are felt to be suitable for expansion in the county and this guides the orientation of its advertising and attendance at exhibitions. The county council is concerned too to help promote local firms, probably putting more emphasis on this than Sheffield as far as British exhibitions are concerned.

Nottinghamshire's main promotional work in the past has been limited to the marketing of its own property and the distribution of information about other available property (issuing a bi-monthly Property and Sites Register). It has prepared some short leaflets, carried out some national advertising and attended a small number of exhibitions (for example, Interidex on the Department of Industry stand), but has until recently not attempted to launch a major publicity campaign mainly because of its success in the provision of land and premises, particularly in the Ashfield area. Unlike Sheffield it cannot follow up a major campaign with the offer of land and this induces some caution. Since 1978, however, the promotional side has expanded with the appointment of a part-time consultant to attract investment from abroad and elsewhere in Britain. The county has used the success of Nottingham Forest Football Club in the European Cup to promote the area, organising exhibitions in the cities visited by the club, as well as several others. The 1978/9 promotional budget of £12,800 was to be doubled in 1979/80.

Nottingham's involvement in promotional activity has also increased since its Industrial and Commercial Development Unit was set up in December 1976, particularly after the appointment of a full-time officer in 1978. The Unit prepares registers of all industrial sites and industrial and commercial property, has begun to take part in relevant exhibitions (for example, Furnex at the National Exhibition Centre, 1978) to attract new industry, and is beginning to build up a set of leaflets based on a brochure entitled 'Nottingham . . . known for the company it keeps'.

Fenland's advertising campaign is helped by contributions from developers and Cambridgeshire County Council. It keeps records and printed descriptions of most available property and supplies to inquirers a printed booklet of local details ('Industry in Fenland'). Like the others it advertises in the specialist press, but has taken part only in one small exhibition in Cambridge, along with Cambridgeshire and the Council for Small Industries in Rural Areas. It was also planning to take part in the East of England Show through the Mid-Anglia Industrial Development Association, in whose foundation the district's Industrial Development Officer played an important part. Since Fenland's resources are far smaller than those of the other authorities it is most concerned with intra-regional moves.

At the bottom end of the scale Cambridgeshire and Peterborough are involved in promotional activity only to a very small degree. The former has prepared a register of available property, largely to help deal with inquiries, whilst the latter is concerned to market its own property, mainly locally. In addition Peterborough district can rely extensively on the Development Corporation's efforts to make the town widely known to developers. Both authorities also have minor inputs into the promotion of tourism, providing or helping with the provision of tourist information.

Several local authorities have policies designed to boost tourism as part of their moves to increase service employment. Most authorities co-operate with their regional tourist boards and some carry out their own promotional activity, helping to encourage weekend trips from Holland, for example, in the case of Nottingham. Nottinghamshire's publicity (like Nottingham's own) has emphasised the facilities of the city as well as the National Water Sports Centre at Holme Pierrepont and various country parks. Much of the tourist publicity produced has a dual purpose, to attract tourists if possible and to improve the general reputation of the authority and its area. Sheffield, for example, is unlikely ever to become a major tourist centre, but is clearly concerned to make itself more attractive in the eyes of potential investors.

Closely related to the objective of attracting tourists to fill hotels is the more easily quantifiable search for conference custom. The two largest district councils are particularly proud of their records in attracting conference business. In both cases the publicity office or department works closely with local hotels and helps with publicity. Sheffield, as befits its size and the greater difficulty of presenting itself as a conference centre in competition with the traditional spa and coastal towns, gives greater resources to the task, but the intention is the same – to keep hotel rooms filled and even to encourage the opening of new hotels.

Information and advice
All the active authorities employ an industrial development officer of some sort, although his title and functions are rarely identical. Only in Peterborough, where the Development Corporation is so important, is there no officer specifically designated as responsible for industrial development – even Cambridgeshire has an officer in the planning department working part-time on such matters, although with no distinctive title. Clearly some of the activities discussed elsewhere are also the responsibility of the various industrial development officers, but one of their tasks everywhere is the provision of information and advice. Industrial development officers usually act as contacts for local firms and potential new industry and they help them by explaining council procedure, for example, on planning, and by helping to

overcome any similar obstacles such as the completion of forms applying for government grants. They tend to see themselves as spokesmen for industrialists within the authority, trying to represent their interests in decision-taking. They emphasise the need for personal contact with employers rather than the simple provision of advertising and information material.

Nottinghamshire provides a good example of the advice work which can be offered, even to large companies. The possibility of a development by Kodak was first raised in 1972,[23] and the present assistant director of the economic development division of the department of planning and transportation met representatives of the company at that time. He was able to suggest possible sites in the 'growth zone' which had been identified as suitable for large-scale prestige development in the Mansfield/Alfreton Interim Master Plan 1971. Kodak had looked at other sites elsewhere in the country at the request of the Department of Industry which would have preferred the project to be sited in one of the Development Areas. These were all considered unsuitable because the process Kodak proposed to use would be harmed by atmospheric pollution. One of the sites in the county (Annesley) proved to be the best on this and other grounds.

Officers of the Economic Development Division encouraged the development from the outset and in the event the county and district councils both favoured the project. Co-operation between the local authorities and the firm was necessary, because the site was on good agricultural land and in the Sketch Green Belt which meant that many safeguards to protect the environment required early discussion. The issues were presented to county, district and parish councillors and a series of public participation exercises were carried out by Kodak in co-operation with the local authorities and the press. The application was a substantial departure from the approved Development Plan and was called in by the secretary of state. He ruled however that the county could itself determine the application, provided it was satisfied that full public consultation had taken place. Kodak was advised throughout the planning process on the stages to be gone through for planning clearance and how best to prepare the proposals. This development covers 93 hectares and is expected to take place gradually over the next twenty years, providing employment for 4,000 people in the 1990s and the planning permission had to encompass this long-term and gradual evolution. Such a development is important for the county since it will help to balance a gradual decline in employment in mining and textiles in the surrounding communities.

When firms are planning to move or thinking of moving to a new area with existing staff, some authorities are able to offer detailed information and assistance to the movers and this is generally organised by publicity departments. This has been true particularly of Sheffield and

Nottingham. In Sheffield the two important moves by the Midland Bank and the Manpower Services Commission to offices in the city were accompanied by seminars in London and Sheffield on housing, education and other local facilities, and coach trips were organised to show what the city was like and the types of housing available. Only in a small number of cases (for example, where government departments are being relocated) are existing employees or their representatives extensively consulted, but such activities are generally held to be useful even if a decision has already been made, because they are expected to help in the attraction of others. Sheffield has used the Midland Bank move as a major feature in its promotional literature. An article from *Trade & Industry* was reprinted in 'Development Sheffield', for example, in which the manager of the Sheffield division of the Midland Bank International was quoted as saying that 'given that we had to move, we couldn't have gone to a better place'.[24]

Business advice of a more technical nature is also offered by some local authorities. South Yorkshire's Economic Services Section has in the past prepared details of available European Community grants and helps with advice (with others in the Employment Promotion Unit) on the availability of central government assistance. Nottinghamshire has now appointed a full-time liaison officer to advise and assist small and medium-sized firms wishing to expand or set up business for the first time, apparently taking on a role similar to the Department of Industry's Small Firms Information Centres. Many industrial development officers perform a similar if less extensive service, even helping with the completion of applications for regional development grants and other assistance. Local authority officers argue that small firms tend to be discouraged by the complex procedures of the Department of Industry and are likely to approach them first. The Department of Industry is, however, sceptical about this, fearing that the advice given may sometimes be misguided because some local authorities tend to forget that selective assistance is discretionary and that it may not be available at the level expected.

It is increasingly common for polytechnics, which nominally come under local authority education departments, to have advisory units for small firms. These units often offer technical production advice, management advice and accountancy assistance not always available to small firms. Sheffield Polytechnic and Trent Polytechnic (in Nottingham) offer such services. This activity, however, owes more to pressures from inside the polytechnics than to policy initiatives from the local authorities. For similar reasons, in Sheffield the City Library provides an extensive and specialist information service dealing with commercial and technical inquiries from local industry.

Incentives and Subsidies

The possibility of offering financial incentives to industry similar to those provided by central government is one which has interested a number of local authorities but few have been able to take much action for legal and financial reasons. Some, like Tyne and Wear County Council, have successfully sought additional powers under private Acts[25] and one of the authorities studied here (South Yorkshire) was seeking additional powers in a local bill. Even without extra powers, however, councils can offer some incentives.

The local authority provision of land and premises itself, coupled with the compiling of a register of other available commercial and industrial property, can be held to provide something in the nature of an incentive to industrialists by reducing their search and construction costs. Notwithstanding the formal position under statute local authorities tend to take a fairly flexible view of what is a commercial rent. They allow the usual commercial concessions, including preliminary rent-free periods, but sometimes extend them a little further because they allow themselves a longer period to break even on their investments than private developers and rents may, therefore, be slightly lower. They also take slightly greater risks than private developers without increasing rent levels to compensate. Even the commitment to the construction of smaller factory units described above is a form of subsidy on account of the greater commercial risk involved with small firms. Where private developers set up an industrial estate they look for 'blue-chip' tenants to give security, but local authorities (like South Yorkshire which bought Aldham from its original developers) are prepared to accept less obviously secure firms and yet to charge the same rents. The rates of return expected by local authorities are usually lower than those for private developers.

In the long run, however, the councils involved have all succeeded in generating income from their industrial property. Sheffield's advance factory units were intended to have a rate of return of 10 per cent, Nottinghamshire's development activities are self-financing over a fairly short period, and even in South Yorkshire, where there is a willingness in principle to subsidise rents, there has been no need to do so. In none of the areas examined did local authorities have serious difficulties in letting most sites and premises. Where problems have arisen price reductions were not regarded as likely to have much effect and in the case of medium-sized and larger firms it must be remembered that rent is usually a relatively small part of the total costs of a new development.

Subsidies are more likely to have a more important part to play in the case of very small firms, chiefly because such firms are usually used to low rent levels and may be prepared to accept less attractive working conditions in return for their maintenance. Local authorities are able to subsidise rents on short-term leases (less than seven years), Nottingham's 'house-shells' for industrial use are let on a weekly basis, and in

1978 when they first came on to the market it was estimated by the Department of Technical Services that £10 would be an economic weekly rent. But in fact the rents were set at less than £6. Under the inner city programmes in Sheffield and Nottingham it is likely that the government will help subsidise initial rents on factory units to encourage local firms.

One of the difficulties in assessing the extent of council subsidisation is that the full costs of assembly, preparation and reclamation carried out by local authorities on derelict and semi-derelict land are not reflected in the rents or prices charged for it. This is because these costs are to a large extent the result of other council policies and are, therefore, generally met out of other budgets, sometimes with the help of government grants. Nottingham's industrial estates, for example, are not expected to meet these full costs. But nor can an accurate estimate be made of the market price for such estates, since they would almost certainly not have been prepared under market conditions. In these circumstances local authorities are playing a different role. They are providing land and premises which would otherwise not be provided and then calculating approximately what the market rates would have been had there been a market in such land, a somewhat uncertain procedure at best.

Local authority industrial mortgages may be useful to some firms, but they can usually be given only if development is taking place on land which was sold or is owned by the council or it is in areas designated under the Inner Urban Areas Act.[26] Some authorities (such as Sheffield) see no need for such loans, which are likely to be only a last resort for firms and may even encourage insecure development. Most of the local authorities in this study do not own sufficient land to make the granting of mortgages a regular possibility and local authority mortgage rates have in any case not been significantly better than commercial ones. Where some allowance for mortgages was made in authorities' budgets (Peterborough, Fenland, Nottinghamshire and South Yorkshire) there had been no recent borrowings. Nevertheless, South Yorkshire is now prepared to give mortgages of up to thirty years' duration to small firms, particularly in its Job Priority Areas.

South Yorkshire has developed a significantly greater interest than the other authorities in offering incentives to industry with the ultimate aim of topping up the financial assistance available in an Intermediate Area to the levels of the Development Areas. The CRIS (County Regional Investment Scheme) was an early attempt to provide direct assistance, and under it £2m. was made available from the county's £50m. superannuation fund to 'provide equity finance of between £100,000 and £250,000 to unquoted companies with good growth potential and sound management, earning minimum pre-tax profits of approximately £50,000 per annum. All investment propositions will be assessed on a strictly commercial basis.'[27] This scheme has been unsuccessful and no investment has been made under it in the county because loans have to come under the same detailed scrutiny as other superannuation fund investment and this is often more strict than the conditions imposed by commercial sources. Yet many of those applying for loans had already been refused loans from commercial sources and were applying to the council for this reason. But the scheme was an attempt to escape from restrictions on equity investment by local authorities and did provide the opportunity to direct some less experienced applicants to more appropriate sources of funds.

The county council has now developed further plans for offering financial aid to small firms (defined as employing up to about fifty workers) in its Job Priority Areas and other areas with high levels of unemployment. This aid, given for the first time in 1979, is in the form of loans (up to £20,000), interest relief grants on loans for plant and equipment (up to a maximum of £1,000 per annum), and consultancy grants to help with product design, marketing, finance and legal advice relating to patents and licensing agreements (up to a maximum of £500). These forms of aid are clearly modelled on some of those offered by central government, but the sums involved are much lower.

Another financial incentive sometimes used by local authorities is to vary the level of rates. On property which is occupied this is possible only on the basis of powers under s. 137 of the Local Government Act and none of our authorities has made use of this possibility. It is more common to reduce rate levels on empty property; Sheffield, for example, reduced the percentage rate on empty non-domestic property to 75 per cent in April 1978. It was felt that charging the full rate was discouraging speculative development (particularly in office building) and that more of such development was needed if office development was to be increased.

The local authority and the economic infrastructure

All local authority activities have in principle an economic dimension because they are concerned with the buying and selling of goods, the provision of services and the employment of labour. But only some of these normal activities are consciously regarded by councils as means of affecting the wider economic environment of their area by influencing the level of local employment and incomes. The kind of local authority action which can be brought under this heading falls into two types – first, direct involvement through ordering policies, capital spending, employment and municipal enterprise, and secondly, the provision of economically beneficial infrastructure.

Deliberate intervention with an economic development motive of the first type is very rare, since it tends to clash with the traditional emphasis on providing services at the lowest direct cost (a requirement which has some legal backing too in many fields of local spending). Local authorities have limited scope to buy locally produced goods, for example, but such a preference can be of only marginal importance. In Sheffield's council canteens all cutlery is locally made, though this is as much for reasons of civic pride as on economic grounds, and Nottinghamshire, with its dependence on mining employment, heats council property with coal (although concessionary rates also make this an attractive commercial proposition).

More important is the fact that local government expenditure in the construction sector can have a substantial impact on local employment. Recently there have been significant cuts in building programmes by most authorities and this has resulted in a continuing loss of jobs for building workers and those in associated industries. Some local authorities have tried to resist reductions in capital programmes for employment and other reasons, but counter-pressures from central government and to some extent from ratepayers have been strong. Overall it is striking that in relation to economic development the conscious management of levels of capital spending for employment reasons has been rare. There is, however, awareness of the problem. This is well illustrated in the case of Nottinghamshire where the programme was to be cut from £10m. in 1974/5 to £5m. in 1980/1 (at November 1976 prices). The number of building workers employed on county council contracts was expected to fall from 750 in 1978 to 300 in 1979/80 and an officers' report to a council committee suggested that 'against the proper desire to reduce the rate burden in order partly to make commercial concerns more able to compete there must be the counter-balancing factor that by curtailing the programme the Council may be doing more harm than good in its avowed objective of stimulating the local economy'.[28] In the present climate of retrenchment it is easier for councils and their officers to identify the difficulties created by reducing capital spending than to act against them.

Similar problems arise in respect of direct council employment. Local authorities are major employers in all the areas concerned in this study and in the more rural areas they are usually the largest single employers. In general, however, councils do not view their own employment as a significant element in the local economy to be manipulated in a counter-cyclical fashion.[29] A partial exception to this is the commitment expressed by most of these authorities to avoid or limit staff redundancies. But even this has to be viewed in the context of local authority attempts to increase efficiency and reduce staff costs which have usually resulted in the acceptance of a policy of natural wastage and the careful monitoring of any replacement appointments. The care on redundancies seems to owe more to the need to preserve a reputation as good employers than to economic criteria related to levels of employment.

Most of the councils have taken up the various employment creation schemes sponsored since 1975 by the Manpower Services Commission,[30] and South Yorkshire submitted more proposals than most other counties in the country. Local authorities, however, had reservations about the schemes, particularly at a time when they have been forced to reduce their own spending on activities regarded as important. As the Association of Metropolitan Authorities commented: 'By definition the schemes have to involve work which would not otherwise be carried out by . . . the local authority and have a maximum duration of six months. Although in some cases the projects carried out are useful, often they are a very low priority compared with other local government activities.'[31]

Municipal enterprise is no longer as common as it was in the interwar years, but many local authorities are still directly involved in the operation of specialised commercial concerns ancillary to their normal statutory responsibilities. These are often held to perform a useful function in the local economy. But all of these activities are expected to yield some measure of commercial return and there is rarely a commitment to large-scale subsidy in the long term. Arguments of this sort apply to the small local authority port maintained by Fenland at Wisbech which brings about £100,000 into the area each year and supports some associated employment for lorry drivers and warehousemen. Discussions have been held with the British Waterways Board and others to assess the feasibility of developing Wisbech as Peterborough's port.[32] Similarly, even though it is used chiefly for holiday traffic Nottinghamshire and Nottingham both have shares (two and one respectively out of a total of eight) in the East Midland Airport, justified on the ground that the presence of a local airport assists in the economic promotion of neighbouring authorities and is a source of convenience for local businessmen.

Two of the authorities studied own shares in commercial concerns, but only in one case was this held to be of real economic importance. South Yorkshire's Passenger Transport Executive owns several small transport firms, including one supplying garage services, but these were acquired incidentally to the Executive's main activities and are being operated solely to raise revenue to support the Executive's major public transport services. They will be sold if they are not revenue-producing. Nottinghamshire on the other hand purchased shares (10 per cent) in 1975 in Horizon Midlands, a tour operator, as part of an effort to save the concern when it was in danger of take-over by a Spanish company. The purchase (made in virtue of powers under s. 137 of the Local Government Act 1972) contributed to the maintenance of traffic at the East Midlands Airport where Horizon Midlands was a major operator. If the take-over had been successful it was feared that many of the company's package tours would have been transferred to other airports. In no instance has shareholding by local authorities been used as a method of directing industry or of assuming a role in relation to industry analogous to that of the National Enterprise Board at the national level.

The significance of the second type of direct involvement – infrastructural provision – is hard to assess in respect of its bearing on economic objectives and policies. Most economic activity would clearly be impossible without the provision of infrastructure by local authorities. But this does not mean that they set infrastructural expenditure within an economic development framework: such expenditure and the associated programmes can just as easily be treated as the provision of a range of services for the local population justified in social terms or as action in discharge of responsibilities conferred by the centre. Thus it remains to be established in each case whether the provision of infrastructure is seen by members of a local authority as part of their attempts to influence the local economy.

It is often argued that a sympathetic housing policy can encourage firms to move into what is for them a new area. All of the authorities studied were prepared to offer housing to 'key workers' to help new firms establish themselves, although in Peterborough's case most of such housing is supplied by the Development Corporation. Yet in fact none of them suffers from a serious housing shortage and thus the demand for 'key worker' housing is bound to be limited (for example, at only 12–24 houses per annum in Sheffield). Sheffield's housing department has in the past planned to provide executive housing in order to make the city more attractive to incoming firms and has included development proposals to this effect in its Housing Investment Programmes. These have however been rejected by the Department of the Environment on the grounds that private builders are best able to carry out developments of this sort.

Under the impact of growing economic pressures the education service has been brought into the consideration of what action local authorities can take to stimulate development. It has now become common for education authorities to consult representatives of local industry when preparing syllabuses and courses. Colleges of Further Education often use Training Services Agency funds to run specialist (retraining) courses designed to help young people find employment. Generally, however, education departments are reacting to the demands of others, servicing industry rather than initiating policies to attract it. The principal exceptions to this are the local Careers Services which offer employment advice to young people. One of the responses to increasing unemployment (reflected in Sheffield and Nottinghamshire, for example) has been the increased employment of Careers Officers, partly because of the need to deal with more unemployed young people and partly because it is felt that more attention to individual cases may help them to find jobs.

The provision of transportation services probably has the most direct bearing on industry, however, since such services affect both the distribution of goods and access to places of employment by employees. Four of the authorities examined have public transport responsibilities (South Yorkshire, Nottinghamshire, Cambridgeshire and Nottingham) and two of these (South Yorkshire and Nottingham) have direct responsibility for the provision of bus services. Whilst all four authorities were committed to providing facilities or ensuring the provision of facilities by others (for example, the National Bus Company) for travel to work services, their policies to this end differed significantly. Only South Yorkshire was using its transport powers (through its Passenger Transport Executive) as a deliberate instrument of economic management. In the structure plan and elsewhere the council argues that its cheap fares policy should make it easier for the residents of South Yorkshire's mining areas to find jobs in the bigger urban centres without sharp increases in their travel costs.[33] In contrast to South Yorkshire the other authorities are concerned to reduce subsidies to public transport as much as possible, although some support is given to routes in isolated rural areas. Nottingham's transport department is trying to move towards full commercial viability as soon as possible.

All of the authorities concerned with road construction (the counties) have taken the view that roads likely to support economic development should be given priority. Sometimes this has simply meant the rephasing of schemes which in any case are not scheduled to be carried out for several years to come. Cambridgeshire's shift of emphasis has perhaps been the clearest, with a commitment to major schemes in the Fens area (for example, on the Fens link road) and plans for several bypasses where road links are currently very poor, but similar influences have been at work in Nottinghamshire.

The parking policies of local authorities often arouse controversy and are frequently criticised by industry and commerce. It has been argued by traders that parking difficulties discourage customers and in one case it was stated by a local businessman that restrictions on parking facilities had resulted in a firm giving up plans for development because its workforce would find access difficult. Although schemes to restrict city centre car traffic are bound to come into conflict with the desire to facilitate access by car to city centre shops and offices, most of the authorities try to take shopping and business problems into account. Nottingham in particular is committed to major city-centre car-parking provision, but the other two cities also have extensive parking facilities. In Nottingham it was felt by some officers and councillors that an earlier 'zone and collar' experiment designed to reduce city centre car traffic and to increase the use of buses had given the city a bad reputation among developers and potential employers. They were concerned to change this reputation for hostility to private cars.

Advocacy and persuasion: other levels of government

Since much of the action taken by local authorities to influence the economy is overshadowed by the decisions of central government departments many councils attempt as a matter of course to put pressure on them as well as implementing their own policies locally. Before reorganisation Sheffield County Borough made a submission to the Hunt Committee[34] arguing that the city should be given Intermediate Area status and it made further submissions before being granted such status. Similarly, whilst Nottinghamshire was reluctant to push too hard for additional Intermediate Areas because it feared that this might mean the loss of some existing Intermediate Areas, it did support Newark's case for such status.[35]

Sheffield, Nottingham and South Yorkshire all made submissions under the Inner Urban Areas Act to the Department of the Environment with a view to gaining programme area or even partnership status.[36] These submissions were partially successful, with all the authorities mentioned becoming programme authorities (including all four of South Yorkshire's districts). Yet none was given partnership status along with the added support that promises.

Cambridgeshire and Fenland have managed to win Special Investment Area status for the Fens area from the Development Commission on the basis of proposals submitted by Cambridgeshire's County Planning Officer and this has given COSIRA added scope for action in the area and brought extra resources, mainly in the form of advance factories. In 1977 Peterborough opposed a reduction in the new towns's projected population and in the event the targets were reduced by less than had originally been feared.

The presentation of reports to the government is often accompanied by further pressures through Members of Parliament (particularly in the case of Sheffield) and consultations with civil servants or politicians. South Yorkshire, for example, took the opportunity of a visit by the Secretary of State for the Department of the Environment in early 1978 to impress on him the problems of the Dearne Valley and the advantages of supporting the Sheffield and South Yorkshire Navigation Scheme. Fenland used its Member of Parliament to win increased aid for Wisbech after the floods of February 1978 and took the same opportunity to emphasise the increasing economic problems of the area. On many issues of broader policy, such as the need for additional resources to go to the inner cities or to deprived rural areas, the councils feed their ideas through the local authority associations. Fenland, for example, through its representative on the Council of the Association of District Councils has played an important part in drawing attention to the need for economic regeneration in rural areas.[37]

Planning and Economic Development Activity

The manner in which the planning function has generally been reinterpreted to embrace a more or less explicit concern with economic prospects and policies for improving them is referred to in Chapters 2 and 6. It is, however, appropriate to conclude this survey of actual activities undertaken for economic development purposes with some reference to this shift of emphasis and some comments on the ways in which planning departments are in virtue of their basic functions of land use control and management necessarily involved in a measure of economic policy-making. Here the concern is, however, with powers and the ways in which they are used and not with the organisation of planning functions, a topic taken up in the next chapter.

The introduction of structure planning undoubtedly encouraged planning departments to try to move away from a more narrowly defined concern with land use. The subsequent creation of new county authorities, and in particular of the metropolitan authorities, pointed in the same direction. Despite the continued emphasis by the Department of the Environment on structure plans as tools of broad land use allocation and of transport planning as defined in statute and circular, the structure plans have provided new scope for planners and encouraged councils to look at wider economic factors at work in their areas. In some cases too the structure plans have offered a chance to planning departments and county authorities to bring together in one document a summary (to which the authority can regularly refer) of the existing structure of and the changing pressures on the county. In some authorities (notably the metropolitan counties) the structure plan has been a central corporate document, dealing with the problems and tasks facing each major department. It has also sometimes been used as a lever to gain extra resources and concessions from central government.

South Yorkshire's structure plan provides a clear example of a planning department moving out of its traditional role. Not only does it list specific areas to be given priority, but it also outlines some of the policies needed to ensure that meaning can be attached to such priorities. It discusses the actions required from the various departments of the local authority and from other local authorities, and was the basis for more detailed departmental proposals. The structure plan contained bids for additional resources, both explicitly in claims that the Dearne Valley be given Development Area status, and in the assessment of the financial resources needed to implement the plan. This estimated that to reverse previous alleged misallocations of resources significantly increased government funds would be needed in South Yorkshire and key sector spending on economic development would have to be permitted. Even if all the claims advanced in the structure plan are not accepted, its authors hope to have made an impact on central government by drawing attention to the county's special needs.

In Cambridgeshire the structure plan does not play as important a part as in South Yorkshire, but its preparation nevertheless represented a new departure. Like South Yorkshire the county was newly constituted by reorganisation and the structure plan process presented an opportunity to prepare an overall picture of the area. For the first time an economic problem in the Fens area was identified and the plan proposed that the council should take that area's problems into account in all its decisions involving resource allocation. The third of the structure plans in this group of local authorities, that of Nottinghamshire, is closest in form to that preferred by the Department of the Environment, being constructed primarily as a land use document. It is seen by officers and councillors as a statutorily necessary document rather than as one crucial for the authority's policy-making. Specific planning work (such as the Deprived Area Study published in 1975) has been more important than the structure plan, partly because of the varied nature of the county. Unlike South Yorkshire it does not possess a more or less homogeneous economic and social structure and, unlike Cambridgeshire, there is no obvious pattern of growth and decline in different areas.

At the district council level the picture of planning aims and methods is much more diverse. For the districts there are difficulties in using planning powers in support of economic policy which are in some respects more serious than those affecting the counties. Individual district plans are based on detailed surveys of land use and take account of other socio-economic factors. But the gains made from the ability to examine a small area in some detail tend to be outweighed, at least in the economic sphere, by the fact that the areas are generally too small to constitute anything approaching viable economic units. One result of this and of the plans' importance in the framework of development control is a continuing strong emphasis on land use control. Local plans tend to have the character of a grid awaiting the insertion of particular planning applications, rather than that of documents to be used positively for stimulating a particular course of development.

Nevertheless, in Nottingham work on local plans for the inner city has helped identify economic problems and the department has put forward proposals to help development in such areas (for example, the proposal for 'house-shells' development). In Fenland the planning department's regular contact with developers has made it the leading economic department and the process of town planning and the extensive planning literature outlining the problems of the Fens towns has emphasised this.

It has often been argued in the past that planning controls were widely used to discourage industrial activity and to restrain economic development in the interests of environmental improvement. Whilst it is difficult to assess the general validity of such a criticism, there is certainly evidence to show that planning procedures are now less often applied with this bias. In these case studies all the district planning departments are now committed to giving industrial and commercial planning applications, and particularly those for extensions, sympathetic consideration and to processing them as fast as possible. This often means reducing the consideration period to six weeks and giving industrial applications priority over others. In order to guard against rejection on technical grounds planning departments, particularly in the larger districts, encourage firms wishing to carry out development to discuss their proposals with them before submitting planning applications. Planning officers, one of whom usually operates as first point of contact for developers and firms, will try to suggest alternative sites if the one proposed is unsuitable. In cases of large-scale development proposals some authorities may even, as does Sheffield, call the Planning Committee together for an informal meeting at which the proposals can be discussed and modified before submission, thus significantly reducing the risks of rejection. County planning departments generally follow the same sort of approach, but their direct involvement with development control is much smaller. In some cases applications for additional mineral working which might previously have been rejected are now being accepted.

Even in Sheffield the planning and architectural department's planning section has not only given approval to most industrial development applications, but is concerned to ensure that there is always a stock of speculative office building available in the city centre to ensure that new employers can move in. In Sheffield too the local plan process is the most developed. One draft district plan claims that 'it provides a basis for co-ordinating development and solutions to local problems'.[38] Most departments with any interest at stake are involved in the consultations on these plans, which also include extensive work in community forums and with local industrialists. At present district plans essentially summarise what other departments already intend to do, but 'programming maps' in future plans are intended to indicate this more consistently. Like some structure plans these local plans may become an important method of committing departments to action and by providing detailed statements of available land may be useful sources of guidance for local industry. Sheffield's planning section is also directly involved in the Comprehensive Development Area Scheme at Mosborough, for which it is the co-ordinating department. It has laid down the structure of development and has drawn up integrated plans for housing and economic development, although the economic recession of the 1970s has made it difficult to ensure that employment keeps pace with population growth.

However, planning departments cannot give up their traditional controlling functions and all of those visited emphasised that on some matters they would still have to impose careful control. In several cases refusal had been given to large-scale supermarket planning applications because of their likely effect on other shopping facilities and employment, and there was little doubt that planning applications for obtrusive industries would be scrutinised very carefully. Examples of industries of this sort include some chemical plants and car manufacturing plans. Fenland, for example, would probably not want any large-scale development which was likely to change that district's predominantly agricultural nature.

Even if it is accepted that planning procedures and policies have contributed to a reduction in the number of small firms in inner city areas the current relaxation of controls cannot of itself be expected to bring them back, particularly as redevelopment has removed many of the premises which previously housed them. Most larger firms and many small firms would prefer to be in new premises, often on greenfield sites with good access to the national transport system rather than in the confined spaces of the cities. Most planning authorities do not at present face the problem of having too little land available with planning permission. On the contrary it is not uncommon for there to be too much of it (1,000 acres in Sheffield) and in the wrong places. Thus changes in traditional planning policies quickly run up against the limits inherent in planning control itself.

NOTES

1 W. Hampton, *Democracy and Community* (London: OUP, 1970), p. 38.
2 *South Yorkshire Statistics* (South Yorkshire County Council, 1976).
3 The Future of Sheffield's Cutlery Industry (City of Sheffield Metropolitan District Council, 1977).
4 'Development Sheffield' (Sheffield City Promotion Committee, Winter 1977).
5 *South Yorkshire Structure Plan, Report of Survey*, Vol. 2 (South Yorkshire County Council, 1978).
6 See *Nottinghamshire Structure Plan* (Nottinghamshire County Council, 1978).
7 They are to lose Intermediate Area status by 1982.
8 See, for example, 'The Inner City' (City of Nottingham, 1977) and *Deprived Area Study* (Nottinghamshire County Council, 1975).
9 *Cambridgeshire Structure Plan. Report of Survey. Consultation Draft* (Cambridgeshire County Council, 1976), pp. 13 and 14. Employment in England and Wales rose by 0·5 per cent between the same years.
10 ibid., p. 43.
11 *Cambridgeshire Structure Plan. Report of Survey*, op. cit., p. 50.
12 *Nottinghamshire/Derbyshire Sub-Regional Study* (Nottinghamshire County Council, Nottingham County Borough Council, Derbyshire County Council and Derby County Borough Council), approved 1970. This led to the more detailed *Mansfield/Alfreton Plan* (Nottinghamshire and Derbyshire County Councils), approved 1971.
13 *South Yorkshire Structure Plan. Written Statement* (South Yorkshire County Council, 1978), ch. 6.
14 'The Creation of Employment Opportunities' (South Yorkshire County Council, 1977). (N.B. This was based on the earlier Draft Structure Plan.)

15   Employment, Development and Publicity Sub-Committee, Corporate and Financial Plans (South Yorkshire County Council, 1977 and 1978).

16   Objectives (City of Sheffield Metropolitan District Council, November 1977).

17   Ironically Cambridgeshire, which does not provide land for industrial development, owns a significant amount of economically useful agricultural land in the form of a smallholding estate. With 1,400 tenants and covering 48,000 acres this is the largest owned by any local authority. The existence of the estate is intended to encourage the continued entrance of small farmers into agriculture, although the number of new entrants is relatively small.

18   Industrial Land Availability Schedule (City of Nottingham, February 1978).

19   Employment, Development and Publicity Sub-Committee, Corporate and Financial Plan (South Yorkshire County Council, 1978), pp. 24–5. This figure includes Carcroft which it manages jointly with Doncaster MDC and which was inherited from the West Riding County Council.

20   Such 'partnership' arrangements have now been extended to statutory undertakers and private developers owning land.

21   In addition to any construction under the inner city programme.

22   Corporate and Financial Plan (1978), op. cit., p. 28. The repeal of the Community Land Act is likely to make this impossible as the county hoped to use the Community Land Scheme as its main source of capital funds.

23   At this time (that is, before local government reorganisation) the county's economic development work was organised differently, but the present assistant director already had the responsibility for economic development.

24   'Development Sheffield', op. cit., p. 18.

25   See P. B. Rogers and C. R. Smith, *The Local Authority's Role in Economic Development; the Tyne & Wear Act 1976*, Regional Studies, Vol. 11 (Oxford: Pergamon, 1977), pp. 153–63.

26   Up to 75 per cent of the development's value under the Local Authorities (Land) Act 1963 and 90 per cent in designated areas under the Inner Urban Areas Act 1978. Authorities with powers under the latter Act include Sheffield, South Yorkshire, Nottingham and Nottinghamshire (in the Nottingham area).

27   *County Regional Investment Scheme, Funds for Industry* (South Yorkshire County Superannuation Fund), leaflet.

28   Report of the Officers' Review Board to the Accounts and Review Committee on Unemployment (Nottinghamshire County Council, 1978), p. 9.

29   This provides an interesting contrast with the activities of those local authorities which carried out public works in the 1920s. The construction of a new road from Birmingham to Wolverhampton in 1924–7, for example, was undertaken primarily for employment reasons.

30   Including the Job Creation Programme and Work Experience Programme now replaced by the Youth Opportunities Programme and the Selective Temporary Employment Programme. In June 1979 the budgets allocated to these schemes were cut significantly.

31   'Priorities for Progress: Local Government and Economic Recovery' (London: Association of Metropolitan Authorities, October 1978), p. 4.

32   See 'River Nene Improvement Study. From the Wash to an Inland Port at Peterborough' (London: British Waterways Board, 1978).

33   South Yorkshire's arguments for a free or cheap public transport system are not restricted to these employment-related ones, but cover a wide range of social issues discussed in detail in the county structure plan and elsewhere.

34   *The Intermediate Areas. Report of a Committee under the Chairmanship of Sir Joseph Hunt*, Cmnd 3998 (London: HMSO, 1969).

35   Nottinghamshire's fears seem to have been justified and the county's Intermediate Areas are to be down-graded. South Yorkshire is to face a similar fate but parts are to be up-graded to Development Area status.

36   'The Future of England's Fourth Largest City' (City of Sheffield Metropolitan District Council, n.d.). 'The Inner City' (City of Nottingham, 1977), op. cit. South Yorkshire prepared a submission arguing that both Sheffield's inner city and the Dearne Valley area should be recognised as inner cities for the purpose of the Act, although of course the Dearne Valley is not an inner city.

37   See, for example, 'Rural Recovery: Strategy for Survival' (London: Association of District Councils, 1978).

38   Chapeltown/High Green Draft District Plan (City of Sheffield Metropolitan District Council, n.d.), p. 2.

Chapter 4

ADMINISTRATIVE AND POLITICAL ORGANISATION: CONFLICT AND CO-OPERATION

Notwithstanding a number of formal requirements local authorities enjoy wide discretion in deciding what kind of organisation to adopt for carrying out their functions.[1] This autonomy of local authorities in respect of their internal administrative and committee structures renders generalisation about how they perform various tasks and with what effectiveness a hazardous undertaking. In some degree every local authority is unique.

Whilst there are in fact many important similarities in the forms of internal organisation adopted by local authorities, the range of variation in organisation is likely to be particularly wide in a field like economic development. This is because the task itself is defined somewhat differently from one authority to another and it may take shape within different related functional areas. And of one point there can be no doubt: the economic development work of local authorities fits uneasily into a system of separate departments.

THE ADMINISTRATIVE ORGANISATION OF ECONOMIC DEVELOPMENT

We shall start by looking at the different ways in which economic activities have been grafted on to the administrative structures of the local authorities involved in this study. In some cases the economic promotion function has been made the responsibility of officers from several departments working together; in others it has been entrusted to officers in one department only. However, in all the more active authorities it was decided to give one officer the main responsibility for co-ordinating and initiating action. As a rule a council's economic activity involves some degree of interdepartmental co-operation and in some authorities it is fitted into a system of corporate management. All of the authorities have Management Teams of chief officers, or Chief Officers' Groups, at which discussions of economic policy and activity take place, but such bodies are operating within widely different organisational contexts and their actual importance varies significantly from one authority to another.

Nevertheless, in most authorities a single department was entrusted with the main responsibility for economic activity. In three cases the responsibility rested with the planning department and in two it was with the estates department as economic promotion work had grown out of the estates management function. This adaptive approach is to be expected. Instead of setting up a new organisation to deal with newly-identified problems, local authorities show a preference for adapting existing organisations to handle fresh tasks. Indeed, even this remark may imply a rather more systematic approach to organisational development than exists, since each department and even sections within departments have distinctive responses to changing problems which reflect their own primary interests and professional skills.

At the county level it was found that the primary responsibility is usually with the planning department. This was clearest in Nottinghamshire which has one of the most developed organisations for economic activity in the form of the economic development division of the county's department of planning and transportation.

There are two main reasons for this organisational preference. First, at the county level an interest in economic measures tends to arise out of the strategic planning function. The structure plans of both South Yorkshire and Cambridgeshire had played an important part in identifying an economic dimension in planning policy, whilst in Nottinghamshire the Derbyshire—Nottinghamshire Sub-regional Study had had a similar role before local government reorganisation. Secondly, county land ownership (apart from agricultural land in the case of Cambridgeshire and land needed for council offices, depots and schools) tends to be on a fairly small scale, so that economic activities cannot be evolved out of existing methods of land management. Thus, when the possibility of economic development work comes on to the agenda it is likely straightaway to have a direct bearing on planning policies. Similar factors applied in Fenland district where the Industrial Development Officer works in the Planning and Architectural Services Department, but with no staff of his own. In this case the district owns so little land that it does not even have an estates officer, whilst the planning department is the only one directly in contact with local industry on a regular basis. But another factor of some influence at the district level is the fact that the operation by planning departments of development control with its connotations of scrutiny and restriction makes it harder to see them as the natural home for activities directed to industrial growth. County planners, on the other hand, have a more obvious interest in identifying economic development prospects since their main responsibilities are directed to setting up the structure plan and have little direct connection with the exercise of planning controls.

Where authorities have inherited large amounts of land and are already significant suppliers of land for development it is likely that the economic promotion function will be based on the existing estates management role. This was clearest cut in Sheffield, where the Industrial Development Office is in the Estates Surveyor's department and, despite an important degree of operational freedom, works closely with other parts of that department. Based as it is in this well-established estates function, Sheffield's economic development work showed a more pronounced commercial orientation than was found elsewhere. In Nottingham district, too, where an interdepartmental unit has been set up, and the estates function has been absorbed into the Department of Technical Services, many of the decisions on development made within that department are as important as the actions taken by the unit itself.

In Peterborough the position is distorted by the district's relationship with the Development Corporation. But here too the authority's own economic development work is carried out by a small estates unit under the Legal and Administrative Officer. Within the Development Corporation it should be noted that the estates department plays the most important part in the programme of employment promotion, providing 250,000 sq. ft of industrial space each year and offering large quantities of serviced land and almost any custom-built premises which are required. The Development Corporation owns undeveloped land on an even larger scale than Sheffield and the development and management of land lies at the heart of its strategy. The ability of a Development Corporation to link planning, housing and land management policies puts into sharp relief some of the limitations affecting local authority programmes of development. Local councils seldom have a Development Corporation's single-mindedness of purpose and certainly do not have comparable resources.

Only in two cases (South Yorkshire and Nottingham) was economic activity organised through units made up of officers from different departments. Some of the officers attached to these non-departmental units have a full-time commitment, but for others the work is only part of a wider range of duties. In these cases, too, albeit in different ways, organisational changes have often reflected marginal shifts in emphasis, despite the fact that the thinking behind these units was inherently supra-departmental. A brief glance at the reasons given for setting up special units helps to indicate both the elements of continuity and change.

Joint units offer the prospect of keeping down the costs of introducing an economic programme and obviate the need to employ new staff, a point of some importance when there is concern about the levels of local government staffing. This consideration weighed heavily with Nottingham which had a strong political commitment to financial economy. But in South Yorkshire too, where the political outlook was different, the foundation of the Employment Promotion Unit helped to secure more efficient use of manpower by allowing the Public Relations Officer also to become the Employment Promotion Officer. His economic responsibilities increased as the public relations job of creating a corporate identity for the new county council began to occupy less of his time. From a more activist standpoint, where there is no clear existing departmental responsibility on which to build, units like these make it possible to start work fairly quickly. In both of the cases just referred to the formation of the units quickly resulted in action and helped to make economic promotional activity an accepted part of the authorities' work.

The view that cross-departmental organisations make it possible to use different professional skills and to have access to information from different departments was particularly important in South Yorkshire, but was also relevant in Nottingham district. There much of the information on land availability and economic matters comes from the representative of the planning department; financial and community land advice comes from the representative of the city treasury; and most of the publicity work is undertaken by the representative from the Publicity and Information Office. In South Yorkshire the Employment Promotion Unit's nominated officers have developed close relationships with each other, and the most important of them work in neighbouring offices (in the planning department) rather than in their own departments. They include officers from the planning department, the Estates Office, the Publicity Office and the leader of the Unit. The head of the economic services section of the Treasurer's department also has regular contact, providing extensive information and advice, particularly on the availability of financial assistance from the council for which he is directly responsible.

Units with this cross- or interdepartmental character are in principle intended to influence the work of other departments, since the officers nominated to them (full or part time) also take part in routine departmental discussions. This is chiefly of practical importance for the planning function, since economic development may come into conflict with established planning policies and regular reminders from a planner with a prime commitment to economic development may help overcome some of the problems thought to be associated with restrictive policies of development control. In South Yorkshire officers in the Unit were expected to exert some influence on the environment and engineering departments and links with the planning department were close. Whilst the extent of the EPU's influence in practice is hard to judge and may not measure up to what is implied by the formal structures, there are certainly opportunities for cross-fertilisation between departments which are not very common in local government.

Finally, these forms of joint organisation provide a method of avoiding the growth of power in one single department to an extent that might threaten the overall balance in the administrative structure of the authority concerned. Thus the units often have a direct connection with the Chief Executive as well as links with main departments. The leader of the Employment Promotion Unit in South Yorkshire is responsible both to the County Planning Officer and the Chief Executive, and this ensures the Unit's relative independence as it is not merely a section of the planning department. In Nottingham the Industrial and Commercial Development Officer is directly responsible to the Chief Executive rather than to the department of technical services which has the responsibility for constructing and planning the council's industrial estates and advance factory units, but little direct input into the Industrial and Commercial Development Unit.

It would be misleading to imply that interdepartmental co-operation took place only in South Yorkshire and Nottingham. Since activities of importance to the local economy cut across departmental boundaries drawn for different reasons, most authorities are forced to develop formal and informal methods of internal co-operation. Even in South Yorkshire and Nottingham joint working was not restricted to the activities of the specialist units. In Sheffield, where departmental boundaries are sharply drawn, work was found to be based on close daily co-operation between the Industrial Development Office and the publicity department. Some of the latter's budget was intended to be spent on promotional material for the attraction of industry, commerce, tourism and conference business and one of the publicity department's officers spent most of his time working with the Industrial Development Officer on the organisation of these matters. In Nottinghamshire county too there was regular and close co-operation between the economic development division and the Estates Office on the purchase and lease of land and premises and between it and the Publicity Office on promotional and advertising material.[2] But the internal links with planners and engineers in the planning and transportation department were also important. The assistant director responsible for the economic development division was able to comment on plans at an early stage and seek help on matters like the construction of access roads.

CORPORATE PLANNING

A distinction should be made at this stage between the co-ordination of the activities of local authorities and the corporate development of policy within them. The need for the former has been appreciated in local government for a long time, but the latter has only in recent years begun to gain any prominence. Often the two have become inextricably linked in the minds of officers and councillors, and corporate planning has been seen as part of a general concern to improve the efficiency of local government through better co-ordination. J. D. Stewart argues that 'The emphasis has been on the control and co-ordination of policies that remain separate in origin rather than on the co-ordination of the processes which lead up to those policies, on the efficiency of policy implementation rather than on the effectiveness of policy formulation.'[3] Clearly the two concerns cannot be completely divorced: an effective system of corporate planning should contribute to the improved co-ordination of activities as the division of authorities into watertight departments is eroded. But the distinction remains important, particularly as it has become common for the terminology and organisational forms of corporate planning to be used by many local authorities without a sufficiently clear understanding of what they are meant to signify.

The formal and informal links discussed above in the fairly narrowly defined field of economic development, that is, the provision of land and premises and the use of publicity to attract industrial and commercial investment, are more concerned with practical ways of ensuring co-operation between officers and departments to minimise conflict in this field than with any broader attempts to formulate a clear authority-wide policy, let alone one which might manage the process of social and economic change within the authority area. But all the authorities studied here have also taken up some elements of corporate planning even if the extent and impact of this trend vary significantly. In most cases the practice of corporate management has been linked closely with the determination of the annual budget so that the budget in effect provides the main corporate focus. Longer-term policy planning remained more elusive in all the authorities visited.

The structure of corporate planning is at its most developed in South Yorkshire, where there is an Economic Development Programme Area Team of officers from those departments represented in the Employment Promotion Unit itself (including the department of administration). This team includes more senior staff than those in the Unit and is charged with discussing broad policy questions rather than problems of implementation. It is through this Programme Area Team, with the help of the department of administration's Corporate Planning Unit and a major input from the Employment Promotion Officer, that a Corporate and Financial Plan for the Programme Area (that is, employment, development and publicity) is prepared. This plan outlines proposals for future activity, states problems and describes progress. As well as containing proposals for the Unit and the sub-committee to which it is responsible, it has discussed policies for the Environment and Highways and the Passenger Transport Committees. Financial estimates, prioritisation of schemes and justifications for policies have been included. Although the first Corporate and Financial Plan for the Employment, Development and Publicity Sub-committee was rather tentative, and it has remained difficult to influence other departments and committees, the plan for 1978 was much clearer. South Yorkshire's structure plan has also been an important part of the corporate planning process, particularly in relation to economic development, and the work of the planning department in identifying industrial and employment problems and possible solutions has provided the basis for subsequent programmes.[4]

In the other authorities corporate planning has been pushed forward less vigorously and been directly mainly towards establishing methods of work that encourage departments to operate within a broader policy and priorities framework, to feed in new ideas for working co-operation and to highlight areas of functional overlap. In Cambridgeshire the Chief Executive has played an important role as an advocate of a more integrated approach to policy-making, including economic policy, by encouraging departments and their chief officers to recognise the interdependence of their functions. Here the development of an economic policy was being pursued in a deliberately cautious fashion: informal working discussions, some organisational adaptation and the impact of structure plan preparation have so far been the main factors edging the authority towards some kind of economic policy commitment. This has meant that decisions with an economic thrust are still taken on an *ad hoc* basis, for example the granting of aid to Fenland district, the examination of possible development schemes in the county, the greater emphasis in the roads programme on economic needs. If and when a more formal policy commitment emerges, it appears likely that it will be based on an aggregation of existing measures.

The ideas of corporate planning do not yet appear to have had a decisive impact on the authorities which used to be county boroughs, Nottingham and Sheffield. The departments and committees have retained much of their independence, although there have been developments cutting across departmental boundaries, for example, in the formulation of policies for the inner city areas. In both authorities, but more particularly in Sheffield, the Chief Executive's principal role has been that of persuasion. In Nottingham the Chief Executive has played an important part in preparing and outlining proposals for economic activity and the creation of the Industrial and Commercial Development Unit itself has opened the way to a broader approach by the council. In Sheffield the first steps were taken with the publication of a set of 'Objectives',[5] which included a section outlining the activities of several departments which were relevant to the employment sector. The committee structure, which will be referred to later, brings different departments together in the discussion of economic problems and this arrangement, whilst not always achieving either a corporate approach or even co-operation, means that there is wide agreement that economic issues are relevant to a range of departments. Some of Sheffield's officers expressed the fear that a more extensive corporate structure with formal interdepartmental groups and increased commitment by all departments to joint working would restrict the existing scope for action by slowing down the decision-making process on immediate issues of land development and disposal and by encouraging departments with limited experience to intervene unnecessarily. In Sheffield's case at least and as long as the authority's economic development and promotional work is seen as requiring specialised activities dependent on specific departmental skills, there is clearly some justification for such a view. Similar views were expressed by officers in other authorities, including some with a stronger commitment to corporate planning than found in Sheffield.

Chief Executives often use economic activity as a sector in which to introduce or emphasise a new corporate dimension. In principle one of the most important tasks of Chief Executives and their Management Teams is to resolve conflicts fruitfully, using and balancing professional skills and enthusiasm. Such resolution of conflicts between different specialists may produce a better result than the pursuit of a policy by the one or the other specialist in isolation. But to be done successfully there must be an effective system of monitoring and information-gathering for the Chief Executive as well as a consistent interest from him or his staff in the work of the various departments. The existence of a corporate staff responsible to the Chief Executive and superimposed on existing functions and staff can, however, create its own problems since the involvement of the Chief Executive may sometimes result in fears that he is trying to intervene too much at the expense of existing departments. In one of the cases examined here the Chief Executive's staff were regarded with some suspicion by the departments. More generally, a corporate system is often regarded as a means of generating paper, carrying the risk of eroding the departmental incentive to take initiatives as a result of absorption into the work (and talk) of interdepartmental groups.

ORGANISATIONAL DEVELOPMENT

The organisation of local economic policy by different authorities cannot be classified simply. Each case has developed from and within its own experience and under the influence of a complex interplay of forces. Even the authority most committed to a centralised policy approach – South Yorkshire – has been influenced by the availability of suitable land, even outside those areas initially identified as priorities and it has reacted to immediate pressures not at first identified in broader policy statements, such as the call for import controls for some industries in its area. Similarly, the authority most clearly committed to a decentralised approach – Sheffield – could not carry out the activities to which it is committed without extensive interdepartmental co-operation. In none of the authorities was there a completely fragmented approach to economic policy, because in each the policy is discussed by the Management Team, whilst the Chief Executive maintains at least a watching brief and often much more than that. Leading councillors (usually through Policy and Resources Committee) are also aware of the need for a more integrated approach to policy-making. To this extent at least, the debates about local government management and administration which have been so prominent in recent years have had an effect.

Certain general conclusions based on a very small group of cases, but augmented by a more general consideration of other authorities, can be drawn about the varied approaches to economic development policy. The level of involvement of metropolitan authorities is likely to be greater than that of the non-metropolitan.[6] This is to be expected given the predominant structural characteristics and problems of the metro-politan authorities. However, it should also be noted that the most extensive programmes of economic development and promotion are most likely to be found at metropolitan district level, whilst the metro-politan counties are likely to find it hard to mount a major programme even if, as in the case of South Yorkshire, they are keen to do so. This reflects their relative lack of financial and other resources. Indeed, some of the larger non-metropolitan counties (such as Nottingham-shire) may actually outstrip some of the metropolitan counties in the scale of their economic activity.

In none of the cases examined here has the local authority set up an officially recognised economic development or promotion department. This tends to be ruled out on account of the existing distribution of relevant functions amongst departments (for example, planning, estates, the Chief Executive), the dependence of economic action on other sectors of local authority work, and the need to use financial and manpower resources prudently. The new functions normally develop from within the existing framework rather than being organised according to some model designed specially for them. Local govern-ment reorganisation did not by any means entail a thorough-going upheaval of all existing functions and organisation and many long-established structures have survived. It is not easy to introduce new organisational forms into an existing and well-entrenched depart-mental structure and tradition. Nor need it be the most appropriate response to the raising of new claims on resources, as is indicated below. Nevertheless, there has been some shift towards a more distinc-tive status for economic activity.

Most of the local authorities examined here had begun to develop some form of specialist section or had appointed a specialist officer.

Nor is the increase in industrial development officers a phenomenon restricted to our cases.[7] This feature of the organisational response is by no means surprising: it demonstrates that the local authority is reacting to some new task, initially at least, by creating a new kind of post or designating a new responsibility and, in principle, this need not reflect any major resource commitment. In most cases the work begins by the nomination of an existing officer as industrial development officer or by the nomination of several officers (usually from different departments) to an industrial development unit. Initially such nomination is almost always of a part-time nature, but gradually the work of industrial development becomes the central task for those concerned, often becoming a full-time activity. Similarly, the work undertaken becomes increasingly specialised, so that the original officers either develop the necessary skills, outgrowing many of the professional links with their parent departments, or new appointments from outside the local authority are made to fill new specialist posts. In Nottinghamshire, for example, although the assistant director responsible for economic development is a trained planner, most of his work is now directed towards developers and involves negotiations about industrial estates and factory units. His team is increasingly made up of non-planning specialists such as engineers with the skills necessary for organising construction programmes and, more recently, a liaison officer to provide advice to small and medium-sized firms.

Whether the form of organisation adopted is based on an existing department or on an interdepartmental unit, the officers involved soon begin to develop a specialised view of their role. Whilst they cannot carry through all the council's economic activities the units become identified as responsible for economic development, their main tasks being promotional activity in the widest sense and internal and external advocacy. Their officers increasingly see themselves as acting on behalf of their own offices or units as much as their parent departments. This is particularly important for those whose time is more and more taken up by work within an interdepartmental unit. Whilst these units are not intended, strictly speaking, to take on departmental responsibilities of their own, elements of departmentalism begin to appear and they develop a considerable degree of independence. Their concern becomes increasingly defined in terms of the activity they actually undertake and the clients they assist so that they may become less interested in some of the broad issues of economic development included in their original terms of reference.

CONFLICT OVER GOALS AND THE ALLOCATION OF
RESPONSIBILITIES

Local authority administration is characterised by divisions along professional and departmental lines. Most local authority functions are associated with specific professional skills and interests which have their own specialist qualifications – for example, legal, financial and town planning – and this is accompanied, despite numerous reports urging otherwise, by the continued lack of a developed managerial specialism. Most Chief Executives still have a legal or accountancy background. The different approaches of separate departments and offices are likely to conflict in varying degrees with the development of economic activity or, perhaps more accurately in some cases, the development of such an activity will clash with the existing functions of these departments. How conflict emerges and the forms it takes depends considerably on the location of the economic development function within the existing structure.

Treasurer's and planning departments are two principal departments with which industrial development offices might be expected to face conflicts over goals. But in practice, such conflict is rarely of great importance, in part at least because of the wide political and administrative consensus on goals and their general nature. Treasurers do not appear to have put obstacles in the way of a growth of economic activities, except to the extent that they must underline the limited availability of finance. Such restrictions tend to be only irritants since economic development budgets are generally small. Indeed, only in one of the seven authorities has there been any cut in the budget. This was not significant and was subsequently more than restored. In most of the authorities spending on economic development actually increased. In South Yorkshire, for example, revenue spending on economic development was expected to rise from negligible levels in 1977/8 to over £0·5m. in 1979/80, whilst capital spending (including £0·25m. in Aid to Industrialists) was expected to rise still more decisively to nearly £3·5m. (the bulk of this being intended to come from Community Land Act sources).[8] Revenue spending in real terms in 1979/80 was expected to be 9 per cent higher than 1978/9.

The need to reduce public spending which has been imposed by central government policy is a reflection of national economic problems which have produced *inter alia* high levels of unemployment locally. Therefore, whilst often accepting reductions in various sectors of traditional spending, local authorities have looked for other ways of counteracting the underlying economic problems and this has tended to make them look sympathetically at their own employment promotion budgets. Only in one of the seven cases were financial considerations said to be important in restraining the development of economic activity and there the possibility of realising existing capital assets was being suggested as a way of raising finance for this purpose. The economic policy sector is a new one at a time when local authorities have few areas of expansion and it is one to which local authority chief officers and councillors are usually well disposed on political as well as economic grounds. Thus there is some willingness to allocate funds to it and otherwise restricted departments are likely to regard it as a potential area of growth.

Nevertheless, the Department of the Environment's method of distributing local government finance under the 1974–9 Labour government had some effect on the local levels of economic activity. The general bias of the Rate Support Grant needs element distribution formula towards urban authorities no doubt helped authorities like South Yorkshire and Sheffield to avoid some of the worst problems of retrenchment.[9] Nottinghamshire, too, because it has in the past received all the needs element for the county area and is an education authority, works within a large budget and can therefore afford to spend relatively large sums on economic development despite its reluctance to use the Community Land Act. The two other districts examined face rather more serious problems – Fenland's total budget is very small (a promotional budget of £11,000, including £4–5,000 from outside sources) and Nottingham's is small for an authority of its size. Despite the major differences between the small rural authority and the large urban one neither has had much financial scope for expanding economic development programmes and each has, therefore, been careful about such commitments.

Two further financial points should be made. First, restrictions on the locally determined sector discouraged action by smaller authorities which did not wish to make use of the Community Land Act. In contrast larger ones (particularly those already owning land) were able to find other sources of finance for development, often on land they already owned, or which was supplied by other authorities. Some councils have spent from revenue or existing capital funds, whilst others have entered into lease/lease back arrangements with private developers, particularly to encourage commercial development, as for example in Peterborough. Secondly, much economic development work actually provides a return to the authority and this reduces long-run costs. The income from the provision of land and premises can be ploughed back into further development and the sums borrowed can often be paid off without using money from the General Rate Fund.

As argued above, planning departments in most authorities (particularly the counties) have played a major part in identifying an economic development function, although at district council level their development control function tends to have an inhibiting effect. Whatever the broad goals accepted in the pursuit of economic development, it is likely that in practice there will be some conflict between planners and industrial development officers (IDOs.). At county level the more ambitious aims of some structure plans are likely to be modified by the necessarily opportunistic approach which IDOs have to adopt. This has not, however, resulted in major disputes in the cases under review, largely because the approach of the IDOs has been endorsed by councillors and has had at least the acquiescence of the planners.

At district level conflict is rather more difficult to avoid since all industrial development officers see it as one of their major tasks to act as spokesmen within the authority for those likely to undertake industrial development. They believe that this is particularly necessary in order to win over the planners. Although representatives of all the planning departments emphasised that they attached far more priority to industrial development than in the past and were prepared to allow most of it, the very process of scrutinising plans and applying some body of agreed criteria to them which lie outside the concerns of the applicant is bound to carry the risk of conflict with developers. The professional goals of planners generally contrast significantly with the practice of IDOs whose goals tend to be defined in the terms used by their clients, that is, local firms and potential new arrivals.

In the county cases criticism of planning departments from officers in other departments has been common. They have been seen as trying to expand into economic development in order to compensate for their lack of major development control functions and to gain some compensation for the cyclical nature of structure planning. Only in one case had the planning department been given complete responsibility for economic development and there the department had much wider responsibilities, of which planning was only a part. Planning departments seem to be viewed by the staff of many other departments as sources of initiation and new ideas, but not as action-oriented bodies. Needless to say this is not an interpretation which planners generally accept.

COMMITTEES AND COUNCILLORS

In all the case studies it was found that the main responsibility for economic activity and policy at the level of the council and its committees has followed fairly closely the way in which administrative responsibility was allocated, that is to say, it has come into the sphere of the Policy and Resources Committee, the Planning Committee or the Estates Committee. Needless to say, a statement of how committee responsibility is allocated does not show what degree of general political commitment a council has to economic policies. This can only be seen from a more detailed examination of the ways in which activities are pursued.

The authority concentrating responsibility for economic activity in one committee most clearly was the South Yorkshire Metropolitan County where an Employment, Development and Publicity Sub-Committee of the Policy Committee dealt with most of the work. This sub-committee was made up of leading councillors, since only those on the Policy Committee could serve on it. As the activity is interdepartmental the sub-committee can and does receive reports from all interested departments (including the department of administration, the Treasurer's department and the planning department). It has also dealt with all the council's other publicity and public relations activity, since the Employment Promotion Officer is also the Publicity Officer. Even in South Yorkshire, therefore, which has the most integrated approach, the legacy of past administrative decisions has left its mark on committee structures.

The sub-committee was set up to emphasise the importance attached by the Labour Party leadership of the council to economic development work. The standing of the sub-committee can be seen in the fact that it alone of all sub-committees considers and approves a Corporate and Financial Plan covering its own area of responsibility. South Yorkshire's other Corporate and Financial Plans are prepared for full committees. From the point of view of some officers the identification of economic development as a separate programme area with its own corporate plan serves the additional purpose of encouraging the development of programme area rather than departmentally based plans. Other committees do, however, become involved on some matters. On the politically controversial issues of supporting a delegation pleading for import controls in the cutlery industry and the form of the programme of financial assistance to small firms, for example, decisions were made by the Budget Sub-Committee which also operates as the executive of the majority party group and is the most powerful political body in the South Yorkshire council.

Only in one other authority studied (Nottingham) was economic activity a direct responsibility of the Policy and Resources Committee, but elsewhere it is common for that committee to have statements included in its terms of reference to the effect that its duties include (as in Cambridgeshire) the consideration of 'the broad social and economic needs of the area and matters of comprehensive importance to the area including the contents of structure plans'.[10] In other words most Policy and Resources Committees have a residual concern with economic policy which may be brought into play if sufficient pressure is felt. In Nottingham where the policy objectives for economic activity were approved by the Policy and Resources Committee, there was little involvement by this committee in the detailed work associated with the pursuit of the objectives. Much of this has indeed to be approved by other committees: the Land Committee, for example, which is not a sub-committee of Policy and Resources, considers any land-related policies.[11]

In Nottinghamshire, Fenland and Cambridgeshire economic activity falls under planning committees. Nottinghamshire's Environment

Committee is in charge of the work of the planning and transportation department and although a sub-committee of the Policy and General Purposes Committee has now been set up to oversee the promotional side of the council's economic activity, the Environment Committee remains central, particularly with regard to the advance factory and industrial estate programmes. In Fenland the Planning and Development Committee deals with development control and other issues appropriate to a district planning authority as well as with economic development, but the committee chairman is also leader of the majority group so that the political leadership maintains a close interest in economic measures. Most decisions on the purchase and lease of land as well as the provision of finance have to be confirmed by the Policy and Resources Committee. The position in Cambridgeshire is less clear, but as economic issues have been raised in the preparation of the structure plan most of the relevant policy discussions have been at the Planning Committee in the first instance. If economic issues become important to council policy then the Policy and Resources Committee is likely to become more closely involved.

In two authorities (Sheffield and Peterborough) the oversight of economic activity was left mainly to Estates Committees.[12] Sheffield's internal organisation is complex and in some respects confusing. It is the outcome of pragmatic organisational responses over the years to perceived problems. As departments have increased their areas of activity, so the responsibilities of existing committees have been extended to cover them. The work of the Industrial Development Office is supervised by the Corporate Estates Committee, since it is part of the Estates Surveyor's department and much of its work is concerned with the provision of land and premises. Detailed reports on the council's economic development work are made annually by the Estates Surveyor. A great deal of the Industrial Development Office's promotional work, however, cannot be divorced from that of the publicity department and most of that is the responsibility of the City Promotion Committee. Joint reports to each committee are now prepared, specifying from which committee's budget spending is to come. This makes it difficult for councillors to monitor effectively or to form an overall picture of the economic activity being undertaken. But the basic decision to support such activity has been made and the council committees are concerned principally to ensure that budgets are not exceeded.

The picture is complicated further by the existence of an Industrial Development Advisory Committee which is made up of local trade unionists, Members of Parliament, employers from both industry and commerce, officers from government departments, other interested parties (including a local business journalist) and half of the councillors on the City Promotion Committee. This advisory committee's terms of reference include the discussion of any matters affecting Sheffield's industry and employment. Although its decisions cannot bind the council, they are reported to the City Promotion Committee, and thus represent an input into the council's decision-making. Since all of the leading officers involved in economic activity attend the Industrial Development Advisory Committee it constitutes a forum where ideas can be discussed across institutional and professional boundaries.[13]

Sheffield's Policy Committee has also begun to intervene more directly in economic matters through sub-committees concerned with the problems of the inner city and work opportunities, mainly to counteract youth unemployment. The latter sub-committee has now been expanded into an Employment Advisory Committee to help build contact with the national Manpower Services Commission, particularly in looking at the Government's various employment creation programmes and at the connections between education and the labour supply. Like the other advisory committees this one was intended to include relevant representatives from outside the council.

LOCAL POLITICAL LEADERSHIP AND ECONOMIC POLICY-MAKING

Without sympathy and support from the political leadership it is virtually impossible for even the most committed council officer to launch a programme of economic action. In reverse, however committed leading councillors may be, they require the support of their officers if an effective programme is to be devised and put into effect. In some of the authorities examined the political leadership has played a very important part as a source of initiatives and continuing support for an employment-generating programme.

There are few pronounced differences between the major political parties in the economic development field. In each authority there has been broad agreement on what the main economic issues are, accompanied in some cases by minor differences in emphasis and disagreement on methods. The main contrasts between authorities seem to have little to do with party control. This was confirmed in discussion with spokesmen of the minority party in all the authorities visited. The authorities themselves showed substantial variation in political composition, yet this appeared to have no significant effect in explaining such policy differences as could be discerned.[14] In most cases political disputes take place on a limited number of clearly understood issues, such as the sale of council housing, the level of subsidy for bus services or the level of bus fares, whilst issues like economic development and employment promotion arouse little or no controversy.

It is often difficult to detect the source of the first initiative for local authority intervention. In most of the cases economic activity had begun in the late 1960s or early 1970s, and its historical course is hard to trace, being mixed up with many different aspects of each local authority's work. In South Yorkshire, however, which was a new authority, there can be little doubt that the initial political commitment to economic action had a big effect. The need to carry out policies to improve the local economic situation was prominent in the Labour Party's 1973 county election manifesto and this was the key document passed to the Chief Executive of the new authority on his appointment.

A similar commitment has existed elsewhere, though expressed less forcibly on the whole. This was so in Sheffield and Nottinghamshire, for example, where at various stages the officers concerned with economic and industrial development were offered increased budgets to encourage an expansion in their activities. In Sheffield much of the political initiative expressed itself through the creation of specialist committees and in some of the ideas arising from the Industrial Development Advisory Committee, including the decision to send delegations to London in support of local industries. Councillors in Nottinghamshire have taken the initiative on a number of important issues, such as the decision to invest in Horizon Midlands, the proposal for a Development Company and the idea of a salesman for the county which first appeared in a Conservative Party election manifesto.

The evidence of initiatives proceeding from the political side does not take us back to the traditional model of the elected representatives as the major source of policy, with officers simply as executants advising them how best to put their proposals into practice. And in present conditions there is no doubt that the initiating role of councillors has diminished in favour of a facilitative role, one in which they take up, perhaps amend and then endorse policy proposals thought out and developed by a council's officers. This trend does not exclude the possibility of councillors enunciating the broadest of objectives which set the limits within which officers must develop operationally effective policies. But it does mean that the councillors' most important contribution is made in reacting to proposals put forward by the administration and in facilitating their adoption in viable and acceptable forms.

In most of the cases studied here the development of officer and councillor sensitivity to economic needs proceeded in parallel. In South Yorkshire Metropolitan County the preparation of the structure plan played a big part in forming the policy background to decisions on a pattern of economic activity and the leading councillors were closely involved in discussions with the planners. In Fenland district the development of an industrial policy was the product of both officer and councillor concern, stemming from a series of regional planning documents which emphasised the problems of the Fen towns.[15] It was the continuation of policies pursued before reorganisation by Wisbech Municipal Borough and March Urban District Council which had been experienced by many officers and councillors of the new authority.

The character of economic development work is such that officers are bound to have a major voice in both policy-making and implementation. The lack of political controversy and the relatively low budgets allocated to the activity help to ensure this. Except in South Yorkshire it is a function only handled as part (often a minor part) of the responsibilities of another committee (or even committees). In all the local authorities the committees were concerned only to exercise a general supervision and, whilst a policy input may be possible if and when larger issues come up for decision, the officers involved were the main driving force. Councillors can and do have some influence, but the fact that a great deal of the work of their officers depends first on identifying firms which plan to develop and secondly on reaching some agreement with them, ensures that this must be limited principally to the facilitative role discussed above. Once economic development is identified as a specialised activity, then the scope for policy initiatives by a committee diminishes.

RELATIONSHIPS BETWEEN LOCAL AUTHORITIES

Co-operation between local authorities on economic issues is severely limited, in part because they are competing with each other for the attention of potential developers. The joint work which takes place is either of such a broad nature that possibilities of conflict are irrelevant or the relationship between the authorities involved is clearly an unequal one.

The former type of co-operation is well illustrated in the permanent and semi-permanent local authority planning bodies which exist at regional level. Since the emphasis has traditionally been restricted to commenting on regional strategies and reacting to policy statements made by Economic Planning Councils, it seems probable that these bodies will decline in significance now that the Planning Councils have been dissolved. Local authorities find it difficult to speak with a regional voice because it is unclear how far that will be to the advantage of individual authorities, except where changes are sought in the application of the Department of Industry's regional policy. Thus in the mid 1970s the West Midlands Planning Authorities Conference emphasised the theme that changes were needed in industrial development certificate control which was said to be restricting regional growth. [16] For none of the authorities visited was there such a clear-cut regional issue. South Yorkshire was probably most effective in using the Yorkshire and Humberside Strategic Conference as a channel for its early criticisms of the Economic Planning Council's regional strategy. Ironically, perhaps, since the East Midlands is recognised as having a very weak regional identity and the Economic Planning Council had not even prepared a regional strategy, the greatest degree of co-operation on planning issues was achieved between Derbyshire, Nottinghamshire, Derby and Nottingham in the early 1970s when the Sub-Regional Strategy for Mansfield—Alfreton was being prepared by a joint planning team. The extent of co-operation has fallen sharply since local government reorganisation and the Sub-Regional Strategy (at least as far as Nottinghamshire is concerned) has lost most of its policy significance.

Only in one of the regions (Yorkshire and Humberside) considered in this study is there a standing Development Association, in part financed by central government (£30,000 per annum), but mainly by local authorities (£120,000: 1977/8 figures). This Association is intended to carry out activities which individual authorities could not carry out on their own. The central government support has been intended to encourage joint work and to discourage unnecessary duplication and wasteful competition between local authorities for new industry. For both these reasons the Association has aimed mainly at the attraction of inward investment, concentrating on advertising, exhibitions and visits elsewhere in Britain and in Europe. Until recently both Sheffield and South Yorkshire were members.[17] But the strains of co-operative work can be seen in South Yorkshire's case – as it has built up its own activity it has been less prepared, given the limited finance available, to fund another body and it has now decided to withdraw from the Development Association and to apply the subscriptions (£25,570 in 1978/9)[18] to its own activity.

An attempt (initiated by Fenland) to create a similar local authority body on a more modest scale in East Anglia has had limited success. A number of authorities[19] have agreed to co-operate in the Mid-Anglia Industrial Development Association, to exchange experience and to refer to other members inquiries from developers which cannot be met by the authority to which they are first made. Despite its small budget it planned to have a stand at the East of England Show in 1979.

The two-tier system of local government in England has left economic activity as a concern of both levels and in itself this could be expected to generate serious conflicts over both goals and the division of responsibility between the tiers. Such has been the division of functions between the tiers that the extent of conflict and competition varies from case to case according to local custom or agreement and the degree of accommodation reached between the tiers over time. But it is only where districts are relatively weak financially and in other resources, and where county and district policies coincide that extensive practical co-operation takes place, as has been the case for Fenland and most of Nottinghamshire's districts. Cambridgeshire has helped Fenland and East Cambridgeshire in carrying out economic development, both directly and by exerting pressure on the Council for Small Industries in Rural Areas and the Development Commission, whilst Nottinghamshire has entered into partnerships with several of its district authorities to develop industrial estates and advance factories, providing finance on a scale not practicable for individual districts. In South Yorkshire too the county and Doncaster MDC work together in managing an estate at Carcroft and the county has organised seminars on planning for industry in conjunction with most of its districts. Even where co-operation does take place, however, districts often seem hesitant, fearing that they will lose some of their powers and policy interests to the county.

Planning has been one of the central areas of conflict since 1974. Some county planners have been reluctant to give up detailed development control work, while district planners have objected to the overall control implicitly held by the counties.[20] District councils have objected to structure plans as being too detailed and specific since this increases the number of development control matters which might have to be referred to the county level for decision. There have been and remain major policy disagreements in South Yorkshire (particularly between Sheffield and the county planning department) and similar arguments took place over the early drafts of the Nottinghamshire structure plan. Some accommodation has now been achieved, largely because the county planning authorities have withdrawn from a concern with detailed planning policies, partly to avoid unnecessary conflict and partly because the definition of what constitutes 'strategic planning' is becoming clearer and more restricted. Most county authorities now consider very few planning applications except for mineral working.

Planning has provided some serious disputes on matters of economic policy. Sheffield objected particularly strongly to South Yorkshire's system of Job Priority Areas and Environmental Priority Areas which, it was argued, was likely to penalise Sheffield and development there. In Nottinghamshire, Nottingham challenged proposals in early drafts of the structure plan for development to be centred on the Mansfield – Alfreton 'growth zone'. In Cambridgeshire there has until recently been less controversy, but the county has challenged some of the Development Corporation's proposals for development at Castor and the city council has objected strongly in return.[21] Most of these policy conflicts stem from the two-tier system which is inherently likely to encourage divergence of interests. At its simplest this can be expressed as follows: county councils are concerned with larger areas and as a result of spending restrictions and the spatially distributive nature of structure plans, are likely to identify particular areas for additional assistance. But district councils are interested primarily in their own development prospects, rarely accepting that any other area of the county can be more deserving than their own.

These problems have extended into the economic development field, particularly in the case of the larger ex-county borough authorities which have often refused to co-operate to more than a minimum extent. Nottinghamshire has now agreed to concentrate its economic development work outside the City of Nottingham. Although Sheffield has expressed concern that the South Yorkshire structure plan proposed to concentrate development outside the city, objections would also be raised if the county launched a significant programme of activity inside the boundaries of Sheffield. Officers argued that inexperienced intervention by South Yorkshire might upset the city's delicate land and property market. These disagreements reflect both the potential conflict over goals described in the previous paragraph and are also an indication of the institutionalised conflict over responsibilities. Those authorities which used to be county boroughs have been concerned continually to emphasise their independence and generally remain reluctant to co-operate, not only for economic reasons but also because they object to the additional constraints involved in such organised co-operation. It is significant that the boundaries of neither Sheffield nor Nottingham were greatly altered by the reorganisation of local government so that their political and administrative traditions have been maintained. Nottingham was one of the leading members (despite its then Conservative majority) in the campaign to secure the return of some powers from the county level to the larger districts.

RELATIONSHIPS WITH GOVERNMENT BODIES ABOVE THE LOCAL LEVEL

Most local authority contacts with bodies at regional or national level are with departments of central government. A major concern of each is to influence the activities and policies of the others and so they are to some extent in a permanent negotiating relationship. There is a process of regular interaction as local authorities prepare spending plans such as the Housing Investment Programmes, the Transport Policies and Programmes, inner city plans, and so on, all of which are considered by central government departments, usually through regional offices, but sometimes (as with the inner city plans) by special joint committees of central and local government.

For the Department of the Environment the supervision of the preparation of county structure plans is a vital element in the planning process since it provides its main source of overall control. The Department at regional level is involved throughout: advising, guiding, prodding and ultimately, after the Examination in Public, deciding whether to confirm or modify the plan. A process of negotiation takes place in which the county and the Department make some accommodation, although the last word rests with the latter. The Department of the Environment has accepted the inclusion (usually in lower case) of some reference in structure plans to policies adopted by counties and falling outside the planning field as strictly defined. But it has generally tried to modify plans like that of South Yorkshire which in its view have strayed too far from land use considerations.[22] Exceptionally, having failed to influence South Yorkshire's structure plan at an early stage, the Department sent an officer from London to challenge its financial implications and projections at the Examination in Public. The Department was unable to challenge the proposed system of Job and Environmental Priority Areas at this Examination because it was also acting in a semi-judicial capacity, but it could challenge the financial estimates proposed for carrying out policies in support of the plan. The Economic Planning Council was left to challenge the policies themselves as contrary to the approved Regional Strategy. But it should be borne in mind that the Planning Council was itself advised by a board of civil servants from the Department of the Environment and the Department of Industry, so that the Department's modesty at the Examination in Public did not stop the communication of its views through another body.

As far as economic activity is concerned the main regular contact with central government is in the planning field. All government departments with an economic interest, including the Ministry of Agriculture, Fisheries and Food and the Department of Industry, make comments on the structure plans and many are important sources of information for local planning departments in their plan preparation. This contact, of course, is mainly at county level. Districts are less regularly involved with government departments on planning issues, although their plans may also be called in for consideration by the Department of the Environment in exceptional circumstances. Because local authorities have no statutory economic function, the department responsible for them has had no effective monitoring procedures and no formal consultative process on economic issues. Just as traditional local authority organisation finds it difficult to adjust to a newly discovered economic function, so the central government organisation accustomed to the supervision of the familiar local government responsibilities does not find it easy to adapt to new activities.

The absence of a clear statutory framework for economic support policies means, therefore, that there is less scope for the kind of detailed central controls which have been built into many other policy sectors. In this context it is striking, for example, that neither the Department of the Environment nor the Department of Industry has a clear picture of activities being carried out by individual local authorities in the economic development field. They have no normal way of gathering details of economic development budgets, nor (and this is perhaps more important) details of local authority industrial estates, although civil servants in regional offices may have details of some of them as a result of their local knowledge. Of course, this should not be taken to imply that local authorities are free to undertake whatever they wish. The lack of specific powers does restrict them, at least to the extent of creating doubt about what can be done in some cases. South Yorkshire's proposed General Powers Bill, for example, includes powers intended to ease the pursuit of an economic policy or at least to render it less exposed to challenge. Some authorities complained that the Community Land Act made economic activity more difficult by stopping the sale of freehold land by local authorities, but others including South Yorkshire made extensive use of the Act's powers and the loans provided under it. Only where the Community Land Act was used extensively, as in South Yorkshire, have regional offices of the Department of the Environment been able to discuss local authority economic activity in relation to the Department's own policies and programmes.

The policies of the Department of the Environment have ensured that counties have been discouraged from trying to use structure plans as overall corporate planning documents, economic plans or programmes, or to include proposals for changes in government policy. This should perhaps more properly be seen as a constraint on local authority planners since the authority remains free to prepare any 'plan' it wishes, provided it is not intended to be a statutory planning document. Such a view, however, which is put forward by some members of the Department of the Environment, appears to be somewhat disingenuous, for it overlooks the way in which local government operates. Local authority policies, as much as their budgets, generally develop on an incremental basis, growing out of long-established or statutory activities. If the statutory planning process cannot be developed to cover wider issues, then a quite separate process of planning is required. But members of few other local government departments will be prepared to accept increased functions for the planning department (or indeed any other planning unit) unless these functions are supported by legislation of some sort. At a time of financial stringency the defence of existing functions is more likely than acceptance of a new and rather nebulous non-statutory 'planning' role. The debates of the 1960s have, moreover, left planning departments and planners in an exposed position. New possibilities have apparently opened up, but it is uncertain how far these have been legitimised in the eyes of councillors and many other officers too, whilst the financial and political environment has become more inhospitable.

Despite the local economic importance of many of the policies of the Department of Industry, particularly its regional policy, there is little regular contact between that Department and local authorities. The Department's civil servants also appear to have decided that local authority activities are unlikely to challenge seriously the effectiveness of their own programmes, although the Department's Invest in Britain Bureau has been set up to co-ordinate promotional activity abroad and it discourages local authority campaigns except through the main government-backed Development Associations. Even so, the Bureau is unable or unwilling to apply sanctions to local authorities such as Sheffield which operate abroad on a relatively large scale.

In all regions, however, there are regular meetings of county and district Chief Executives with the regional offices of the Department of the Environment to exchange views. These discussions have increasingly included economic questions such as those raised in the Department of the Environment circular 71/77 on the Industrial Strategy for which the Department of Industry was also responsible. This circular encouraged local authorities to be more sympathetic to industrial requirements and development, and to appoint Industrial Liaison Officers. Whilst all of the authorities studied claimed that the circular had had no significant effect on their own activities, there has been an increase in the appointment or designation of such officers in all regions since it appeared. This may be a coincidence since the circular caught a tide of opinion already on the move. Nevertheless, the circular is generally agreed to have marked a watershed in the development of local economic activity by endorsing its growing importance. It was accepted by some planning officers that it had on occasion been useful as a text to put before councillors who might otherwise have taken a negative view of an economic development programme.

The extent of local authority contact with other levels of government depends principally on their ability to control and influence council activity, on the availability of resources from them and the advantages to be had from influencing them. Similar considerations apply to those centrally funded bodies which are not strictly under central government control, such as the Economic Planning Councils (now abolished) and the Council for Small Industries in Rural Areas which have been referred to above in different contexts. Local authority contact with the Economic Planning Councils was fairly regular and they always included several local authority representatives. But in no case did the local authority see its relationship with the Economic Planning Council as a very important one. Some authorities expressed hostility towards the Councils, some felt they performed no useful function and others saw them as relevant only in so far as they could be used to present a regional case to central government. It is unlikely that local authorities shed many tears over their dissolution.

The Council for Small Industries in Rural Areas (COSIRA) has no direct connection with the statutory functions of local authorities, but its advisory committees always include officers or councillors from local authorities and local authority officers have increasingly sought discussions with its County Organisers. As indicated earlier Cambridgeshire and Fenland have been closely involved with COSIRA in the development of a Special Investment Area. If additional resources are available locally officers are eager to retain contact. Similar considerations apply to the development of increased formal and informal contact between local authorities and the Manpower Services Commission (MSC) since the Commission has had additional resources for employment creation and training programmes, the local deployment of which might assist in reducing unemployment. Officers have become increasingly concerned to take part in the MSC's own District Manpower Committees, and in at least one case efforts have been made to involve the MSC in the authority's own committee structure.

RELATIONSHIPS WITH LOCAL INDUSTRIAL AND
COMMERCIAL INTERESTS

The links between local authorities and economic actors range from informal and social contacts with officers and councillors to formalised meetings with representative organisations. The former are probably more important but more difficult to identify, whilst the latter are easy to identify but are often occasions for symbolic concern with little impact on policy-making.

Trade union interest in local authority policies has been small, except where job loss or major cuts in services have been involved. Attempts by Nottinghamshire's planners to encourage trade union comments on the structure plan, for example, were unsuccessful and this has been the experience elsewhere. When the council took an interest in the problems of mining in the east of the county and threatened to refuse planning permission for mining developments in the south unless guarantees of employment were given for employees in the older mines, the National Union of Mineworkers made it clear that council intervention was not welcome since the issue was solely one for negotiation between the union and the Coal Board.

In Sheffield and South Yorkshire the local trade unions have had an influence on the development of an economic policy, but there the importance of informal links has been particularly noticeable. In South Yorkshire, for example, the concern for economic and environmental matters has almost certainly been heightened by the local importance of the National Union of Mineworkers and the past experience of pit closures. Many of the county councillors from outside Sheffield are employed by or have been employed by the National Coal Board and they reflect this experience. But direct pressure from the union is more difficult to identify since the union's fears are shared by its members who are councillors. In Sheffield there is a remarkable overlap between the District Labour Party and the Trades Council, which until the early 1970s were united in one body and still share many of the same officers (including a full-time secretary). Many leading members of the City Trades Council are full-time trade union officials and members of the

City council. The idea for an Industrial Development Advisory Committee was originally raised by the Trades Council which had its own sub-committee on industrial problems and has played an important part in raising issues through the Industrial Development Advisory Committee.

Employers' organisations at local level – Chambers of Commerce – regularly make submissions to councils on issues of concern, usually the operation of planning and transportation policies. They are also more likely than Trades Councils to comment on planning policies in some detail because in the major cities they generally have larger staffs and are more directly affected by such policies. In South Yorkshire and Sheffield the major Chamber of Commerce is in Sheffield and generally supports the work of Sheffield's Industrial Development Officer and Publicity Officer. The Chamber has co-operated closely with these officers on relevant schemes (including several exhibitions and a visit to the west coast of America), and it is represented on the Industrial Development Advisory Committee. It also co-operates in South Yorkshire's work, being particularly committed to its campaign on the Sheffield and South Yorkshire Navigation. But it has consistently and vociferously opposed the county's public transport policy.

The experience of the Nottinghamshire Chamber of Commerce, based in Nottingham, is similar. It has regular meetings with representatives of both the county and city and has made a financial contribution to the city's Industrial and Commercial Development Unit. The Chamber is now involved in the county's Economic Forum, and is particularly keen to maintain informal contacts with officers.

Formal consultation takes place in all authorities, but it is not felt to be very important in any of them. Neither Chambers of Commerce nor the trade unions, it was widely argued, fully understand local authorities. They cannot devote a great deal of attention to local policies and activities and in any event they have other interests to pursue. This division is still clearer when local authority contacts with employer and trade union organisations above the local level are considered. Nottinghamshire's Economic Forum, which includes representatives from the Regional Confederation of British Industry and the Regional Trades Union Congress, seems to represent the maximum level of interest. Regional organisations of this type are more concerned with central than local government and share the weaknesses of most English regional institutions, having few full-time staff and a weak sense of regional identity. They are often consulted on issues such as structure planning, but local authorities are more interested in individual firms or public bodies which can supply extra resources. Regional bodies tend to exist in parallel with councils so that each is tolerant of the other, but neither has a great deal of influence over the other. For most local authorities it is their ability to deal with individual cases which is a measure of their own success, and these are the clients to which much local authority activity is directed. In particular there is close co-operation with estate agents and developers, especially in Sheffield, Nottingham and Fenland. In the latter district there is even a joint publicity fund with developers and the county council to help promote the area. Where industrial development officers have been appointed one of their main functions has been to encourage local co-operation with industry and where possible local authority planning departments have involved local firms, particularly in the preparation of district plans on which their views have been sought.

The relationship between local authorities and their 'clients' in the economic sphere is an unusual one. Councils have no powers to direct industry and commerce, despite their ability to impose restrictions and suggest alternatives. They are in a particularly weak position with regard to large firms, whose investment decisions are unlikely to be influenced by the marginal financial impact of local authority incentives. With such firms local authorities are in the position of supplicants, hoping in a variety of ways to indicate their sympathetic attitudes to development and to draw the firms' attention to their existence. From the point of view of large firms the main services which local authorities can perform are, first, to improve the range of information at their disposal on the basis of which investment and locational decisions are made, and secondly, to resist the temptation to restrict the firm's operation once it is under way. There is little need for a close and continuing relationship.

It is, therefore, understandable that many local authorities should argue that their main contribution lies in assisting small and medium-sized firms. An orientation towards these firms allows local authorities to have a 'client' group which has its own problems and many of whose members are (at least in principle) tied to the local authority area. The provision of assistance to small firms is now seen by planners to be creditable in itself almost without reference to any additional employment which may ensue. The harsh reality of local authority inability significantly to influence larger firms is masked in the policy justifications that large firms grow from small ones and that Britain's small firms sector should be expanded. Even with small firms, of course, local authority relationships are by no means unproblematical. Councils and their staffs are not on the whole well-qualified judges of entre-preneurial skill and it is difficult to see how they can generate the enthusiasm necessary to encourage the growth of new enterprises. Nevertheless, industrial development officers give many signs of being well suited to providing a more or less efficient estate agency and property development service to small firms which does not seem to be coming from any other source.

NOTES

1 The appointment of certain officers and the creation of some committees is required by statute. Education authorities, for example, must have both an education committee and a chief education officer. There are similar requirements for the appointment of officers responsible for planning, finance and social services among others.

2 The need for some of this co-operation on publicity matters may no longer exist now that the division includes an officer with specific responsibilities for promotional work.

3 J. D. Stewart, *The Responsive Local Authority* (London: Knight, 1974), p. 13.

4 See, for example, 'The Creation of Employment Opportunities' (South Yorkshire County Council, 1977), and Employment, Development and Publicity Sub-committee, Corporate and Financial Plan (South Yorkshire County Council, 1977).

5 Objectives (City of Sheffield Metropolitan District Council, November 1977).

6 This impression is confirmed by N. Falk, *Local Authorities and Industrial Development: Results of a Survey* (London: Urbed, 1978).

7 It is also reflected in the results of Falk's survey, ibid.

8 Employment, Development and Publicity Sub-Committee, Corporate and Financial Plan (South Yorkshire County Council, 1978). This included proposed spending beyond the guidelines. The total capital expenditure 1979/80 to 1983/4 proposed was to be nearly £13m. The repeal of the Community Land Act will, of course, make such a budget very difficult to achieve.

9 The changes to the system first introduced in 1979–80 can be expected to reduce the room for manoeuvre enjoyed by urban authorities, particularly in the context of the Local Government Planning and Land Bill 1980.

10 Cambridgeshire County Council, Yearbook 1977–78, p. 187.

11 Until recently Nottingham's main resource committees (Finance and Land) were not sub-committees of Policy and Resources (P & R), but joint meetings were frequent and the chairman of P & R was vice-chairman of Finance, whose chairman was vice-chairman of P & R. Since May 1979, when Labour regained control, the structure has been altered, and the central committee is now the Policy and Finance Committee.

12 In Peterborough to Policy and Resources Committee's Finance and Property Sub-Committee.

13 Several authorities are now setting up similar bodies or looking into other possibilities. Nottinghamshire's Economic Forum is a good example.

14 During 1977/8 the party political composition of the councils concerned was as follows:

	Conservative	Labour	Liberal	Vacant	Other
South Yorkshire	31	62	2	—	5
Sheffield	22	63	5	—	—
Nottinghamshire	66	20	1	—	2
Nottingham	40	14	—	—	1
Cambridgeshire	56	7	1	—	4
Peterborough	26	20	1	—	1
Fenland	25	7	1	2	5

15 See, for example, *The Small Towns Study* (East Anglia Consultative Committee and East Anglia Economic Planning Council, 1972).

16 See, for example, *Current Developments in the Economy of the West Midlands Region* (West Midlands Planning Authorities Conference, April 1975).

17 Subscriptions may be paid either by individual districts, so that if all in one county affiliate then the county too is a member, or by the county on its own behalf and on

behalf of its districts. In the past South Yorkshire has affiliated on behalf of its districts.

18   Corporate and Financial Plan (1978), op. cit., p. 13.

19   Fenland, Cambridge, Peterborough, Huntingdon, Kings Lynn and Forest Heath District Councils, and Cambridgeshire County Council.

20   Until recently counties had the rarely used power under Schedule 16 (para. 19) of the Local Government Act 1972 to direct a district planning authority to grant or refuse a planning application in cases where the consideration of such an application might affect its own position as a local planning authority (for example, where there might be conflict with the structure plan). Government proposals (announced in July 1979) will remove the right to make most directions of this sort.

21   The controversy over the development at Castor also provides an interesting example of the impact which the third tier (parish council) can have in exceptional cases. Castor Parish Council has consistently opposed the proposed development and has been strongly supported by local residents. Both the city and county councillors representing the area have supported the parish council's position, but have usually been in a small minority on their respective councils. Peterborough City Council is particularly strongly committed to the development. The county's Planning Committee was, however, sympathetic to the parish case, partly as a consequence of resentment that scarce resources were being diverted to the new town and partly because the county council includes several councillors from rural areas with little interest in further urban development. Although the development is now expected to take place the episode has shown how a parish council can use differences of interest between two higher levels of local government to its own advantage.

22   Largely as a result of DoE policy, in the key diagram (Fig. 51) of the structure plan finally approved (December 1979) for South Yorkshire all reference to Job Priority Areas has been removed, to be replaced by less specific 'areas of greatest potential for industrial development.'

Chapter 5

ECONOMIC POLICY-MAKING BY LOCAL AUTHORITIES IN THE FEDERAL REPUBLIC OF GERMANY

Whereas Great Britain possesses a centralised pattern of government, the Federal Republic is, as its name makes clear, a federal state. To this basic constitutional condition making for a decentralised system of government we must also add the guarantee of local self-government contained in art. 28(2) of the Basic Law: 'Local authorities are to be guaranteed the right to regulate all matters concerning the local community within the framework of law and on their own responsibility.' In principle, therefore, the German local authority appears to enjoy far more autonomy than the British and operates within a dispersed and decentralised structure of government. Nevertheless, as we shall see, it is doubtful whether in practice the formal constitutional differences have a decisive impact on what local authorities can actually undertake in the sector of activity with which this study deals. Moreover, there are tendencies at work in Germany which in the opinion of many observers are bringing local authorities more and more within the ambit of policies determined at the state level, thus diminishing in significant ways the differences between the two countries which might be inferred from their different constitutional foundations.

In the Federal Republic economic promotion at the local level is one of the few genuinely autonomous activities in the sense that it is not prescribed by statute as a task which must be carried out. Historically its origins as a local concern lie far back in the past, but it received a new impulse during the postwar phase of reconstruction, much of which involved local authority investment in urban infrastructure and the application of local planning powers. The rapid growth of industry, especially in the larger urban areas, reinforced a general local authority concern with economic development and its consequences. As early as 1961 the KGSt, a local authority advisory body for administrative organisation,[1] had developed an organisational model within which economic policy was recognised as a functional area fitting local administrative structures. This model was widely applied.

Given the economic policies successfully pursued in the Federal Republic after 1949 and the emphasis in them on sustaining the framework for a market economy, it is not surprising that the field of economic action open to local authorities came to be fairly narrowly circumscribed in practice. Economic policy at the local level was seen essentially as supportive, that is to say, in terms of promotional and developmental programmes intended to encourage patterns of economic growth and industrial investment determined largely by agents beyond local control and operating under market conditions. This is no doubt one reason why no attempt has been made to supplement the general competence by the provision of a specific statutory framework for local economic action: it has remained a sphere in which local authorities must themselves decide what needs to be done and what is practicable within existing resources and other constraints. Acting under their general competence they have to decide what seems best suited to advancing the economic well-being of the local areas and their inhabitants.

In the light of what has just been said it is not surprising that the level of economic development effort by German local authorities has been closely related to prevailing economic conditions. In the early postwar years much local authority effort went into infrastructural measures designed *inter alia* to encourage rapid industrial reconstruction. Then, during the period of high economic growth rates from the mid 1950s onwards local authorities could enjoy rising revenues without paying much attention to explicit economic development measures. It is only during the past decade when growth has slowed down and localised structural problems have become more common that economic development in the sense of actively encouraging industrial and commercial investment has become a more important policy sector for local authorities.

In respect of the kinds of action which local authorities can undertake to stimulate economic development, it has to be remembered that the local authority is not in a strong initiating position. Basically it can offer inducements – chiefly certain services and land – but in doing so it is competing with other authorities. The private entrepreneur may benefit from such competition, but it is rare that the local authority gains advantages from the competition between entrepreneurs. Moreover, whilst infrastructural services, some financial support and technical advice have been shown to play a part in locational decisions by enterprises, it is also known that these factors are seldom decisive in tipping the scales in favour of new investment. Thus it is almost inevitable that the local authority is in its economic activities forced into a reactive role: it appraises a situation, tries to devise measures which offer some prospect of influencing external agents in that situation, and hopes that its inducements will have some effect on entrepreneurial behaviour.

We have referred so far to the dependence of local authorities on actors in the largely private economy. In addition, however, the German local authority operates within the framework of Federal and *Land* economic policy-making. This now includes the elements of both macro-economic demand management and of structural policy. The former has a major impact on what are held to be appropriate levels of public expenditure locally, whilst the latter includes regional development programmes which directly influence the kind of opportunities open to individual local authorities. Amongst structural policies broadly considered we must include town development policy, a sector which has gained new importance during the past decade. Its significance in relation to local economic activities lies in the fact that under national legislation grants are made to local authorities for land assembly and purchase as well as for the servicing of sites. Thus, in outline there are three principal dimensions of state action and intervention affecting local economic policies:

(i)   support grants under town development powers;
(ii) regional economic development programmes, including both purely *Land* programmes and Federal government–*Land* joint programmes;
(iii) development programmes under general counter-cyclical demand management policies as well as in the shape of specific structure policies, the addressees being chiefly businesses but including local authorities too.

It is worth underlining the fact that most of the responsibility under the first two headings falls on the *Land* administrations, even though funds may come directly from the Federal government. The pattern of governmental relationships within which the local authority finds itself does not, however, have a vertical hierarchical form. It is much more a pattern of interdependence between the different levels, with the realisation of policies pursued by each level depending extensively on how far they prove to be adaptable to objectives and interests already well established at one or more levels of the system. This fact of interdependence has been underlined recently by the diminishing impact of overall national demand management policies. As a result more emphasis has been given to the kind of decentralised action represented by industrial support measures initiated by *Land* governments or local authorities.

THE LEGAL BASIS OF LOCAL ECONOMIC POLICY

The notion of a general competence enjoyed by local authorities reaches back at least to the reforms pioneered in Prussia in 1808 by Baron vom Stein. It was reaffirmed in art. 28(2) of the Basic Law. The counterpart of a general local authority competence is, however, the recognition of the state's[2] duty to exercise oversight of the legality of all local government action. In other words there is in Germany something like 'tutelle administrative'. The supervision of local authorities exercised by the *Länder* administrations divides up into legal and administrative oversight: *Rechtaufsicht* and *Fachaufsicht*. The former rests on a general power vested in state authorities and is directed to ensuring that local authorities act correctly within the law. The latter depends usually on specific statutory provisions or operates when the local authority is acting as an agent of the state level and, of course, it allows the state authority to scrutinise local decisions in detail. Legal oversight, which is narrow in scope, applies generally to all local activity, whilst the range of general administrative oversight has tended to increase as a result of specific legislation encouraging or requiring local authority activity on behalf of the state level of government. In the case of the all-purpose municipalities and counties (*Kreise*) legal oversight is exercised by the provincial administrative president, a field officer appointed by the *Land* Interior Ministry, whilst much of the technical, administrative oversight is usually exercised by the appropriate representatives of the ministry responsible for the activities concerned, usually also located in offices of the provincial administration (*Regierungsbezirk*). For local authorities falling within the area of a county authority, it is the latter acting in a state capacity that exercises legal oversight.

Whilst local authorities are in principle entitled to take whatever action they regard as desirable for the economic benefit of their areas, in reality, however, the range of possibilities open to the local authority is limited, both by resource availability and by the needs to exercise its powers within the law. In other words, a local authority could not get away with action held to be legally inappropriate for such a public body. This general restriction can be taken to rule out action involving acceptance of business risks or the provision of direct subsidies to firms. There is too some sensitivity in relation to the external effects of local economic development policies and the general understanding is that local economic development has to be pursued in a restrained way. Nevertheless the local authorities are spared the need often felt in Britain to be able to point to specific powers contained in statutes before taking action and their economic role has emerged quite naturally on the basis of the general responsibility for the well-being of local inhabitants.

There is some variation in the internal organisation of German local authorities. Broadly speaking, it is possible to distinguish between unitary and dualist systems. The former is exemplified by those local authority constitutions embodying an elected local council, itself choosing a mayor and assistants who both head the administration and preside over the council. An important variation in South Germany is the institution of the directly elected mayor or lord mayor who acts as the chief executive authority and presides over the council as well. The dualist system finds expression in the juxtaposition of a council and a collegial executive, the latter being appointed by the council for a fixed period, or in the system found in North Rhine-Westphalia under which the council elects a mayor to preside over its meetings and appoints an administrative director and assistants who assume executive responsibility. It is important to note, however, that regardless of constitutional variations from one *Land* to another there is in German local government always a clear definition of who is in charge of administration and policy implementation. The executive power is reasonably well differentiated from the deliberative and legislative.

Decisions on bigger questions have always to be confirmed by the councils, and under the local government system in North Rhine-Westphalia far more than formal confirmation is usually needed. The preparation of such decisions generally takes place in functional committees, some of which under the North Rhine-Westphalia constitutional codes for local government must be set up, for example an executive committee and a finance committee. But the establishment of many of these specialised committees remains within the discretion of the local authority and which are deemed necessary depends a lot on the size of the authority and the type of problems it faces. Committees are established by the council, usually on a basis that guarantees proportional representation of all political groups on it.

Committees are essentially preparatory organs. They can in theory be given delegated powers of decision, but this is rare and most decisions are taken at least formally by the full council. This is reflected in the frequency of council meetings. The 'urgent decision procedure' is of some importance, since this permits both the executive committee and the mayor (in association with at least one council member) to decide matters of urgency without prior reference to the council.

A sharp separation between local authority and state-provided services can no longer be made. The centre of gravity of the local functions lies, however, in the provision of the essentially local social infrastructure and services. In contrast, the *Land* level of government is already much more concerned with functions calling for planning and control over areas larger than those of individual local authorities. Some of these functions are chiefly regulatory, whilst others involve service provision with infrastructural support from local authorities, for example in the education sector.

In respect of the degree of local responsibility which can be claimed three types of task can be distinguished, viz.:

(i)   autonomous local activities, the extent and range of which depends on local resources and decisions;
(ii) mandatory tasks, usually required by federal law;

(iii)   agency tasks performed by local authorities on behalf of the state
         and subject to administrative supervision by the *Land* authorities
         as well as to the general supervision of legality which applies to (i)
         and (ii) also.

The second and third categories nowadays constitute at least 80 per cent
of all local government activities. The function under review in this
study does, however, belong to the remaining 20 per cent or so for
which in principle local authorities assume full responsibility themselves.

Technically local authorities enjoy budgetary autonomy. On the
revenue or resources side they depend chiefly on the rates levied on
land, on the business tax, on a supplement to the payroll tax[3] and on a
guaranteed share of national income tax. In respect of these taxes, with
the exception of the last one, the local authorities can affect the local
yield by varying, where appropriate, the rate at which the tax is levied.
Usually variation of tax rates is possible only within a fairly narrow
band and is not indulged in frequently.

Under the local government finance reforms of 1969 steps were taken
to reduce the dominance of the business tax in local government
financing. For the future 40 per cent of the proceeds of this tax were to
be passed on to the *Länder* and the Federation, whilst in compensation
local government received a 14 per cent share of national income tax. It
was hoped that these measures would integrate local authorities more
effectively into a structure of national expenditure planning and
revenue projections as well as permit a more restricted, but for that
reason more effective, pattern of revenue equalisation between authorities through the redistribution of resources between rich and poor
Länder. In fact these objectives have not been fully achieved.[4] The local
government share of total tax revenues has risen less than was expected
as a result of the reforms, whilst the dependence of local authorities on
the business tax has remained relatively high (41·4 per cent of total local
revenue from taxes in 1975 as against 42 per cent share for income tax).
The business tax is, of course, particularly sensitive to fluctuations in
the level of economic prosperity. The proportion of local resources
derived from state contributions has continued to rise, reaching about
28 per cent of total income in 1977. These state contributions fall
broadly into two categories: there are block grants, serving *inter alia*
equalisation purposes, and specific grants. In North Rhine-Westphalia
the latter have tended to rise relative to the general grants, thus facilitating opportunities for the *Land* government to influence investment
decisions by local authorities. Indirectly at least this has implications
for economic development measures undertaken by local authorities.

THE PLANNING SYSTEM

The German planning system can be viewed as a four-tier hierarchy, viz.:

Federal spatial planning
Land planning
Regional planning
Local development controls and building regulations.

In principle at least this hierarchy corresponds to an increasing amount of detail in the extent of the regulation and control provided for. At the Federal level legislation establishes general principles of spatial planning which are to be taken account of by the *Länder* in drawing up their development plans (level number two). At regional level the *Land* governments establish more detailed development priorities and these in turn have to be followed by local authorities exercising direct control over development in particular areas.

Many German local authorities maintain town development plans which extend beyond straightforward control of building and the use of land, although this is not a legal requirement. Such plans are aimed at the integration of various local sectoral development plans in order to provide a basis for a coherent process of urban planning. In theory at least this provides a favourable framework for decisions on economic measures. In practice, however, the process of physical planning and the operation of building controls tend to assume the dominant role in the activity of local planning. Local authorities have under Federal building law a duty to exercise their planning powers 'in the interests of orderly urban development'. They are required to establish comprehensive land use plans as well as much more detailed building plans for specific areas. The former is intended essentially as a framework plan, prescribing what kinds of development are acceptable. The latter is a specific determination by the local authority of the kind of building standards, conditions as to use, densities, and so on which have to be observed by developers. Not surprisingly the building plan has turned out to be a somewhat rigid instrument and local authorities frequently seek to escape from the attendant difficulties by failing to establish such plans, thus remaining free to deal with proposals for development on an *ad hoc* basis.[5]

In North Rhine-Westphalia local planning is linked with *Land* planning through the regional development plans, which are intended to facilitate something like balanced regional development within the *Land* as a whole. Advisory bodies drawn from local authority representatives exist at provincial administrative office[6] level to express views on these area or regional plans. The local authorities are required to take account of *Land* regional development plan priorities in their own planning and they are further tied in to the state level of government in virtue of their duty to align their investment programmes with those of the *Land* and the Federal government over a five year period.

THE CASE STUDIES

Five local authorities in North Rhine-Westphalia were chosen for study. The criteria used for selection were the same as those used in England, subject to allowance being made for differences in institutional structure and for the fact that North Rhine-Westphalia is characterised by an unusual concentration of population and industry in the Ruhr area. The five cities selected were Essen, Bielefeld, Gelsenkirchen, Recklinghausen and Gütersloh. Table 5.1 shows these cases in relation to a number of basic selection criteria.

Table 5.1   *Economic indicators[a] of cities selected*

	Size class[b]	Unemployment level	Tax resources per capita	Level of local authority debt per capita
Essen	I	Medium	Medium	High
Gelsenkirchen	II	High	Low	High
Bielefeld	II	Low	High	High
Recklinghausen	III	Low	Low	Low
Gütersloh	IV	Low	High	Low

[a] Measured in relation to all local authorities with more than 50,000 inhabitants in North Rhine-Westphalia.
[b] Size classes: I = over 500,000 population
                          II = 200,000–500,000 population
                          III = 100,000–200,000 population
                          IV = 50,000–100,000 population.

Essen, with 670,000 inhabitants, was the largest of the cities examined. It is a major centre and comes within the administrative area of the Düsseldorf provincial administration (*Regierungsbezirk*). The contemporary economic structure of Essen illustrates the transition which has taken place from being one of the major European centres of the iron, steel and coal industries to becoming a city whose employment is dominated by the service sector. Earlier local policy measures have given Essen one of the best infrastructures in the country and this, in combination with the changes in the pattern of employment in favour of the electronics and machine tool industries as well as the service sector, means that the city is not regarded as being in need of state-supported economic development action. Nevertheless, the city has relatively lower revenues per head than Cologne or nearby Düsseldorf and unemployment is above the national average, reflecting the fact that the adaptation of the employment structure to the decline of heavy industry has not yet been successfully concluded.

The Social Democratic Party (SPD) has 47 out of 83 seats on the Essen City Council, a majority position that it enjoys in all other Ruhr cities.[7] On the other hand the council Committee for Economic Affairs and Estates is presided over by a member of the Christian Democratic Union (CDU), a fact which illustrates the readiness of the political parties to permit something like a proportional distribution of council positions.

The economic position of Gelsenkirchen and of Recklinghausen is substantially less favourable than that of Essen. Gelsenkirchen (pop. 317,980) is an all-purpose authority which has not been able to absorb all the effects on employment of the structural crisis in the mining industry which began in the 1960s. Recklinghausen (pop. 120,000) has had a similar experience. Both towns have lower than average local tax resources. Whilst the indebtedness of Gelsenkirchen has recently risen rapidly, this reflecting substantial local investment, Recklinghausen's debt has risen much more slowly and at a rate below that of the increase in tax resources. The industrial structure of the two towns differs significantly despite shared characteristics: in Gelsenkirchen heavy industry accounted for one-third of employment in 1975, but chemicals and other manufacturing activities were already in second place. In contrast Recklinghausen has experienced far less diversification. Both cities qualify as priority centres for state economic development assistance. Under the joint Federal–*Land* programme for regional development Recklinghausen receives a support rate of 20 per cent, whereas Gelsenkirchen qualifies for only 12 per cent.

The SPD has a clear majority on the councils of both cities: 43 out of 67 councillors in Gelsenkirchen, 32 out of 59 in Recklinghausen. The committees concerned with economic policy in both towns are chaired by members of the majority party. Recklinghausen and Gelsenkirchen are within the *Land* administrative province centred on Münster. The former is no longer an all-purpose authority (that is, one similar in status to a pre-1974 county borough in Britain), but has been brought within the surrounding county authority.[8]

Bielefeld (an all-purpose authority) and Gütersloh (subject to a county authority) have populations respectively of 314,000 and 77,000 inhabitants and face completely different economic conditions from those prevailing in the Ruhr cities. Both have above average tax resources and below average unemployment rates, with Gütersloh consistently having an unemployment level below 3 per cent. Both towns are marked by a well-balanced employment structure in which the level of industrial employment is very high (principally machine tools in Bielefeld and electronics in Gütersloh). Local authority indebtedness in Bielefeld corresponds to the level in Essen, whilst Gütersloh shows a lower level of municipal debt than any of the other cases.

Bielefeld's council has recently had a slight SPD majority and that party as a result works in coalition with the Free Democratic Party. As in Essen, however, the Estates Committee which looks after some aspects of economic policy is chaired by a CDU member, although there is also an Economic Affairs Committee chaired by the SPD Lord Mayor. In Gütersloh the last local elections produced a shift in favour of the CDU, members of which preside over both committees dealing with economic affairs.

In summary all three cases in the Ruhr basin reveal similar economic characteristics and problems. Their basic industries tend to be highly sensitive to fluctuations in the economy, the industrial structure is still in varying degrees insufficiently varied and not highly adaptable, population movements have reduced local purchasing power, and environmental factors tend to be unfavourable. Bielefeld and Gütersloh reveal more or less contrasting conditions with a positive score in respect of most of the factors which present difficulties for the Ruhr cities. On the other hand, the growth of the tertiary sector in Essen should not be overlooked (now over 50 per cent of total employment) and even in Recklinghausen there is a similar trend. Variations in industrial structure between the five cases are reflected too in the tax base, particularly in respect of the business tax which is plainly more buoyant in Bielefeld and Gütersloh than in the three Ruhr cities. All the latter suffer to some extent from the disadvantages of having too much industry with relatively low rates of turnover.

GOALS, ACTIVITIES AND METHODS

The process of town development planning has resulted in the preparation of more or less detailed statements of goals embracing *inter alia* economic activity and the promotion of employment. What was said about goals in the course of the case studies did, however, often qualify the extent of agreement and similarity found in the general written statements. Broadly speaking goals were presented under four headings. There was the provision or maintenance of employment opportunities, often joined with the improvement of labour productivity; there was further the achievement of greater diversification in job outlets, or more generally improvement in the prevailing structure of employment; less prominent but nevertheless important was the strengthening of the local tax base; and finally there were goals related to improvement of locational factors, including infrastructure likely to benefit potential investors. Without doubt, however, those goals relating to the creation of employment and structural improvement were dominant.

Of the cities investigated Essen had made the most sophisticated attempt to apply labour market analysis to its investment promotion policy and to integrate the results with its town development planning. One consequence was the emphasis on providing for growth in the service sector. Bielefeld worked on similar assumptions, but owing to its more favourable position could afford to be more selective with respect to the types of industrial development it would encourage (with a preference for high skill industries). In contrast Gelsenkirchen was constrained to place less emphasis in practice on structural improvement and to encourage whatever job opportunities come along. Recklinghausen chose to emphasise the need to encourage industry with good growth prospects and with high ratios of capital to labour, although again in practice it is not well placed to react in a discriminating manner. Gütersloh is exceptional in being able to emphasise locational goals, chiefly in order to maintain and improve an existing well-balanced structure of employment. Unusually, Gütersloh is an area where shortages of skilled labour are apparent, a fact which leads existing employers to take a critical view of any policy of encouraging new development likely to make additional demands for highly skilled labour.

While the aims attributed to current economic policies reveal considerable similarities, it can be seen that they differ in detail, and what is more important, acquire different senses in different circumstances. Employment promotion in Gelsenkirchen is directed fundamentally to maintaining the existing working population, whilst in Gütersloh and to some extent in Bielefeld employment promotion can in practice take second place to measures intended to improve the attractiveness of these cities and thus to preserve their existing patterns of economic activity.

When one turns to the possibility of using these goals as guidelines for a process of steering or guiding the local economy, it becomes evident that they cannot operate in this way. In practice the emphasis in day-to-day administration is on the maintenance of existing firms and on facilitating such movement of employment opportunities within the local authority areas as enterprises want to achieve for economic reasons. This becomes a delicate matter when, as in Essen, clearance and redevelopment policies are being followed which may in some cases require the relocation of businesses and thus entail the risk of movement out of the local authority area.

However, despite the emphasis in practice on maintaining the existing structure of employment, the goals do in principle point to the need to attract new industries. In other words they point to a situation which cannot be achieved merely by some kind of redistribution of what is already available, but calls for additional sources of employment. In this context it is worth noting that the formal goals do lead to excessive emphasis being placed on manufacturing or industrial employment and not enough on measures to increase the service sector, even though it has been shown that this is the sector which is increasing most consistently in the majority of the cases examined. In fact a wide variety of measures is taken by many local authorities to encourage the growth of service employment, for example in the hotel and tourism branches and to some extent in relation to office employment. But such measures are not often viewed as an integral part of economic development policy, being often generated by particular sections of the local government administration which may have little direct concern with overall employment opportunities and the prospects for the future development of the local economic structure.

Both this investigation and other wider-ranging surveys have shown that in order to have any serious chance of attracting industrial investment a local authority needs to be able (a) to offer land and/or buildings, (b) to have an adequate labour supply, and (c) to possess an effective transport system, especially with regard to its links with the national transport network. The order of priority amongst these conditions shows some variation, probably reflecting differences in the economic strength of different areas. For example, the availability of land may receive a lower rating in places where unemployment is low and no special measures of support for economic development are in force.

The availability of financial incentives is held to have some effect, but is by no means decisive. In addition local authorities do not themselves dispose of important financial incentives. These are determined chiefly at the state level and thus operate as a general factor in the economic environment, giving to some areas an advantage which may be regarded as compensation for existing structural and locational weaknesses. Furthermore, general financial incentives do not affect substantially the relative immobility of much industrial activity, and this fact alone tends to confer more importance on the factor of availability of land and sites.

In considering the activities of land provision, improvements in infrastructure and labour supply it is evident that whatever a local authority can undertake in these directions requires the co-operative action of many services other than those of the local economic development office. The latter is likely to take the lead in acting as a focal point for advice to businesses on land availability, local planning conditions, services which may be provided, and so on. It may engage in negotiations on particular sites, although decisions are bound to require support from the estates offices. Detailed information about planning may be called for and provided, whilst internally the economic development services will as necessary provide appreciations of the implications of particular industrial development measures.

In all the cases investigated the provision of advice about local conditions to potential employers (or to firms contemplating relocation or expansion) took up much of the time of the economic development officers. In particular it was found that smaller firms wanted assistance in dealing with planning or building controls. Often the economic development officer is able to accelerate decisions on building applications. Advice is also needed, where applicable, on state financial aid, the terms on which it is given and how to secure it.

It has already been stressed that land is a decisive factor. Whilst the supply of industrial land is in global terms strictly limited, in practice there is an excess of offers over demand in the Federal Republic. Thus the local authority is rarely in the quasi-monopolistic position that might be suggested by the non-substitutability of most sites and the overall constraints on supply. Instead there is scope for competition between authorities, and, of course, competition between different sources of supply in a single local area.

In the cases studied there are, however, differences determined by the structure of the area, past development and geography. Bielefeld and Gütersloh have only very limited amounts of land available for development, whilst Essen, Gelsenkirchen and Recklinghausen (and especially the last two) cannot find takers for all the sites that can be offered. Budgetary allocations for land purchase have been raised, for example, to 3m. DM in 1978 in Gelsenkirchen and Recklinghausen. Bielefeld has proposed to go far beyond such figures (to 20m. DM in 1978), chiefly because only after territorial extension in 1973 did it become possible for the city to engage in an active land policy. Both Essen and Bielefeld are engaged in extensive urban renewal programmes entailed by the relocation of many businesses on environmental grounds. This imposes a need for the provision of alternative sites if existing industry is to be retained. It also means that some flexibility in the pricing of land becomes necessary, since if businesses can secure elsewhere both lower land prices and state assistance, they are more likely to move out. In two of the cases studied, Gelsenkirchen and Recklinghausen, grants from the *Land* government for acquisition and servicing of the land by the local authority were available, but little use had been made of this facility. The reasons appeared to be the restrictive conditions attaching to such grants and the risks of financial loss if it proved impossible to dispose quickly of the sites so acquired to investors. Sale of land by local authorities is the rule, whereas leasing is quite exceptional.

Very little interest has been shown in the erection and leasing of industrial premises, chiefly for small firms. Potential users tend to dislike leasing. Essen and Bielefeld have considered such possibilities, but only in Bielefeld was action taken within the context of clearance and redevelopment schemes, and then without success.

Most of the forms of direct financial aid in support of industrial investment depend upon state legislation and action, though some involve transfers to the local authorities. This is true, for example, of the grants towards the acquisition and servicing of land under the 1971 urban renewal legislation which has been extended to embrace industrial and commercial promotion. In making such grants the *Land* government is guided chiefly by regional development considerations which also govern the provision of special concessions on depreciation allowances to firms undertaking new investment. In relation to financial support provided by the local authorities this chiefly occurs in the form of land sales below the market price, reductions in or rebates on contributions payable for land servicing, provision of favourable rates by municipal public utilities, and defraying of interest charges on the costs of establishing an enterprise on a new site.

There is no doubt that price variations in the offering of sites play a significant part in the repertoire of incentives offered by local authorities. But the matter is treated with discretion, partly for fear of undermining each local authority's ability to compete with its neighbours, partly because there are legal conditions requiring local authorities to ensure a proper return on land sales and to respect the public interest in their pricing policies. It is, therefore, a matter of some argument how far they can legitimately go in offering land for sale at prices below a strict market valuation. It has been observed too in Essen and elsewhere that the provision of land on favourable terms for the relocation of firms tends to raise demand, since firms are then prompted to purchase against future expansion needs and to contemplate rationalisation measures that are often land intensive. The intervention of the state supervisory authority in relation to land sale prices is rare: one case only of a critical comment was revealed in the course of this study. *De facto*, therefore, the *Land* administration accepts that local authorities can act in ways that run counter to its own priorities in relation to the distribution of industrial investment.

The manipulation or adjustment of land prices is apparently a more important method of attracting investment than any of the other possibilities of local support just mentioned, although rebates on servicing costs, for example, might just as easily be taken account of in calculating the price of a site as in any direct concession.

German local authorities attach great importance to infrastructure and to the provision of basic services for land available for development. This was regarded as vital by all the cities concerned in this study. But the extent to which improvement of the local service infrastructure can be achieved depends to some extent on the state of physical planning and building control requirements. What this means is that the servicing of land and works necessary for that purpose are intended to proceed only on the basis of established planning conditions. In Essen physical planning has been carried forward energetically, so that the framework for much infrastructural work exists. This is not so in Gelsenkirchen and Recklinghausen where comprehensive development plans have not yet been realised. The provision of transport facilities is in part a state responsibility, but with major contributions from local authorities. Very substantial priority has been attached both to the improvement of transport facilities within cities as well as to the development of a national rapid transit system by road and rail to which most important urban centres are linked.

It is worth noting that very little use is made of cost-benefit analysis in the application of economic development policies. Little attempt is made to compare the externalities involved in one type of development with those arising from another. It was argued, especially in the Ruhr cities, that such analysis would be superfluous in conditions in which it is desirable to accept practically any form of development which offers itself. This view is, however, rather more typical of the political side of local government than of the administrative. In the case of new developments the administrative services did show some readiness to go through the elements of a cost-benefit analysis, though rarely able to impose this on the political leadership.

Much effort goes into trying to attract new industry and in particular larger firms. Yet in reality most economic development taking place arises from the relocation and expansion of already well-established firms. The emphasis on larger firms may turn out to underestimate the continuing importance in current conditions of stimulating the establishment of new and smaller enterprises.

There are many other aspects of local authority activity which clearly have indirect economic effects. Much of the effort devoted to improving the social and cultural environment can be justified in terms of its impact on the attractiveness of a city to those contemplating the establishment of a business there or a movement to it in order to take up offers of employment. The same applies to vocational training facilities, although most local authorities prefer to see these in purely social and educational terms. The provision of sites for private housing (usually to individuals wishing to build) can also be treated as an indirect method of contributing to economic development, since it may be used as a way of influencing the labour market, for example, by facilitating mobility or, as in one case, encouraging the retention of skilled labour. But German local authorities have no direct concern with the provision of housing in the manner of their British counterparts.

ADMINISTRATIVE SOLUTIONS

The cases studied revealed a high degree of organisational diversity. In two cases there was what can be called the 'office' solution, in two others the 'administrative division' solution. Essen had in 1978 established an office (*Amt*) for economic development which is located within the department (*Dezernat*) for economic and legal affairs. From 1972 to 1977 economic measures had been the responsibility of the estates office which comes within the same department. In contrast Bielefeld in 1978 dissolved its office for economic development and tourism, retaining economic development as a division within the estates office. Under both forms of organisation the economic development function came within the department for economic affairs, estates and land management.

Gelsenkirchen has never had a separate office for economic development. The function is discharged by a division of the office for town development planning which is directly responsible to the city chief executive. In Recklinghausen an attempt is being made to treat economic development and town planning as distinct offices within a technical department to which other functions are entrusted also.

Gütersloh is the exception in that its organisation chart contains no mention of economic development as a separate function. And in response to questions it was stated quite definitely that so long as the market proved capable of providing a satisfactory level of activity there was no need to set up a special local authority organisation for economic activities.

The organisational arrangements in Bielefeld and Gelsenkirchen represent a minority view of how best to organise the economic functions of local authorities. In contrast according to the findings of a broadly based survey[9] 58 per cent of cities prefer to establish an office for economic development rather than rely on a division subordinate to some other functional office. On the other hand some kind of link with estates offices and with the finance or treasurer's office, usually via inclusion in the same department, is quite common.

There is general recognition that economic development is a cross-cutting function, the discharge of which depends on co-operation from related sectors of local administration. In Bielefeld, Gelsenkirchen and Essen some effort is made to reduce co-ordination demands by extending the competence of the economic policy units themselves. In Recklinghausen there was reliance on co-ordination within the departmental structure, whilst in Gelsenkirchen the direct relationship between economic development and the head of the city administration was intended to facilitate inter-office co-ordination. In both Gelsenkirchen and Recklinghausen regular meetings of the heads of offices or divisions with functions related to economic development are held. At the top level, that is, that of departmental heads, there was in all the cases studied a marked trend towards institutionalising regular meetings with the aim of facilitating co-ordination both in policy determination and implementation.

There were everywhere signs that the head of administration or chief executive took a close interest in economic measures and in Gelsenkirchen he is formally responsible for the economic development office and its work. It appears that the involvement of chief executives stems in part from a genuine concern with economic problems, but in part from the fact that the promotion of industrial development often requires urgent decisions on land sales and other forms of support. These matters are usually of some political sensitivity and thus the head of the administration tends to be brought in. It is also noticeable that in the expansion of economic development offices there is a tendency to appoint qualified staff on contract rather than create new posts for career officials: this underlines the need for a kind of professional experience not usually gained in the regular local government service.

It was evident in all the German cases studied that the function of economic development has expanded in recent years and this has had an impact on the organisational arrangements and forms of co-operation between services. Promotional activity to attract industry has increased as has acquisition of land for disposal to firms, whilst at the same time economic development offices have been playing a more active role in physical planning, at any rate in relation to the designation of areas suitable for development. Generally, economic development and building control functions have been closely linked, and in three of the cases examined it was clear that the city planning offices had lost power in favour of the economic policy-makers. There is, however, much variation in the balance struck between economic development functions and building control: in the cases studied it was favourable to economic development, but other research suggests that this is not always the case. [10]

The evidence gathered indicated that the economic development function had been extended in several ways. For example, in Essen the economic development office has made contracts for acquisition and sale of industrial and commercial sites; in Gelsenkirchen the same office has been involved jointly with other branches of the local administration in such agreements; in both Essen and Gelsenkirchen the economic development office has undertaken site development prior to offering land for industrial use; and in Essen, Gelsenkirchen and Bielefeld the economic development office has undertaken activity in relation to establishment of building plans for industrial sites. The economic development offices have also tended to become partners in the procedures for approval of commercial development schemes, and have in three of the cases studied acquired the right to be consulted in the determination of all commercial building plans.

The staffs employed on economic development remain small, however. In Essen and Gelsenkirchen they number seven in both towns (with only two at the level of the higher civil service grade), and in

Bielefeld there are five, in Recklinghausen three. Gütersloh employs no staff specifically charged with economic development work. Other studies show that the staffing levels in the larger cities examined are more or less average for the country as a whole having regard to population variations. But Gelsenkirchen is plainly devoting more staff resources to economic promotion than its size alone would warrant.

An alternative to the conventional methods of organisation which has often been discussed is the private law development company. This device is held to offer greater flexibility than normal public service organisation and it had been considered by the cities under review here. But only in one case was the matter seriously pursued, and even then the decision finally went in favour of an office in the city administration. Nevertheless, there are some ten urban development companies in the Federal Republic and thirty-five regional companies of the same kind. Several of these undertake a variety of commercial activities as well as seeking to attract industrial investment. There is some ground for believing that links with the local authorities concerned are loose, and it is not at all clear that this type of company does offer substantial advantages over direct promotional activity by the local authority.

THE ROLE OF COUNCILLORS IN THE ECONOMIC POLICY FIELD

Economic development is not a controversial policy area. There is general agreement on the need to counteract unemployment as far as is possible and on the importance of maintaining a given level of economic well-being. Thus there was no serious sign of dispute between political parties on objectives. The high degree of political consensus appears to facilitate direct intervention by political leaders who quite often initiate proposals or quickly take over suggestions put forward by the administration.

On the other hand, when it is a question of developing a programme or devising administrative schemes for action in support of economic development it is the administrative officers who normally take the initiative and exert the most influence. Since the top administrative positions are mainly held by political appointees the process of securing political backing usually goes forward without difficulty. It is customary too on many occasions to secure 'preliminary' agreement in the council or political parties before an important issue is actually put forward for decision. This is often a useful procedure in the case of giving support to industrial investment decisions since it tends to facilitate rapid action.

Though the political leaders are plainly interested in the bigger individual cases and in the general direction of economic development policy, there is no evidence that the political parties attempt to lay down detailed criteria according to which particular investment projects might be judged. Basically the political side leaves wide discretion to the administration to take what it can get in the way of new or additional development.

In all the cases examined there were committees of the councils charged with the oversight of economic development, though in some this responsibility was discharged alongside other functions. Additionally there were other functional committees involved in the economic sector. In Essen there is a single committee for economic affairs and sites; in Bielefeld the economic development committee co-operates with an estates committee; in Gelsenkirchen the economic responsibilities fall to an estates committee and to one for town development; in Recklinghausen the economics committee exists alongside a committee for building sites; and in Gütersloh both a sites committee and a planning committee prepare for decision matters classified elsewhere as economic development. Evidence derived from other studies indicates that the frequency with which committees meet varies positively with the size of town; in a big city a council committee may meet once a week and the full council too will meet very much more frequently than in Britain.

In all the cases studied the economic development offices report to the sites or estates committees as well as to their own committees, where that applies. The close involvement of estates committees provides an indication of the importance attaching to the fixing of prices for the disposal of sites, although there is no evidence that estates committees normally exert a decisive control over pricing policy. On the contrary, on the whole they ratify the proposals of the administrative officers.

The attitudes expressed by council members underlined the fact that they attribute a lot of importance to economic development, and indeed put it before most other local functions. In other words, it is something very much to the forefront of their thinking about local priorities. No doubt purely political considerations influenced this judgement. But it is symptomatic of the attention currently paid to economic activities that in Bielefeld a special economic development committee has been set up under the chairmanship of the Lord Mayor,[11] so that it can be used, rather unconventionally, as a forum for discussion with local businessmen and for the provision of advice. In Recklinghausen efforts are also being made to give much more political prominence to the economic role of the local authority and in this way to win the sympathy of potential investors.

There were hardly any signs of conflict between the council and the administration except in those circumstances in which particular economic interest groups have been strongly represented in the council and thus sought to push or defend their own interests. In the Ruhr cities the reluctance of the mining interests to dispose of land except on the most favourable terms often constitutes a problem on which the administration does not always get full support from the political parties in which there are divided interests.

THE LOCAL FINANCIAL SYSTEM AND PLANNING: EFFECTS ON ECONOMIC DEVELOPMENT

In so far as carrying out a policy depends on resources and these resources are derived from local sources of revenue, a local authority has an incentive to act in ways that will tend to increase the yield of the business tax. Whilst in none of the cases studied was it claimed that economic development was viewed as a direct means of improving the revenue yield in this way, nevertheless there is no doubt that economic development is regarded favourably because *inter alia* it tends to have this effect. It improves the tax base. On the other hand the effect is relatively long term: business turnover fluctuates substantially in the short term and it is unrealistic for a local authority to look for any sure rise in revenue yield as an immediate consequence of its success in attracting industry. Thus we cannot speak of a close link between economic development and the local financial system, although this is not to overlook the fact that ultimately local resources are significantly affected by the level of business activity and of incomes earned locally.

In the cases examined the officers of the treasurer's department were clearly conscious of economic activity as a cost in the short run. They tended to stress the expenditure that has to be incurred immediately for site acquisitions or servicing as well as the financial risks involved in, for example, the holding of land for industrial development for any length of time.

Practically no use was made of the facility open to local authorities of varying within permitted limits the rates of property and business taxes. This was not regarded as an effective way of influencing entrepreneurial decisions, and in any event there is no evidence that such variations in local rates of tax are prominent factors in investment calculations.

In all the cities studied there had been a tendency towards integrating economic development policies with the process of land use planning. What this means in practice, however, is that physical planning has to adapt itself to the need for flexibility inherent in an economic development policy which aims at realising whatever opportunities for industrial and commercial development present themselves. As already indicated, the planning process has at local level two stages, the preparation of land use plans and the establishment of detailed building schemes laying down conditions to be observed in specific areas. This second stage is in many respects a source of rigidity, and it is not surprising that local authorities often prefer to delay the preparation of such plans so that *ad hoc* decisions can then more easily be taken. Under

Federal building law it is permissible, in the absence of building plans, to give development approval in advance of such plans, and this practice was often adopted by the authorities investigated. On the other hand it does entail the disadvantage of reducing the prospect of securing approval from the *Land* authorities for grants towards the costs of site servicing. The local authorities complained furthermore of the complexity and slowness of the process of securing approval for their building plans, a situation which affected economic development proposals adversely.

Basically, however, planning considerations can only impede local authority economic development policies if the local authority allows this to happen or if they derive externally from such limitations as may be imposed by the *Land* supervisory authorities. These could come into play if local planning were held to be in conflict with priorities in *Land* planning or if the *Land* authority imposed restrictions via its approval of statutory building plans for specific areas. In fact there was no conclusive evidence of efforts by the *Land* supervisory authorities to restrict local authority allocations of land for industrial and commercial development, and in so far as the *Land* has intervened it has done so in some cases for the purpose of restricting the amounts of land designated for residential development.

To sum up, the impact of economic development needs on the land use planning system has been in the direction of subordinating its future-oriented perspectives to the need to be able to respond quickly to proposals for development offering prospect of immediate employment benefits. Carefully thought out schemes for comprehensive and balanced development have had to give way to more pragmatic step-by-step methods of solving current problems.

EXTERNAL RELATIONS IN THE ECONOMIC DEVELOPMENT FIELD

A sceptical view of co-operation between local authorities is generally taken, chiefly because they see themselves as in competition with each other. This is particular marked in the Ruhr area where adjacent cities are keen to attract such limited new investment as is available and of necessity are keenly aware of their competitive relationships.

The chambers of industry and trade are obviously closely concerned with economic measures, and in Essen the chamber worked closely with the local authority. In Gelsenkirchen too a real effort was made to draw on the advice of the local chamber of trade. But informal relationships between representatives of industry and senior local authority officials tend to be just as important as the more formal links between chambers of trade and local authorities. This was particularly so in the smallest of the cities investigated. More general research confirms the importance of informal ties between industry and commerce on the one hand, and local officials and politicians on the other. Within this pattern of informal relationships the trade unions do not appear to play a prominent part.

Despite the existence of a long-established special purpose association in the Ruhr, the Settlement Association for the Ruhr Coal-Mining Area, the local authorities involved in this study did not look to this body for initiatives in economic development nor were they enthusiastic about co-operative links with it. One explanation of this position is that the Association can only propose measures not likely to benefit disproportionately any single local authority, and this reduces any incentive which authorities might have to look to it for support and action. A company for economic development in North Rhine-Westphalia has been set up by the *Land* government, but is mainly concerned to encourage development in accordance with *Land* regional priorities. Its efforts are also directed chiefly to smaller authorities. Consequently none of the local authorities we studied here was interested in collaborating with it, including those which had qualified for *Land* development area grants.

The extent to which the state (*Land*) authorities can or do intervene in economic matters depends very much on the size of the local authority and on whether it qualifies for special assistance. The larger a local authority is, the less likely it is that the *Land* administrative authority will seek to intervene or put obstacles in the way of local proposals. If the provincial office puts obstacles in the way of a big local authority an attempt may well be made to overcome these by an appeal directly to the responsible minister. In this way party links assume primary importance.

The provincial officers of the *Land* government exercise general legal supervision over economic development policy and have to approve the payment of development grants to firms and for specified purposes to local authorities. Since the whole procedure of establishing building plans is subject to state supervision, the provincial administrative offices are necessarily informed of all local authority economic plans and proposals. In so far as such plans affect land use the provincial administrative office has scope for exerting influence, although this is not to say that it will always try to do so.

Indeed the provincial administration steers on a light rein. This is the case in those circumstances in which in theory it could raise objections on planning grounds. But much the same is true in respect of development grants for which either the private firm or a local authority apply. The provincial office then gives approval and is hardly able to link this with the imposition of any policy requirements of its own. Under the urban renewal legislation of 1971 contributions can now be made to land preparation and servicing for industrial development and this again brings in the provincial offices as approving authorities. Here an effort has been made to bring about more co-operation between the town planning (Interior Ministry) and commercial (Economics Ministry) divisions in the provincial administrations.

Only two of the cases studied were cities within a county (*Kreis*) and thus restricted in some respects in what they could undertake. There was, however, little evidence of any desire to work closely with the *Kreis* administration in economic matters. The *Kreis* level is unlikely to have such an extensive and specialised organisation as the larger towns, particularly in a sector like economic development which has expanded in recent years. The cities within counties are jealous of their powers and for that reason alone prefer to act independently as far as is possible. The position is, however, rather different for smaller local authorities which may welcome *Kreis* support and the benefits available from county promotional activities. Moreover, the smaller authority is unlikely to have either the technical resources or the funds to permit it to embark on a serious programme of economic development.

THE INTERPLAY OF AUTONOMY AND DEPENDENCE

Economic conditions and prospects in each local authority area are highly dependent on what is happening in the national economy as a whole. For this reason alone it would be unrealistic for local authorities to behave as if they could in principle decide autonomously what kind of economic measures best suit their particular needs and circumstances. The authorities examined here fully appreciated these limits and recognised that their economic policies must for the most part be adapted to exploiting such opportunities as prevailing circumstances open up for them. It was striking, however, that in the appreciation of these opportunities local authorities appeared to be strongly influenced by traditional views of economic action as being primarily concerned with encouraging industrial investment. Despite the allocation of a share of income tax yield to them in 1969, a step which might have been expected to prompt a broader view of economic development and of its links with comprehensive urban development needs, it is evident that the older view still dominates this field of policy-making. Success in economic policies is measured by the extent to which new industry is attracted or existing industry maintained. As a result action tends to be geared very closely to the assumed needs of local industry.

It is awareness of problems in the economy – and this means in the first place unemployment at levels above what has in recent years been regarded as equivalent to 'full employment' – that acts as the principal release mechanism for the adoption of a positive attitude towards local economic development. Of course, awareness of problems alone does not imply particular courses of action. In the case of Gütersloh the 'problem' is seen as external to the local area and the policy response to this is basically to maintain existing patterns of activity. In Bielefeld, however, where the problem is not seen as having a marked impact locally, the fact that the city is classed as a central point for sub-regional services and is relatively much larger than Gütersloh results in a more activist view of how economic policy should be pursued and of the purposes it should serve. The three other cases all illustrate how the economic problem is seen in terms of a direct local impact on employment levels. It is this local situation to which the authorities feel compelled to respond and they do so with measures thought appropriate to treating the main problem, that is, unemployment.

Whilst it can be seen that in formulating their policies local authorities may commit themselves to long-term and general goals such as diversification of the local employment structure, development of the tertiary sector of activity and the achievement of balanced urban growth, it has also to be recognised that when taking action they are compelled by political circumstances and by the realities of local economic conditions to work on a shorter-term and *ad hoc* basis. They have to take account of the political concern felt by those affected by unemployment or the threat of it, and they must respond to the interests and preoccupations of the sources of employment in the locality. Thus the typical kind of 'active' economic development policy which emerges in these conditions is one which attempts to mobilise personnel and financial resources to attract or retain industry. This in turn implies an emphasis on making sites available, on providing such financial incentives as are permissible and on developing an active promotional or marketing policy.

These circumstances have resulted in an expansion in the organisational resources devoted to economic activity. The scale of such organisation remains fairly modest, although it has to be remembered that the starting-point was very low. There are variations, however, in the ways in which economic development policy has been organised and adapted to related functions. It is essentially a horizontal, cross-cutting activity and the evidence suggests that it is pursued most effectively when entrusted to an office which forms part of a single department into which the other principal supporting functions are integrated. This means essentially that the estates or land management function and the land use planning function are closely linked with economic development. If this is achieved then the problems of co-ordination tend to be reduced. This way of identifying and locating the economic development function was more evident in the larger cities studied in North Rhine-Westphalia, this in turn being traceable to the effects of size and complexity as well as to well-established habits of specialisation.

Where the economic policy function remains organisationally separate from the town planning responsibilities there has, however, been a tendency for it in turn to acquire direct involvement in the determination of land uses. That is to say, under the impact of the need to attract industry, the town planning function itself has had to take some of its priorities from the economic development offices, and this has been reinforced in some instances by the direct interest in economic measures shown by the head of the local authority administration.

The impact of economic needs has been felt not only on city development generally, but also on the more specific procedures providing for the establishment of building schemes to which development is expected to conform. Here the concern is with flexibility and with retaining a capacity to respond quickly to opportunities for industrial and commercial development which may present themselves and which can be realised only if restrictions inherent in formally approved building schemes can be avoided.

Land availability is a basic conditions for the pursuit of economic development policies and this was emphasised by all the local authorities. On the other hand an adequate supply of sites does not of itself give the local authority much capacity to control the process of attracting investment. This is in part because land is only one factor (though an important one) in the calculations of developers, and in part because local authorities are in competition with each other in the offering of sites. It is unlikely that any single local authority can benefit substantially in its dealings with developers as a result of possessing control of a strictly limited resource, land.

In relation to the availability of financial resources local authorities readily accept classification as development areas since this means that state assistance is payable to developers. On the other hand they show some reluctance to take up grants payable for the preparation and servicing of sites because these are linked with conditions imposed by the state authorities. Such grants also carry financial risks since, if development does not take place, they become repayable. The point of general importance is that the local authorities accept the need to work within a framework of state policies and priorities, but at the same time seek to minimise opportunities for direct state intervention in the exercise of their own policy discretion. Moreover, local authorities are to some extent able to compensate for declining to take up state funds by expanding their own expenditure on site acquisition and preparation. This has happened particularly where the local authority faced a situation of land shortage. Another form of expenditure which has increased is that for promotional work and advertising. The exact extent of this is, however, hard to determine because such activity is undertaken for many purposes other than the attraction of industry and commerce.

With regard to the processes of decision-making it is apparent that economic policy implementation is dominated by the need for flexibility and quick reactions. It is not a policy area which can be programmed in advance by clearly defined operating conditions and generalised statements of goals. Nor is there evidence of a desire to use cost-benefit techniques of analysis, despite the fact that in theory they seem to be called for in relation to employment-generating investment decisions. Local authorities are so sensitive to the risks of losing investment opportunities that they are prepared to accept the additional burden on some of their own services which may flow from neglect of the externalities involved in the opportunistic pursuit of new development. The preference for taking the chances offered and facing indirect costs arising from them later is particularly marked on the political side of local government, and for understandable reasons. The political leadership wants to appear active and to have something to show in the shape of achievement.

More generally, there are many signs that economic development decisions are subject to a centralising effect, that is to say, they tend to be pushed up to the higher levels of the local administration where they can be taken with the minimum of delay. This happens because of the nature of the issues involved, the strength of political interest in such matters and the tendency of firms (especially the larger ones) to address themselves to senior levels in the administration or on the political side in the councils.

In principle there is scope for substantial conflict between urban planning requirements and the needs of a successful economic development policy. The planner is concerned with an overall balance of different factors in the urban environment for the benefit of the inhabitants as a whole. The economic policy-maker is concerned far more narrowly with employment levels and the needs of particular sections of the working population. This conflict rarely assumes a serious form, however. The economic development role has gained more than a foothold in the planning function itself, and the planners tend to accept the priority accorded to employment creation through the attraction of new investment. Thus what might have been a conflict of goals turns out to be much more like an adaptation of the planning process to changed economic priorities.

Another potential area of conflict is in the relations between the local authorities and the *Land* administration. This possibility stems from the fact that the state level is pursuing planning and economic development goals which may be realisable only at the expense of particular local authorities (for example, success in regional development schemes may involve loss of industrial capacity and jobs in a more prosperous area). But in practice the *Land* administration is pursuing a variety of policies amongst which a range of compromises is possible. Moreover, the pattern of public sector services is so complex and multi-layered that there are many opportunities for bargaining between individual local authorities and various parts of the *Land* administrative system.

Additionally political contacts and pressures help to reduce the risk of conflicts which can be resolved only to the serious disadvantage of one or the other of the parties involved. Thus it can be concluded that the importance now attached to positive economic action by the local authorities has induced in the state supervisory organisations much of the flexibility in the application of state policies that has been found to be indispensable by the local authorities in the implementation of their own economic development programmes.

Finally, there is no doubt that local economic policy-making depends crucially for its effectiveness on the behaviour of those agents in the economy to whom incentives and facilities are offered. It is not a policy area which is in any serious way subject to control by the local authorities, nor indeed for that matter by the state level either. For this reason the question of local discretion and of the local authority's scope for taking a policy initiative has to be posed differently from the manner in which it is often put. Conventionally it is held that the discretion of the local authority depends on the extent of state control or intervention and on the quantity of resources available. But in the economic field state intervention and regulation are minimal, whilst there is too no serious and general shortage of what are the most relevant resources at the disposal of local authorities. Consequently, explanation of the recognition by local authorities that their scope for effective economic action is so limited has to be found elsewhere. In the German context the most important explanatory factors appear to be the autonomy of the agents in the economy just referred to, the impact of constraints operating in the economy as a whole and the effects of competition between local authorities.

There is, therefore, a situation in which local authorities are relatively free to devise their own policies and to apply them autonomously. Yet they recognise that success rarely depends extensively on their own decisions. If it is then asked why they nevertheless attach so much importance to economic activity, the answer appears to be that the financial stability of a local authority in the Federal Republic is still seen to depend substantially on the health of local industry and that local authorities continue to take seriously their constitutional role of acting in ways which will further the well-being of their populations.

NOTES

1 *Kommunale Gemeinschaftsstelle für Verwaltungsvereinfachung.* For some comments on this organisation and its work see F. Wagener, 'The Joint Municipal Association for the Rationalisation of Organisation and Management in the Federal Republic of Germany', *Public Administration*, Autumn 1974.

2 It is worth stressing that under the West German system of government the state generally means for local authorities the *Land* governments and their administrative agents. Under the Basic Law the *Länder* can be said to constitute the state for the purposes of executing Federal and *Land* law.

3 This tax, the *Lohnsummensteuer*, was abolished as from January, 1980. The business tax, *Gewerbesteuer*, is assessed on both profits and capital.
4 See 'Entwicklung der kommunalen Steuereinnahmen in Zeitraum, 1961–73, *Deutscher Städtetag – Beiträge zur Finanzpolitik* (Cologne, 1974).
5 For a treatment of the land use planning system in operation see J. J. Hesse, *Organisation kommunaler Entwicklungsplanung* (Stuttgart: Kohlhammer, 1976).
6 Provincial administrative office designates in this chapter the *Regierungspräsident*, a kind of regional prefect, who is responsible for the supervisory functions of the *Land* ministries *vis-à-vis* local authorities.
7 All the details of party strengths are for the period in which the case studies were carried out, that is, 1977/8.
8 The 'county authority' is used here to refer to the *Kreis* which is both a unit of local government with an elected council and officials, and a unit for the exercise of state supervisory powers over *Gemeinden* within the *Kreis* which are not 'kreisfrei' all-purpose authorities. The basic unit of local government remains the *Gemeinde* (inside or outside the *Kreis*) and the *Kreis* is not quite equivalent to a second tier in the system. It has a range of service provision functions, but quite extensively acts to provide services which smaller *Gemeinden* cannot provide singly.
9 B. Wrobel, 'Aufgabenfeld und Organisation kommunaler Wirtschaftsförderungsdienststellen' (draft) (Cologne: Deutsche Institut für Urbanistik, 1978).
10 Wrobel, op. cit.
11 It should be remembered that the Lord Mayer – *Oberbürgermeister* – is not confined to representational functions, but is leader of the council.

Chapter 6

PROGRAMMES AND POLICIES COMPARED

INTRODUCTION

A comparison of what local authorities attempt to do in support of their local economies and of the ways in which they are organised for such activities must begin by recognising major differences and similarities. The differences are most marked when we look at the institutional framework in the two countries. Despite a shared democratic approach the organisation of government in the two countries reveals marked contrasts. Western Germany's government is based on a federal system with strong powers for its *Länder* (provinces or states), whilst Britain provides a fairly clear example of centralised government.

The federal structure significantly restricts the power available to the German national government (the *Bund*) and some of those powers which in England are held centrally belong to the *Länder* in Germany. In addition the local authorities have a formally autonomous status which the *Bund* and the *Länder* must take into account in their own actions. The right of local authority self-government is rooted in constitutional guarantees. In contrast British local government depends on specific or general powers conferred by Parliament in ways which often involve the central government too. As a result local authorities have tended to take a rather narrow view of their powers, fearing the possibility of legal challenge, whilst at the same time the central government has been able or even required to exercise powers of supervision and intervention of indeterminate scope.

When we turn to economic structure and problems there are basic similarities, however. Both Britain and the Federal Republic are advanced industrial countries with a heavy concentration in manufacturing industry and in both private enterprise is still the main basis of economic activity, although more decisively so in the Federal Republic than in Britain. Both face, albeit in different ways and to a different extent, the same sorts of economic pressure and the business cycle tends to affect them at approximately the same time. The same industries (for example, steel, shipbuilding and textiles) are in recession in both countries, and the national governments have intervened to slow down this decline. Most of the population of both countries lives in large urban areas and this very fact produces difficulties for local authorities in the definition of their own local economic areas. Whilst economic structure shows many similarities, there have been differences of emphasis in the ways in which and the extent to which the state intervenes in the economy. There has in the economic system of the Federal Republic been a more consistent stress on market principles and private ownership of productive assets than in Britain. As a result whilst the state has provided extensive support for industry over the years, it has been directed chiefly to the provision of services and to ensuring the viability of enterprises operating under market conditions. In Britain's 'mixed economy' there has been more extensive direct public ownership and greater uncertainty about the terms and objectives of public support to private firms. Thus it is possible to say that along with obvious similarities in economic structure and problems and in the *de facto* acceptance of substantial government intervention in the economy, there have been and remain differences in attitudes towards the objectives and conditions of this intervention.

Within this context attention has been focused in this study on the ways in which institutional forms and methods are adapted and modified to cope with similar problems and the ways in which the institutional structure helps to determine how problems are perceived and what responses should be made to them. For this reason it has been important to examine the constraints and opportunities which exist for local authorities in both countries as they attempt to develop active policy initiatives which are neither simply reactions to pressure from local interests nor merely a response to programmes prepared by the state levels of government.

Despite the restrictions placed on the instruments which German local authorities can use in the economic development field, it remains a major example of local 'self-government' or autonomy. In England, by contrast, the economic area is one where central government has had the main responsibilities and local government has not been expressly brought into the field. Local authority interest and activity have nevertheless been growing so that it is now possible to talk of a kind of convergence in what local authorities actually do in the two countries.

It thus represents a policy area in which the disparity between formal institutions and rules and their operation in practice can be seen quite clearly. In particular, the extent to which higher levels of government are able to supervise German local authorities can be seen and compared with the extent to which English local authorities are able to escape from the restrictions imposed by the Department of the Environment and other departments of the central government in order to develop a policy initiative of their own.

THE POLICY CONTEXT

Local authorities do not operate in a political or governmental vacuum and the development of economic policy by other, more powerful governmental agencies affects the scope for local authority action or at the least sets the framework within which such action has to take place.

In many respects it is the most general of the national government's economic concerns which has the major direct impact on local authorities: this is the commitment to some broad concept of economic management, whether conceived in terms of Keynesian demand management or control over money supply and public sector borrowing. Even in Germany where economic decision-making is more dispersed and the *Länder* retain substantial independence, the 1968 Stability and Growth Law (*Stabilitäts- und Wachstumsgesetz*) states that public bodies should adjust levels of spending according to the state of the business cycle and thus sets local government spending within a broader national framework of economic management.

In both countries local authority spending is a significant proportion of public expenditure, although the existence of provincial governments in Germany reduces its share slightly. Table 6.1 indicates the importance of local capital spending, for example. Inevitably the higher levels of government have attempted to control overall expenditure. This is clearer in Britain, with the recurrent arguments over Rate Support Grant and controls over capital spending, but in Germany attempts have also been made to vary levels of grant. Policies of this sort are generally of less importance in Germany since grants are a less significant source of income (see Table 6.2), and a large proportion of them are for specific purposes.

Table 6.1   *Share of government capital investment (percentages)*

| | Great Britain[a] | | Federal Republic of Germany | | |
	Central government	Local authorities	Bund	Länder	Gemeinden
1961	23·6	76·4	24·5	18·0	57·4
1967	20·1	79·9	23·8	19·0	57·2
1971	23·5	76·5	15·9	18·8	65·3
1975	24·5	75·5	17·0	18·0	65·0
1976	25·4	74·6	15·6	19·0	65·5

[a] The British figures do not include investment by public corporations. This has generally been around the same level as or higher than capital investment by local authorities.
   Sources: Central Statistical Office, *Annual Abstract of Statistics*, 1971 and 1979 (London: HMSO, 1971 and 1978); Gemeindefinanzbericht 1977, in *Der Städtetag*, No. 1, January 1977.

In both countries broad economic management is supported by interventionist policies directed towards more specific targets. These policies have conventionally been divided into regional and industrial policies, although there is sometimes overlap between the two.

Table 6.2   *Sources of local government revenue (percentages)*

	England and Wales[a]				Federal Republic of Germany[b]		
	Govern- ment grants	Tax	Other[c]		Govern- ment grants	Tax	Other[c]
1973/4	39·6	24·6	35·8	1974	23·5	40·5	36·0
1974/5	47·7	24·7	27·6	1975	24·0	40·3	35·7
1975/6	49·6	24·5	25·9	1976	22·5	41·0	36·5
1976/7	49·6	23·8	26·6	1977	22·9	41·8	35·3
1977/8	48·0	24·6	27·3	1978 (est.)	24·8	40·2	35·0

[a] year ending 31 March
[b] year ending 31 December
[c] fees, charges etc. and excluding borrowing.
Sources: Department of the Environment and Welsh Office, *Local Government Financial Statistics, England & Wales*, 1973/4, 1974/5, 1975/6, 1976/7 and 1977/8 (London: HMSO, 1974, 1978 and 1979); Gemeindefinanzbericht 1979, in *Der Städtetag*, No. 2, 1979; own calculations.

The regional policies operated in each country have the aims of improving the economic position of specified areas by increasing employment opportunities and raising income levels in them. Similar methods are used in the two countries since the policies are based on the offer of investment grants to firms in assisted areas (*Fördergebiete* in the German case). The amounts spent on regional policy are probably slightly greater in Britain than in Germany, but this is difficult to assess accurately since not only is there a national scheme in the latter to which the Federal government contributes 50 per cent of the cost and the relevant *Länder* provide the remainder, but the Länder themselves generally have their own separate internal schemes.

There are three principal differences in the forms of regional policy undertaken in the two countries. First, there is no equivalent in Germany to the system of Industrial Development Certificates and such direct control on development would be unacceptable. Secondly, the development areas eligible under the Joint Federal/*Land* policy are identified in more detail than in Britain, being regularly checked against an agreed set of social and economic indicators to ensure that they are still eligible for aid.[1] Thirdly, the existence of a federal system means that there is not a nationally uniform regional policy. In North Rhine-Westphalia, for example, it has been estimated that between 1969 and 1975 two-thirds of the funds spent on regional economic policy came from the *Land*.[2]

Particularly since the mid 1960s the national governments have become involved in a third form of economic intervention, directed towards particular industrial sectors and even particular firms. In Britain this has generally been called an industrial policy and in Germany *'sektorale Strukturpolitik'*. To some extent such policies have provided rationalisations for *ad hoc* intervention to save and reorganise particular firms whose collapse might otherwise have caused large-scale localised unemployment at a politically unacceptable level – for example, the rescues of British Leyland and Rolls Royce in Britain, state assistance to the coal industry in North Rhine-Westphalia and to the shipbuilding industries in both countries. But the two central aspects of the policies are clear: first, they are said to perform a 'fire brigade' function, rescuing industries on a temporary basis until they are able to operate independently again; and secondly, a pump-priming function, intended to help new high technology industries to start the process of self-sustained growth.

The total expenditure by the Federal government on structural support for industry now seems to be a greater proportion of the total government budget than similar spending in Britain (see Table 6.3). In Britain over the years since 1973/4 the proportion has fallen from an initially higher level to only half that of the Federal Republic. But the implications of this should not be exaggerated, since Federal spending represents a smaller proportion of total public expenditure than does central government expenditure in Britain. Spending by the *Länder* would also have to be considered if the proportions were to be comparable. It is, nevertheless, safe to say that in both countries state intervention in support of industry is now of major importance.

Table 6.3 *Government expenditure on industrial policy as a percentage of the total central or Federal government budget*

Great Britain[a, c]		Federal Republic[b]	
1973/4	6·6	1973	4·9
1974/5	5·3	1974	4·6
1975/6	3·3	1975	3·8
1976/7	2·3	1976	3·4
1977/8	2·0	1977	3·1
1978/9 (est.)	2·0	1978 (est.)	4·1

[a] year ending 31 March
[b] year ending 31 December
[c] spending on industrial innovation (including Concorde and the RB211), general support for industry and support for non-transport nationalised industries (principally coal but also the Central Electricity Generating Board).

Sources: The Government's Expenditure Plans 1979–80 to 1982–3, Cmnd 7439 (London: HMSO, 1979). 'Bundesministerium der Finanzen: Finanzbericht (Bonn) 1978 and 1979; *Bericht der Bundesregierung über die Entwicklung der Finanzhilfen und Steuerbegünstigungen*...(4, 5, 6, 7, Subventionsbericht), 1973, 1975, 1977, 1979; own calculations.

There is, however, an important difference in approach. British governments have been ready to prepare overall policies for industrial reorganisation in the Industry Acts passed while both major parties have been in power. The German Federal government is more reluctant to see its industrial intervention as anything but exceptional. This is reflected in the fact that much of the activity in Britain can be justified by reference to one main Act, whereas in Germany several separate laws (such as that covering the reorganisation of the coal industry) have to be used as justification for specific intervention. Whilst the policies of the Department of Industry may be changing under the Conservative government elected in 1979, the extent to which such policy changes in the industrial field will represent a major change of method and direction cannot yet be reliably assessed.

LOCAL AUTHORITIES AND THE LOCAL ECONOMY

In both countries authorities clearly accept that they have an interest in the economic well-being of their areas. Even where they appear relatively inactive in the economic policy area this is usually justified by the argument that some other agency is taking the necessary action, or that the local economic situation is favourable and can be best supported by minimal interference and a sympathetic response to such demands as local industry and commerce may make.

Whilst the response from each authority has varied, the experience of recession has encouraged increased action in both countries. Whether a local authority becomes 'active' and deliberately attempts to influence the local economic situation, depends principally on the extent and type of problems it identifies in its own and surrounding areas. But this identification of a problem need not always be closely related to objective indicators such as unemployment levels.

It would be mistaken to imagine that English councils have never in the past interested themselves in local economic matters. In fact they have sometimes been in the forefront of pressures for change, particularly in the present assisted areas. In the 1920s local authorities were even encouraged by the Commissioner for the Distressed Areas to take action to alleviate unemployment. But the level of consistent interest has been low and only since the late 1960s has there been a dramatic increase in concern.[3] There has been a growing realisation, first in the assisted areas but now more widely, that if local authorities do not act then no other agency[4] is likely to adopt policies oriented specifically towards local problems.

In Germany officers and councillors have seen the growth of activities from a different point of view. They have not had to develop a new role for themselves based on a criticism of other government agencies, but have developed on the basis of existing interests. They have simply taken the view that they themselves have been doing too little (in part reflecting the fiction that local authorities can resolve nationally caused economic problems within their own boundaries) and have responded by increasing their activities in directions already quite familiar.

Local authority concern for the economic well-being of their areas is the product of a complex series of pressures and influences on councillors and officers filtered through council committees, administrative departments, political parties, employer and employee organisations. It is also influenced by the pressures of local opinion, including those expressed in local newspapers, and by the personal experience of the councillors and officers who may, for example, live near or regularly pass significant pockets of industrial dereliction and therefore identify that as a problem.

There is some evidence that the statistics[5] available to English local authorities influence the way in which problems are seen, since they serve as the basis for many policy documents in which the main emphasis is on unemployment levels, problems of industrial structure and even changing population levels. But on the other hand it is clear that problem definition of this sort can only be of secondary importance. For most authorities the existence of a 'problem' is confirmed by an impressionistic consensus among officers and councillors and not by the gathering of statistics or the carrying out of research. The particular indicators used by each authority vary quite significantly according to what is being argued rather than according to the value and reliability of the indicators themselves. It is rare to find an authority claiming that it has few or negligible economic problems, and those figures will be highlighted which appear to indicate the existence of problems.

Local authorities in both countries and particularly in England are problem-oriented bodies. Many of the services they provide are offered in response to more or less clearly understood problems and the expansion of any service which either requires extra finance or a redistribution of resources depends on an acceptance by leading officers and councillors that problems in that sector need to be tackled. In the economic policy area this means that a decline in employment and prosperity or the likelihood of a future decline must be identified. The development of a new activity only takes place as a response to a problem or, more important, something which is seen as such. The attention given to economic development in Britain has therefore not grown as the result of some overall interest in the management of the local economy but rather as the result of pressure from various sources to respond to particular locally experienced problems. Thus despite all the possible mediating factors, it is clear from our cases, and perhaps not surprisingly, that councillors and officers working in authorities whose residents face high levels of unemployment tend to be more interested in the possibilities of economic intervention than those with lower levels.[6]

The definition of problems is affected by two principal filters. First, a local authority's councillors and officers usually share a picture of their area's economic condition and prospects which is hardly influenced at all by party commitments and rarely based on detailed empirical analysis. This image of the local economic condition is most developed where it merges with a tradition of civic pride and a sense of past strength and importance, above all, therefore, in the larger cities in both countries and in England in those which used to be county boroughs. In this context a fear of economic decline tends to be very strong, since that is often associated with a decline in political status too. To a remarkable extent, also, local authority officers and councillors have restricted their perceptions of the local economy to their own administrative boundaries, and this is clearly easier within larger and more homogeneous authorities. The existence of a municipal consciousness of this kind often expresses itself in an identification with the problems facing existing local employers and industries, whose health is also generally taken to imply local prosperity although it need not always bring wealth to a large number of local residents.

This view is linked very closely with the second orientation of officers and councillors, namely, towards the social welfare of those living in the area. Authorities in both countries are concerned to improve the well-being of local residents. This welfare orientation also finds an organisational expression since local authorities in both countries are organised around the provision of particular specialist services to more or less clearly identified client groups. It is, therefore, common for authorities to respond by providing appropriately specialised services to a newly defined group of clients, that is in this case industrialists and developers. The decision to act does not involve any idea of steering industry, but is based rather on the attempt to satisfy the needs of firms as far as possible within the existing local authority functional framework. Such activity is undertaken with the hope that it will bring a positive return to the local authorities in terms of their own wider goals and purposes.

The services provided to firms in each country differ from each other only to a limited extent. But in Britain the decisions over activity relevant to economic development are divided between more service divisions (departments and committees) than tends to be the case in the Federal Republic. More of them seem to have some interest in economic development than do their German equivalents. This is partly because a conscious service orientation towards industry is relatively new in Britain and there is still some uncertainty over the manner in which this particular service can be linked with the other local authority services.

LOCAL AUTHORITY GOALS AND STRATEGIES

In principle policy-making in the economic development field might be expected to follow a relatively simple model of goal formulation, leading in a more or less direct way from goals prepared by the principal councillors and officers down to specific activities probably carried out by middle level officers. This would seem to be still more likely for those English local authorities which have taken up the principles of corporate planning and those German local authorities which are involved in town development planning (*Stadtentwicklungsplanung*).[7]

In reality, however, the contrast between the two possible approaches, one with its emphasis on the definition of goals and their supporting context and the other with its focus on adaptive and incremental policy-making, is rarely very sharp. In England the fact that there is at the political and administrative levels a relatively high degree of dispersion of specialised responsibilities amongst committees, sub-committees and departments, ensures that what effectively counts as economic policy-making is an aggregation of specific activities. Even in Germany, the most systematic town development plan prepared by any of the authorities visited has gaps where economic development was to be discussed. Local authorities in both countries have at their disposal only a limited selection of instruments and those available can rarely be applied in a systematic fashion. In both countries the practical experience of economic development work encourages the establishment of priorities which may in turn influence more broadly stated goals, at least in the process of policy justification. It is thus more accurate to argue that activities search out their own goals than to attempt to maintain the ideal type of: goal → operationalisation → action.

This view of policy-making is confirmed by a review of the goals typically outlined by local authorities in discussing their economic priorities. It should be emphasised too that isolating these is difficult in many cases because several levels of goal are often mixed up in policy documents, yet they are rarely related to each other. At this level of understanding and argument there is a vagueness and generality in both countries. Certainly some connection between goals and activities can be identified in so far as, for example, the preparation of industrial sites is relevant to a goal such as the creation of employment opportunities. But in none of the cases was the success of a local authority's measures assessed rigorously in terms of the achievement of such goals. Conversely, it follows from this that the goals are only of limited relevance in explaining specific decisions on action.

The most important general goals in Germany and England relate to:

  (i)   the reduction of existing levels of unemployment;
 (ii)   the improvement of local employment and industrial structures;
(iii)   the increase of income from locally determined taxes;
(iv)   the increase of the incomes of local residents.

The first of these was the most common. All authorities were concerned to increase levels of employment which is hardly surprising given that the economic problems are generally defined in terms of high unemployment. Some authorities were particularly concerned about low levels of female employment and others with the relative decline of male employment.

Although much of the argument on levels of unemployment is couched in terms of goals, and sometimes even in quantified targets for the reduction of unemployment, particularly in county structure plans in England, in fact much of it represents a justification for specific measures and activities rather than an expression of goals which are intended to determine policies. No local authority in either country was prepared to argue that its actions had resulted in the creation of a specified number of new jobs which would otherwise not have been there.

An interest in the local industrial structure and employment mix was less extensive than that in unemployment, but in both countries there is some emphasis on broadening an area's industrial base, thus improving its long-term economic security. In both countries the industrial sector remains of overwhelming importance, but priorities are often identified within it. In one German case, for example, increased employment in textiles was hoped for, particularly to improve female employment opportunities. More commonly German and English councils identify priorities for growth industries such as electronics. There seems to be a slightly greater interest among English authorities in encouraging an increased service sector. This should not be exaggerated, however, as German councils also have an interest in the attraction of white-collar employment. The difference of emphasis can be explained by the differing importance of tertiary sector employment in each country (see Table 6.4). Despite a slightly faster rate of growth in service employment in Germany, its share remains significantly smaller and the share of industrial employment has barely fallen since 1960.

In Germany, the desire to increase local tax yields from business tax was often cited as a third and less prominent goal of economic

Table 6.4   *Percentage share of employment*

	Great Britain		Federal Republic of Germany	
	1960	*1975*	*1960*	*1975*
Industrial sector	48·8	40·9	48·2	46·0
Service sector	47·0	56·4	37·8	46·7

Source: Report on the Development of the Social Situation in the Community in 1976 (Brussels: EEC, 1977), quoted in P. A. Stone, *Arbeitslosigkeit und Industrieansiedlung in Grossbritannien...*, s. 281, Archiv für Kommunalwissenschaften, 1978.

development policies. Despite the local authority finance reform at the end of the 1960s, increased factory development still brings an increase in local authority income. By contrast increased rate income was not a goal of economic activity for any English authority, partly because the greater degree of central government funding for local English authorities is intended to compensate for differences in the rate yields between councils.

In a few cases in each country the goal of raising the income levels of local residents was expressed, but in no case was it seen as decisive. In Germany the fact that local authorities receive a share of the income tax paid by local residents might have been expected to increase interest in local earnings levels, but a slightly greater interest of this sort probably existed in England. The difficulty of effectively translating such a goal into any sort of proposal for action helped to reduce its importance even at this level of goal formulation.

The differences between the strategies adopted to achieve their goals by local authorities in the two countries seem to be slightly greater than the negligible differences in stated goals. Yet even here they are of emphasis rather than of approach.

Authorities in both countries attempt to attract new development from outside their areas and are keen to attract large-scale prestige developments. New prestige development is seen to be important not only in itself but also as a vital weapon in the process of attracting others. This orientation to new development is slightly stronger in Germany than in England, since those responsible for economic development in German local authorities tend to see large firms as their clients and as targets for their activities.

Conversely, in recent years English local authorities have been particularly concerned with the problems of small firms, and the process of creating new ones. Attempts to influence and assist such firms have been central to their policies. At first sight this provides a sharp contrast with the situation in Germany and is a further example of their apparently greater interest in the retention of existing local industry. There is, however, now an increasing interest in the position of small firms among local German authorities and one can expect this to develop in the future. In the manufacturing sector employment in small firms actually declined at a faster rate in Germany from 1954 to 1968 than in the UK.[8]

There are four main reasons for these differences of emphasis. First, Britain's economic problems have been greater so that there are fewer large firms to attract. They are in any case difficult to attract with the tools available to English local authorities, partly because of the large-scale national system of regional aid which has major firms as its target. Secondly, Britain's small firms' sector has been small since 1945 and has continued to decline in size. Yet it has been identified by some commentators as very important for Britain's future economic and employment hopes, and this analysis seems to have been accepted by both central and local government.[9] Even with the decline in Germany's small firms' sector since the early 1950s, it has been estimated that Germany has 40 per cent more small firms per head of the population than the United Kingdom,[10] and it should be emphasised that the decline in importance of small firms in Germany has been partly the consequence of their growth and of the growth of the German economy, whilst in Britain the disappearance of small firms has been extensively due to closures and economic stagnation.

This has been reinforced by a third factor, since local authorities in England have been blamed even by reports of the central government for the decline of small firms, particularly in the inner cities,[11] and this blame has been directed principally at planning departments, their definition of non-conforming uses and their redevelopment policies.[12] The acceptance of this argument by many councils seems to have had the corollary that local authorities should try to reverse the process.

Finally, local authorities take the 'realistic' view that they can influence small firms more easily than large ones. Small firms are likely to be more constrained in the distances they are prepared to move and may restrict inquiries to their local authority area whilst the first governmental point of contact for a large firm is likely to be the Department of Industry. There is also an important cultural influence because small firms can be identified as local and, therefore, are seen more clearly to be the responsibility of local authorities than are the branch plants of large firms. There is likely to be a regular process of inter-action between the proprietors of small firms and their organisations and council organisation (for example, the position of the Master Cutler in Sheffield with a status similar to that of the Lord Mayor). Considerations like these also apply in Germany, but there the larger firms too seem often to have established local roots and close links with local authorities.

Although local authorities in both countries argue that they want to encourage industrial diversification, at a strategic level they can rarely be selective. Despite the expressed desire of English local authorities for more office employment, for example, they too remain interested primarily in manufacturing industry, for whose needs they and their German counterparts are able to cater more easily. Similarly, although it was stated in some cases that particular industries would not be welcome, in fact the industries mentioned as unsuitable would, in any case, be extremely unlikely to move to those authorities which claimed not to want them. Local authorities usually fight, sometimes between themselves, for whatever development is available.

This means that their main strategy in both countries tends to be opportunistic in the sense that it is affected not only by stated or implicit goals but also, and perhaps more significantly, by the opportunities presented by potential developers. Although local authorities generally see themselves as influencing the investment decisions of firms, in practice they are often in the position of adjusting their policies to suit the firms concerned. They are reacting to demands rather than creating them. To some extent this is the result of the sort of goals which have been identified: they overestimate the potential for local authority intervention so that at the level of implementation officers are left to follow a process of pragmatic adjustment to events. The contrast between the general goals described above and the detailed practice of case by case negotiation discussed below is very noticeable.

ACTIVITIES: THE LOCAL AUTHORITY AS PROMOTER

The activities undertaken in both countries reveal many similarities. Local authorities are committed to encouraging or cajoling firms and other governmental authorities to act and their own economic activities reflect this. When councils actively intervene to alter the local economic situation officers and councillors see themselves primarily as intervening from outside the economic system to influence others. In general, therefore, their own staffing levels are not seen as crucial to local employment and in none of the cases was there any independent interest in job creation or public works programmes intended to reduce unemployment. In England such an interest depended on the offer of central government funds. This provides some contrast to the experience of the 1920s when local authorities hardly saw any other role for themselves on economic matters. The construction of the *Grungürtel* (Green Belt) around Cologne and of a road between Birmingham and Wolverhampton provide major examples of such activity in that period.

(i) *The provision of land and premises*
The provision and preparation of land with planning permission for industry is the most important activity in both countries. It provides a service to potential developers from outside the authority area, but also to existing employers who either want to expand, are tempted to move from small areas in confined inner areas or who are being moved in the course of redevelopment. Local authorities in both countries are involved in land assembly both for industrial and city centre shopping development and some English authorities (such as Sheffield) have attempted to provide developments linking housing and employment, thus moving beyond what is possible for most private developers. Among the German cities in the Ruhr area the fact that the old mining companies controlled a large amount of land was identified as a significant restriction on local authority initiatives.

There are two important differences between the English and German policies on the disposal of land. First, English authorities tend to dispose of land on the basis of long- and short-term leases, whilst German authorities usually sell it freehold. To some extent the English practice was encouraged by the Community Land Act which forbade the sale of council-owned industrial land without the permission of the Secretary of State for the Environment. But even before the Act was passed most local authorities with large land-holdings (such as Sheffield) were reluctant to sell their own land and followed a policy of selling leases. This was due partly to the reluctance of most authorities to dispose of capital assets; partly to the desire to retain some continuing control over the land; and partly to the fact that much of the land was either developed as factory units or was most suitable for small-scale development. Land is often leased for ninety-nine years to large developers, but more commonly for about twenty-five years to smaller firms who cannot afford or do not want the longer leases. Similar (twenty-five years or less) leases are available on many factory units, and rents in these are usually subject to regular review.

The second major difference is that English local authorities are heavily involved in the construction and marketing of advance factories of various sizes, but usually in the smaller sector of the property market. These advance factories are intended principally for small firms such as those affected by planning policies in the inner areas and to those which would otherwise find it difficult to obtain suitable premises. In Germany it is very rare for authorities to be involved even in the provision of industrial estates, and although two of our cases were considering the possibility of converting some older industrial premises for current use by small firms this was still only at a preliminary stage.

The difference in approach can be explained partly by the greater concentration of English authorities on small firms who are likely to be most interested in ready-built units and unlikely to be able to pay large sums for them. But another important factor is that even small firms in Germany are held to have an 'ownership mentality' (*Eigentümermentalität*) which makes them reluctant to rent or lease property. It is for this reason that attempts by some German local authorities to set up industrial estates have generally been unsuccessful.

(ii) *The varying of land prices and rents*
The variation of land prices is the main incentive offered to developers and employers in Germany and the levels are usually agreed in detailed negotiations between firms and appropriate officers of the authority. No single rate of discount is offered by any authority; rather the price negotiated depends on what is acceptable to the potential developer. It is principally for this reason that negotiations must remain confidential,

for otherwise some firms might view their own terms as unfavourable in comparison with those offered to another concern.

Although in practice the land and premises provided by English local authorities are offered at slightly below market rates, there are few private developments with which they can be compared. Most authorities expect to make a reasonable return on their land and premises, and only in one of our cases was there any evidence of significantly reduced rents for premises and that was for a small-scale experimental programme. Similar possibilities exist on some inner city schemes where assistance is expected from the centrally funded Urban Programme, but authorities are reluctant to use their own resources for such activity.

The main reason for this difference between the two countries seems to be that there is more intense competition for mobile industry between German cities. This is reinforced by the legal maxim that local authorities should not make a profit on land sales, whilst in England inter-authority competition remains fairly minor and the doctrine of *ultra vires*, coupled with the financial orthodoxy of most local authority officers and councillors, discourages such a policy. In England it seems to be becoming increasingly difficult for private sources to provide land and premises, particularly for small firms, so that English authorities tend rather to compete in the extent of services they can provide to industry, above all in the form of land and premises. They are sceptical about the impact of reduced land prices and artificially low rents. Whilst authorities in the Federal Republic also compete over what services are supplied, in packages of land and infrastructure, for example, the element of price competition overlays this and sometimes takes on a greater importance.

The differences between the two countries also reflect the wider difference in political approach, which exists at higher levels of government too. German local authorities tend to intervene less directly than English ones. The former are concerned to offer incentives rather than to become involved directly in such activities as the provision of premises. German governmental agencies deliberately try to use means which correspond to market forces (*'marktkonforme Mittel'*) to influence firms, but British politicians and officials appear to be less tied by this concern. The main results of this are that in Germany the price mechanism (including tariffs) is used more extensively than in England and direct involvement (including public ownership) tends to be more common in England.

(iii)   *Other direct or indirect financial help: loans, grants and tax reductions*

Local authorities in both countries attempt in different ways to influence the financial environment within which firms make investment decisions. But the extent of local authority financial assistance (except through the variation of land prices) is limited because local authorities cannot direct sufficient resources to affect significantly the cost of investment and they are sometimes restrained by various legal restrictions. Local authority uncertainty about this sort of activity is reflected in the hesitant and divergent means used.

Some English authorities offer loans (mortgages) to employers to help them carry out development either in specified inner city areas or on council-owned land, but these mortgages have not been extensively used as interest rates have not been particularly favourable and the lack of loan funds has rarely been a problem for those developers to whom an authority might lend. Loans at favourable rates of interest are also made in Germany, but mainly through the *Städtische Sparkassen* (Municipal Savings Banks) which are not directly under local authority control. German local authorities may, however, be prepared to guarantee loans.

In Germany it is common to reduce the charges made for providing services to industrial premises (*Erschliessungskosten*) in order to help attract firms. This is less common in England, partly because some of these services are not the responsibility of the local authorities but, for example in the case of sewers, of the regional water authority.

Direct grants to industry by councils are rare in either country and legally controversial in Germany, but one English county examined here now offers small grants for various purposes to firms employing less than fifty people. This is another indication of the orientation of English local authorities towards small firms, but it is unlikely to be taken up extensively because of the costs involved. One English authority among our cases has attempted to use its employees' superannuation fund to offer equity capital to local firms, but the conditions have been as strict as (and stricter than some) commercial sources so that there has been no local share purchase. Only in one of the English cases have shares been purchased out of normal local authority funds and that was clearly exceptional. German local authorities would be regarded as exceeding their powers if they acquired shares in local firms.

In the past it was possible for German authorities to vary local tax rates in specific cases to help retain industry. Since the late 1960s this has not been strictly legal, but it has been suggested that some authorities have continued to make concessions on an informal basis.[13] In England similar possibilities are also limited, but rate levels on empty property can be varied and in one case it was argued that the reduction of rates on empty office premises had been useful in encouraging continued speculative office development.

(iv) *Promotion and advertising*
At a time of recession advertising and promotion have some attractions,

particularly for councillors. They require little additional manpower or finance to initiate, yet they create an impression that action is being taken. Promotional budgets are currently rising in both countries, but the activity seems to be given more weight in England. Budgets are higher – no active English authority among our cases had an annual advertising budget below £10,000 and some English authorities (including Sheffield) have budgets which are about four times as large. Accurate comparison is, however, difficult because some of the promotional spending undertaken by German authorities falls under the heading of general municipal promotion. Nevertheless, a difference in approach remains. Advertising and promotional activities were not seen as central parts of the German economic development programmes. German local authority officers are often sceptical about the success of such effort, an attitude, moreover, which is shared by at least some industrial development officers in England. Even those authorities which undertake such work extensively agree that it is difficult to assess its impact. German and English local authorities undertake similar forms of advertising, but there is a greater emphasis by the English than the German authorities (particularly the larger ones) on attending industrial and trade exhibitions. This partly reflects the greater emphasis on assisting local industry, since several industrial development officers explained that they wanted to help small firms at relevant exhibitions by providing a stand for and manpower assistance to some of them. Although it remains a luxury for all but the largest authorities, there is also an increasing interest in England in attempts to attract foreign industry and this is less noticeable among German authorities. The problems of the British economy appear to be driving English authorities further afield and attendance at some large British and foreign exhibitions is a reflection of this.

(v) *Professional advice and assistance*
The giving of advice and assistance is not expensive compared with most other local authority activities as it often uses existing staff resources, yet is highly valued by many developers and firms. It is, therefore, not surprising that almost all the authorities in this study saw it to be of great importance. It was noticeable that the more developed and specialist a local authority's economic development office the more extensive the advice and assistance it offered.

This form of activity contains two main elements. First, it may concentrate on help with the local authority's own formal procedures, for example in planning, and emphasis may be put on the importance of ensuring that all the different sections of an authority can be approached through one point of contact. Local authorities have in the past, particularly in England, been criticised by developers for being almost impenetrable, but in both countries developers should now have little difficulty in making contact with the relevant officers. It may, second, also involve the giving of advice on alternative sources of assistance, the availability of resources, land and property and even technical and financial advice.

Such a source of help and information may help to reduce both the search costs of firms wishing to move and make them reluctant to start looking in places where no similar assistance is offered. English industrial development officers often maintain that they are more appropriate sources of advice for small firms than the higher levels of government, which are thought to be remote and inaccessible.

(vi)   *The mobilisation of support from other levels of government*
In both countries local authorities attempt to gain additional resources and favourable decisions from other levels of government – usually central government in England and the *Land* in Germany. Additional resources may be available from those bodies and it is often important for local authority areas to be favourably viewed within national or regional policies if their economic interests are to be advanced. The advocacy role follows clearly from the usual position of local authorities in their regular negotiations with higher levels of government across a wide range of policy areas. They accept that they cannot operate in isolation from these higher levels.

It is common for local authorities to argue and campaign for more favourable status under their respective regional policies – that is, to become '*Schwerpunkte*' in Germany and assisted areas in England – or to attempt to retain such status if there is felt to be a threat of its removal. The effect of such arguments is usually very limited, although there is evidence that national and regional governments have occasionally been influenced by such local authority pressure.

Local authorities also attempt to win extra finance for themselves. This is difficult in respect of the main sources of finance because they are fixed according to nationally agreed criteria. But most English local authorities have attempted to get additional funds under the Job Creation Programme, the Inner City Programme or for the reclamation of land. Similar claims have been made by some German local authorities for land development grants, but these have not always been taken up because they only cover a part of the land and development costs. They commit authorities to expenditure from existing budgets as well as reduce the flexibility of local authority spending, since land purchased with the aid of these grants must be sold within a limited period or the grants must be returned to the *Land* authorities.

There is often significant local authority pressure for public offices to be relocated in their areas, and there are several examples among our cases in both countries. The *Land* development plan of North

Rhine-Westphalia identifies the territorial distribution of such offices as an important instrument of development policy and most local authorities would agree. Similarly many councils have tried to encourage more infrastructural spending by national and regional governments to encourage economic development and employment. Local authorities have pressed for spending on roads (including motorways) (England), universities (particularly Germany), airports (e.g. Bielefeld) and canal improvement (e.g. South Yorkshire). Whilst economic issues are not the only ones involved in the arguments for such infrastructure, they have been important in the statements produced by the local authorities in planning documents and elsewhere.

(vii) *Locally determined infrastructure*
Local authority spending on infrastructure is a particularly nebulous category in the consideration of local economy policy. It is easy for officers and councillors to justify spending in terms of the local economy, even when the main reasons for the spending are unrelated to economic factors. Yet it was quite clear from the cases, as we have stated above, that no local authority in either country expressed keen interest in the possibility of public works schemes. Infrastructural spending undertaken on the grounds that it aids the growth of employment opportunities is generally jsutified on the basis that others (principally private firms) will be encouraged to develop by the improved network of social and economic infrastructure.

In a number of cases local authority statements to the effect that their infrastructural policies were influenced by economic considerations were convincing. In all the English counties visited, for example, particular road schemes have been supported because of their economic implications and similar considerations have weighed heavily in the public transport decisions of some authorities. One authority in each country was involved in the provision of port facilities at least partly to help local industry and employment, and similar considerations apply to the local authority input to the airports at Bielefeld and Castle Donington.

German local authority spending on cultural activities is sometimes also said to help local development prospects and education departments in England claim to take local economic needs into account in preparing courses and syllabuses. But to see such spending as part of an economic policy is to stretch the definition of infrastructure too far. Similarly, despite Sheffield's promotional campaigns emphasising how clean the city now is and hence its suitability for office employment, it would be a mistake to believe that the attraction of new employment was the main aim of the clean air programme which led to the dramatic environmental improvement.

References to the importance of locally determined infrastructure for economic development were, perhaps surprisingly, more common from English authorities. Economic policy is a new departure for them so that they are able to give it a wider definition, particularly in the context of an interest in corporate planning, whereas in Germany *Wirtschaftsförderung* has already acquired a rather more restricted technical meaning. In England this tendency to take a wide-ranging view of economic policy is encouraged by local government's weak financial position which tends to work against new expenditure, except on a limited range of policies which at present do, however, include economic development. It is, therefore, of advantage to a department with little direct economic importance to argue that its infrastructural spending may have significant economic side-effects. In Germany the justification for a great deal of infrastructural spending owes much to a view of the city as a cultural and social centre for a surrounding hinterland, which only implicitly contains the assumption that a pleasant civic environment will assist in the retention and even attraction of employment. Infrastructural spending is, therefore, less likely to be regarded as a direct part of an economic programme; it amounts rather to a series of separate programmes which together improve the social environment and by so doing improve the economic prospects of the area as well.

(viii)   *Planning*

The local authority planning function can clearly have an important influence on the local economy and provides one of the most significant points of contact between the public and the private sectors at local level. In both countries town planning has been embodied chiefly in a system of development control. Whilst there has been similarity of aims, the structure of local authority planning and its relationship to the plans of other levels of government have differed markedly as between Britain and the Federal Republic.

The British planning system is clearly intended now to be flexible and all plans are subject to regular review. Only structure plans have to be approved by the Department of the Environment and local plans prepared by district planning authorities have only to be examined by county planning departments to ensure that they are in conformity with the structure plan, which is broad enough to leave a great deal of discretion to planners at district level. In operational terms the English system still rests chiefly on the approval, modification or rejection of individual planning applications. Many planning authorities approve applications which they feel will help local employment even if they represent major modifications to existing or proposed local plans. Detailed requirements for specific development are not usually made until the planning application stage, and planning departments are therefore able to negotiate with developers at that stage on the basis of only general guidelines.

German planning is at the same time more rigid and more coherent than the British, with clear links between the *Landesentwicklungsplan* (*Land* development plan), the *Gebietsentwicklungsplan* (area development plan)[14] and the *Flächennutzungsplan* (land use plan) right down to the individual *Bebauungsplan* (building plan). All of these plans have a legal status when finally produced. The formal process of amendment is then often time-consuming and action counter to policies expressed in them may be legally challenged if the amendment process has not been completed. *Bebauungspläne* are supposed to be prepared in advance of planning applications, and their amendment may take two or three years. They specify conditions and details which would usually only appear at planning application stage in England. The zoning carried out by local plans falls within the *Flächennutzungsplan*, which generally covers the whole of an authority area with the familiar coloured spaces to indicate housing, industry, commerce, mixed uses, and so on.

The German and English systems of development control do not, however, operate in quite so divergent a way as the formal framework might indicate. German planners try to use their system as flexibly as possible and sometimes consult potential developers before preparing their *Bebauungspläne* and occasionally (despite legal constraints) delay their submission to the *Land* authorities as long as possible in the hope that they will be able to adjust them in the light of planning applications before they become legally binding. This factor has contributed to the fact that few building plans have actually been completed, although each local authority is required to prepare them for the whole of its area. The existence of such plans restricts the possibilities open to local authorities and their preparation requires a significant manpower commitment which most authorities can ill afford.

There are two principal ways in which planning methods and the planning process may be important for the economic development work of local authorities. First, planners and planning documents may attempt to persuade others (both within and outside their authority) to take action. In England planners have, often successfully, convinced other departments that certain economic problems exist and that local authorities can and ought to play some part in solving these. In a number of cases planning departments have been influential in offering new ideas on economic questions and proposing small-scale action for particular problems. The existence of structure plans and local plans has, on balance, helped in this process by providing a focus for the planning department, other departments, leading councillors and committees. In one of the English cases the structure plan played a particularly important part, identified priority areas for economic assistance, acted as a corporate focus for economic activity and was used as a weapon to persuade central government to assist development by providing extra aid. Whether this is the correct way to use a structure plan, according to the Town and Country Planning Act 1971 and various circulars from the Department of the Environment, may be open to question but it gives the plan a direct significance which is often absent elsewhere.

In Germany local authority plans can less easily be used in this way since many of the functions of structure planning (and more) are already the responsibility of the *Land* through its *Land* development plan, particularly at the level of area development plans. Within the local authority much of the focus provided by some planners and plans in England is instead provided by the office of town development, the *Stadtentwicklungsplanungsamt*, where it exists, or by the longer established economic development function wherever this is located.

Secondly, planning powers may be used restrictively or permissively at the development control level. It is easy to see, for example, how a development may be halted by the refusal of planning permission, although more difficult to see how permissive policies will call forth development. Planning rules have now been relaxed in both countries in the hope that past restrictions can be overcome. To a limited extent planning tools can be used as instruments to attract development since firms are more likely to invest where the planning process is quick and the response is sympathetic. But this depends on the continued existence of some planning authorities who are slower and less sympathetic and from whom development might be attracted. The effective handling of planning rules is probably more important in Germany, both because the levels of private investment are higher than in England and because the planning rules are more restrictive and require sympathetic manipulation.

One of the dangers of the increased flexibility accorded to planning in both countries is that it may cease to have any clear purpose, particularly in a period of negligible or nil growth. In other words, planning guidelines may simply be adapted to suit the needs of those making applications and the skills of a planner could be reduced to those of altering plans to suit others or of preparing plans of such generality that almost any development will be acceptable. In practice this danger has not yet been fully realised, but there are already signs in some cases that local authority plans are less important than the negotiations initiated by those who wish to develop.

NOTES

1   These indicators cover the extent of labour reserve, the levels of earnings and infrastructural facilities (including public health, education and roads). See Working Paper D, Annex 1, in 'Conference on Regional Problems in North Rhine-Westphalia and North-West England', Papers by the German Working Party (Anglo-German Foundation for the Study of Industrial Society, 1977), pp. 1–5.
2   ibid., Report of Working Party D, p. 12.

3   See, for example, M. M. Camina, *Local Authorities and the Attraction of Industry*
     (Oxford: Pergamon, 1974); N. Falk, *Local Authorities and Industrial Development:
     Results of a Survey* (London: Urbed, 1978); P. Lawless, 'New approaches to local
     authority economic intervention', *Local Government Studies*, vol. 6, no. 1 (1980);
     and R. Minns and J. Thornley, 'Local authority economic planning: a guide to
     powers and initiatives', in G. Craig *et al.* (eds), *Jobs and Community Action*
     (London: Routledge & Kegan Paul, 1979).
4   Except in the special circumstances of new town development in Britain.
5   The only figures readily available at something approximating to the district level are
     for unemployment. For counties certain figures on earnings and industrial structure
     are also available. Other items have to be estimated from the regional statistics,
     ascertained on the basis of special surveys or extrapolated from outdated census
     figures. See B. Needham, 'Guidelines for a Local Authority Employment Study'
     (Farnborough: Saxon House, 1979), for a discussion of statistical sources which may
     be used by local authorities in the preparation of economic policies.
6   Both high and low levels are defined in terms of each country's experience. No
     attempt is made at internationally ranking authorities since low levels in Britain
     would be high in Germany. See below, Table 7.2.
7   Whilst the principles behind these methods of resource and policy planning are not
     significantly different, the German *Stadtentwicklungsplanung* is generally more
     developed. Many German urban authorities are, for example, able to prepare overall
     Stadtentwicklungspläne for their cities which commit various departments to
     spending programmes in particular areas. *Stadtentwicklungspläne* also include some
     elements which in England might more appropriately be seen as the province of
     planning departments.
8   G. Bannock, *The Smaller Business in Britain and Germany* (London: Wilton House,
     1976), quoted in N. Falk, *Think Small: Enterprise and Economy*, Fabian Tract 483
     (London: Fabian Society, 1978), p. 6. Small firms are defined as those employing
     less than 200 and excluding the self-employed.
9   For some arguments on the importance of small firms for the economy and role
     which local authorities might play, see N. Falk, ibid. and R. Minns and J. Thornley,
     'The Case for MEBs', *New Society*, 2 September 1976.
10 G. Bannock, op. cit., quoted in N. Falk, ibid.
11 See *Policy for the Inner Cities* (London: HMSO, 1977).
12 See, for example, Department of the Environment circular 71/77 on the Industrial
     Strategy.
13 See, for example, 'Hart am Rande der Legalität – Report über Industrieansiedlung
     in Westdeutschland', *Der Spiegel*, no. 10 (1972).
14 This title is used in North Rhine-Westphalia but similar plans are prepared in other
     Länder.

Chapter 7

ORGANISATION AND CO-ORDINATION COMPARED

Local authorities have in both countries used variations in organisational structure as central elements in the mobilisation of their own resources in the economic development field. They are able to introduce such changes independently in accordance with their own judgement of the best way to proceed. This helps to explain the organisational differences between them: there are differing criteria of what makes for efficiency, the length of time authorities have been involved in this field vary, the local economic problem is perceived in different ways by officers and councillors and, more especially in England, there are fragmented methods of goal formulation and decision-making.

The organisation of economic activity in each country takes place within a different administrative tradition. There is no English equivalent to the organisational scheme[1] prepared by the Kommunale Gemeinschaftsstelle für Verwaltungsvereinfachung (or KGSt)[2] and accepted by all German authorities, albeit with a locally determined division of responsibility. Despite the report of the Bains Committee[3] English local authority organisation remains far more irregular and varied, and is based on the local interpretation of those tasks which are undertaken by most authorities.

German organisation is based on eight broad policy areas identified by the KGSt which generally find a local expression as *Dezernate*. These are something like the directorates developed by some English local authorities. Within these large departments the KGSt has identified related specialist areas which are expected to be represented locally as *Ämter* (specialist departments). Economic development (*Wirtschaftsförderung*) is listed as *Amt* 80 within the *Wirtschaft- und Verkehrsdezernat*. In practice the *Ämter* need not be associated with the *Dezernate* suggested in KGSt's organisational model, but the model provides the framework within which decisions on organisational responsibility are made.

In England organisation has instead tended to develop to cope with the provision of particular services, usually those specified by central government. Sometimes these have been amalgamated into wider departments but the organisational structure remains specialist, so that English departments tend to be nearer the larger German *Ämter* in terms of functional responsibility, but closer to the *Dezernate* in terms of their hierarchical importance. German organisation is fairly systematic, at least in principle, with its *Dezernate* and specialist *Ämter*, but in England some departments may be more like the former and some more like the latter. In England there are no widely accepted criteria on the basis of which departments can be differentiated; nor are there guidelines to help with the internal organisational division of existing departments.

The table below (Table 7.1) is intended to illustrate the organisational differences between the two countries. In England economic development has an almost experimental character, arising in any one of several departments and even in the form of an interdepartmental unit, whereas in Germany it has been given a clear organisational home, usually being accorded the status of an *Amt*. In one authority studied it is carried on by a section (*Abteilung*) of another *Amt*, principally so that it can be directly responsible to the *Oberstadtdirektor*,[4] but only in one (the smallest and most prosperous German case) has no separate place been found for economic development in the administrative hierarchy, largely because there the task does not require the commitment of any additional manpower or organisational resources.

Despite these important differences between Germany and England significant similarities can also be identified in the extent of organisation and the reasons for it among the local authorities investigated, even if the range of cases does not justify extensive generalisation.

Cities with large populations which usually also have significant manpower and financial resources, management expertise and a long civic tradition, tend to have the most clearly identified organisation for economic development. This link between population size and organisational response also seems to be reflected among the counties in England, but other external factors such as the degree of urbanisation, the metropolitan/non-metropolitan division and the extent of economic problems play a part here.

Population size and the degree of urbanisation tend to be less important factors in determining organisational response where economic problems are particularly serious, as is shown by the cases of Fenland and Gelsenkirchen. Although Fenland has the lowest level of urbanisation of all the English cases it has its own industrial development officer, whilst the responsible county council – Cambridgeshire – remains reluctant to become involved in economic development activities. Gelsenkirchen, of course, has a larger population than Fenland and is heavily urbanised, but it too has staff levels in its economic development section significantly higher than might have been expected for an authority of its size. In both cases it is clear that the poor economic situation has encouraged organisational innovation and expansion (see Table 7.2).

Table 7.1 *The location of administrative responsibility for economic activity*

County or district/ Gemeinde (listed by order of population size)	Department/a Dezernat	Office/a Amt	Level of responsibility Specialist b section/ Abteilung	Interdepartmental unit /Dezernats- übergreifend	Internal interdepartmental organisation/ Dezernats- übergreifend
1 COUNTIES (ENGLAND ONLY)					
South Yorkshire (Metropolitan) (pop. over 1m.)	Chief Executive (Dept of Administration) County Planning Department. County Treasurer's Department	Estates Surveyor	Economic Services Section	Employment Promotion Unit	Economic Development Programme Area Team
Nottinghamshire (pop. 0·6–1m.)	Clerk of the County Council and Chief Executive. Department of Planning & Transportation	Estates. Publicity	Economic Development Division		Land Officers' Panel
Cambridgeshire (pop. below 0·6m.)	Chief Executive. County Planning Department				Economic Group of Chief Officers (proposed)

DISTRICTS/ GEMEINDE				
Essen	Oberstadtdirektor	Amt für Stadtentwicklungsplanung. Planungsamt		Arbeitsgruppe 'Arbeiten'
	Baudezernat			
	Wirtschafts- und Rechtsdezernat	Amt für Wirtschaftsförderung. Liegenschaftsamt		
City of Sheffield (Metropolitan)	Chief Executive	Publicity Department		
	Estates Surveyor		Industrial Development Office	
	Planning & Design Department	Planning Section		
Bielefeld	Oberstadtdirektor. Baudezernat. Dezernat für Wirtschaftsförderung, Liegenschaft- und Bodenordnung	Planungsamt. Liegenschaftsamt	Abteilung für Wirtschaftsförderung	Arbeitskreis 'Stadtentwicklung'
Gelsenkirchen	Oberstadtdirektor	Amt für Stadtentwicklungsplanung	Abteilung für Wirtschaftsförderung	Arbeitskreis 'Baureif machung städtischer Grundstücke'

County or district / Gemeinde (listed by order of population size)	Level of responsibility				
	Department / Dezernat	Office /[a] Amt	Specialist[b] section / Abteilung	Interdepartmental unit / Dezernats-übergreifend	Internal[c] interdepartmental organisation / Dezernats-übergreifend
	Baudezernat Kämmerei	Planungsamt Leigenschaftsamt			
Nottingham	Town Clerk and Chief Executive	Publicity & Information Office	Industrial & Commercial Development Officer	Industrial & Commercial Development Unit	
	City Planning Department				
(pop. over 0.2m.)	Department of Technical Services	Land Division			
Recklinghausen	Technische Dezernat	Planungsamt Amt für Wirschafts-förderung Liegenschaftsamt			
City of Peterborough[d] (pop. 0.1–0.2m.)	Legal and Administrative Office	Estates Manager and Valuer			Programme Review Group

Gütersloh	Oberstadtdirektor. Dezernat für Stadt- planung und Stadt- entwicklungs- planung	Amt für Stadt- planung und Stadt- entwicklung	Industrial Development Officer
Fenland (pop. below 0.1m.)	Department of Planning and Architectural Services		Industrial Development Officer

---

[a] As explained in the text above, there is no English equivalent for the German distinction between *Dezernate* and *Ämter*. We have, however, tried to provide a distinction by defining an 'office' within an English department as an easily identified part of that department which has also been given some organisational form by the authority concerned. This means that in most cases the English offices are rather less important than the German *Ämter*.

[b] The distinction between office and specialist section is similarly unclear in England, and in the case of Nottinghamshire, for example, the Economic Development Division of the Department of Planning and Transportation could just as well be seen as an office.

[c] We have attempted only to include those internal interdepartmental organisations which are important for the economic development function. In some cases the decision to include any particular working group or regular officers' meeting has had to be somewhat arbitrary.

[d] In the case of Peterborough this table is a little misleading since it ignores the role of the Development Corporation and the relations between it and the local authority. The central government-sponsored Development Corporation currently carries out most of the functions which would usually be associated with local authority economic development, and does so on a greater scale.

Table 7.2 Population, unemployment and staffing levels by authority

Population size	Authority	Unemployment levels (1976)	Non-secretarial staff employed on economic activity (1978)	
			Full-time	Part-time
Large (C)	South Yorkshire Metropolitan County Council	High	3	3
Middle	Gelsenkirchen	High	5 (+2)	—
Small	Fenland	High	1	—
Middle–Small	Peterborough	Middle–High	—	—
Middle–Small	Recklinghausen	Middle–High	3 (+1)	—
Middle (C)	Nottinghamshire County Council	Middle	5 (+2)	—
Middle	Nottingham	Middle	1	4
Large	Essen	Middle	7	—
Small (C)	Cambridgeshire County Council	Low	—	—
Large	Sheffield	Low	3	2
Middle	Bielefeld	Low	3 (+2)	3
Small	Gütersloh	Low	—	—

Notes

(i) Population Size:

Counties:
Large (C)   over 1m.
Middle (C)   0·6–1m.
Small (C)   below 0·6m

Districts/Gemeinde:
Large   over 0·5m.
Middle   0·2–0·5m.
Middle/Small 0·1–0·2m.
Small   below 0·1m.

(ii) Unemployment levels:

Great Britain (5·3%)
High   = over 5·7%
Middle = 5–5·7%
Low   = below 5%

Germany (4·6%)
High   = over 5·2%
Middle = 4·2–5·2%
Low   = below 4·2%

(iii) Staffing: Part-time involvement is particularly difficult to estimate accurately, because the time put in is likely to vary from place to place and officer to officer. No allowance has been made for policy or other input from chief officers nor for occasional co-operation. In some places (e.g.

Nottinghamshire) there have been additional appointments since the case studies were completed. The figures for Sheffield are particularly misleading since a great deal of the work of the publicity department should be seen as related to economic development, as should some of the work of estate management currently carried out by members of the Estate Surveyors' department. The figure of three part-time employees given here is thus almost certainly inadequate to cover real manpower levels.

(iv) *Peterborough:* The staffing figures for Peterborough are misleading since much of the work one would normally associate with economic development is actually undertaken by the new town Development Corporation, which has significant staffing and financial resources.

Some qualifications have to be made to the above conclusions. As we have argued earlier, the response to economic problems is influenced by the reaction of councillors and officers and by the political-administrative culture of the individual authority. Economic and demographic factors can only explain broad differences. Why some authorities sharing similar economic and demographic conditions and even having the same party in control should respond in quite different ways can only be answered on a case by case basis. It should also be emphasised here that the existence of an organisation for economic development does not imply any particular level of success or efficiency; nor does it imply any particular level of resource commitment.

ADMINISTRATIVE RESPONSIBILITY

Table 7.1 does not adequately reflect the overarching interest of either chief executives or *Oberstadtdirektoren* (OSTDs). The fact that economic development is the direct responsibility of the OSTD's *Dezernat* in only one German case is particularly misleading. Both chief executives and OSTDs are extensively involved in the economic decision-making process, often through informal channels. In North Rhine-Westphalia one reason for this happening lies in the political importance of land sales and decisions on land prices: these matters tend to involve the *Oberstadtdirektor* directly as the council's leading administrative and political officer. He will be involved in and informed of most major negotiations with potential employers, and this is supplemented in several cases by the importance (apparently rarer in England) of informal social relations between the *Oberstadtdirektor* and leading local employers. An English chief executive may have a general interest in the work of the economic development officers, but an OSTD is usually more directly involved in decision-making because of the land issue.

In both countries leading officers accept an overall interest in local economic development as part of their concern for the local environment. In Germany this is emphasised by the degree of political responsibility which exists as a result of the election of such officers. Economic development is also seen to be an undertaking which requires a high level of co-operation and co-ordination between *Dezernate* and departments. In Germany the OSTD has always had a co-ordinative role and requires no formal organisational responsibility to act, but in England the Chief Executive's role remains less clear and the growth of an explicit co-ordinative function is more recent. In some cases chief executives have tried to use economic activity as a means of emphasising their supra-departmental role.

Economic development is commonly associated with one or other of the planning or estates departments – planning tends to be the more important in England and estates is generally more important in Germany, but the difference in emphasis is not very great. In England it is common for industrial development officers to be in the planning department or to be associated with it through interdepartmental bodies, but in some cases they may be members of the estates department and will certainly have to work closely with estates officers, usually through some formal organisation. In Germany, economic development is often handled in the same *Dezernat* as the planning or estates function and estates may even be a part of the economic *Dezernat* if one exists. It may also be associated with town development planning which is usually under the *Oberstadtdirektor*.

In both countries the planning and estates functions generate their own interest in economic matters. Both are important for the encouragement of economic development activity because the identification, provision and preparation of industrial sites are central activities in the process of local economic development. Land is crucial for economic development activities in both countries for all authorities, regardless of whether they already own a great deal or not. The former are concerned to manage and service their existing land and the latter must attempt to purchase land as a first step in the process.

Planning departments often play a more significant part in the early stages of the growth of an economic development function than they do as the function increases in importance for the authority and develops its own momentum. At this point questions of land purchase, assembly, development and disposal become vital and estates departments and officers become increasingly important, or their functions are more or less absorbed into those of the economic development unit or department. In Germany planning departments have also lost importance relative to economic development departments and where specialist units have developed in England a similar process can be identified. But it must be remembered that in both countries many of those responsible for economic development have been trained as planners and thus a substantial planning influence remains.

The need to use the skills of officers from several different professions indicates the extent to which some form of co-ordination and integration is needed. In both countries it has become increasingly accepted that local authorities should plan their operations in a more integrated fashion or at least avoid unnecessary duplication and conflict between and within departments. Economic development is a policy area in which interdepartmental co-operation and policy-making is particularly important.

The formal organisation of joint work and policy-making on the administrative side is similar in the two countries. At the top, chaired and directed by the *Oberstadtdirektor* in Germany and chief executive in England, is the *Verwaltungskonferenz* or management team,[5] at which chief officers discuss programmes cutting across departmental boundaries or which have implications for other departments (including, for example, budgetary implications). These bodies range from providing opportunities to achieve necessary compromises between strong departments to being more coherent sources of policy initiative, particularly where the chief executive is able to use them to foster his own policies. The strength of the German *Dezernate* orients *Verwaltungskonferenzen* towards the former of these poles and this is generally true of the English cases too, particularly where there is some reluctance to use the title of management team. In some English authorities, however, the management teams, with the encouragement of the chief executives, have been instrumental in the identification of economic issues as suitable for local government intervention.

At lower levels in both countries economic development work is usually supported by a series of interdepartmental working groups, frequently dealing with particular specialist sectors, such as land purchase, covering specific projects or negotiating with firms and providing complementary professional skills. In some cases working groups are more or less permanent, in others they are only brought together for individual schemes (for example, to prepare the *Flächennutzungsplan* in Essen, or help with the structure plan in two English cases). In England it has become accepted in a limited number of authorities that where programme areas overlap interdepartmental co-operation is needed to encourage policy debate,[6] although the effect of this is uncertain as many officers retain a strong loyalty to their parent departments and professional skills. In two cases permanent interdepartmental bodies or units have also been set up to deal with problems of implementation, partly to save on manpower and partly to avoid excessive fragmentation of effort between departments. No such units exist in Germany. Although they are not intended to make policy, in fact such units generate a direction of their own since the identification of suitable sites for development and the detailed discussions with individual developers are usually of more importance than programmatic guidelines drawn up elsewhere. Unlike working groups in either country these units can make executive decisions.

A great deal of work which would be seen as interdepartmental in England is often carried on within one *Dezernat* in Germany. The regular meetings of *Amtsleiter* (office or section chiefs) are then important for policy discussions and co-ordination. This is particularly important in the three German cases where the economic development responsibility is in the same *Dezernat* as the estates department.

Informal co-operation between officers in different departments and different *Dezernate* and between those in different offices and *Ämter* within the same departments is vital for the pursuit of local economic policy in both countries, particularly at the stage of implementation.

This study showed no significant departure from the results of a recent German survey[7] of local authority economic development activity which indicated that such contact was important in nearly 90 per cent of cases, a significantly greater proportion than those for whom formal interdepartmental groups (at *Amtsleiter* or *Dezernent* level) were important. Similar results were apparent in England, and in one English authority personal co-operation was almost the only effective element of interdepartmental work and was crucial to the achievement of a successful promotional and development campaign.

The day-to-day contacts in both countries between officers respons-ible for the detailed work of economic development and those at a similar level in the planning, estates and publicity fields influence the ways in which policies are implemented at least as much as formal meetings at higher levels of the authorities. In one case it was even argued that an excessive degree of formal integration might restrict the development of joint work.

The organisational identification of economic development in both countries has been accompanied by a trend towards specialisation and professionalisation in the carrying out of the function. In Germany, although there have not yet been major changes in personnel new appointees tend to be recruited from outside the authority with qualifica-tions in subjects such as economics rather than being legally trained administrators (*Verwaltungsbeamten*). The newly appointed specialists rarely fulfil the necessary criteria to become *Beamten* (career officials).[8] A similar trend is observable in England, but here the main interest has been in the attraction of staff whose skills are directly relevant to the promotional aspects of development. Whilst many industrial develop-ment officers were initially trained as planners,[9] it is clear from our cases that the planner's traditional skills are less in demand and that new elements of enterprise are needed together with the ability to apply commercial standards to the potential use of land and premises. Officers attracted from outside local government have included those with experience in advertising and publicity, industrial valuers and chartered surveyors. In both countries industrial development officers and their support staff either require skills which have been developed outside the local government service, or else they begin to develop such skills in the practice of economic development. Detailed specialisation is more common in England because local government had traditionally been based on separate departmentally based professions and the idea of a unified local authority profession closer to the German model of an administrative career is almost unknown. As is well known it is rare for officers in English councils to move from one department to another.

Nowhere among our English cases has economic development been accorded full departmental status, but the daily work of units and support staff seems to be encouraging an increasing loyalty to the group working on economic development rather than the parent department. In both countries those officers working in the field tend to see themselves as in some way different from the rest of the authority with an ability to work alongside and respond to the needs of industry. In several cases they identified with the dynamism of business represented by their industrial clients in contrast to what they saw as the slower moving decision-making process of local government. As already noted, in some German authorities this concern for a separation from the local authority system has resulted in the creation of development companies, backed by the local authority but operating independently to attract private industry.

INTERNAL CONFLICTS

Interdepartmental conflict was not as significant as might have been expected. Nevertheless, the existence of separate departments with their own professional interests involved in regular arguments over resource allocation does encourage some conflict over goals and the distribution of responsibilities. The most important conflicts in each country were with planning departments which at the same time were often also sources of ideas, manpower and other resources.

Traditionally planning in both countries has been interested in physical land use and has been concerned to keep industrial and residential development apart. Planners have aimed to protect the environment of residential areas in particular, but have also increasingly become interested in broader environmental issues. These concerns have been blamed, particularly in England, for some of the difficulties faced by small firms and there is a regular stream of complaints (also expressed in case study interviews with local Chambers of Commerce in both countries) that the planning process is a long and unnecessarily cumbersome one which actively discourages development.

Most planning departments have moved from a crude system of zoning and land use segregation, developing a wider concern for homes and employment. This means that they tend to allow development (such as non-conforming or mixed uses in England) which would previously have been unacceptable. All of the planning departments visited emphasised in varying degrees their concern for economic development and their commitment to allowing firms to develop within flexible guidelines.

Even so, some goal conflict is likely to remain. Planners scrutinise development and measure it against criteria agreed in advance. This continues to put them in a position in which they can be seen to present obstacles for development. The main task of industrial development officers, on the other hand, is unambiguously to assist and encourage industrial and commercial development and this tends to dominate even over-stated employment goals. They are committed to helping developers come through the planning process successfully in their own terms rather than those of the planners, and many industrial development officers in both countries see themselves as spokesmen for industry within the authority on planning and other matters.

Conflicts over areas of responsibility between planners and industrial development officers seem to be more common in the Germal local authorities than in the English. In Germany this form of conflict must be seen against the background of the development of *Stadtentwicklungsplanung* (STEP) which has taken some of the wider interests of planning departments away because it, too, is concerned with spatial distribution of resources throughout the city. STEP has usually been initiated within planning departments, but is now more often located directly under the *Oberstadtdirektor*. Although none of the authorities visited had undertaken any economic planning within its town development plan this has been done by some other authorities and the possibility remains in the background. In several of the German cases the industrial development offices undertook some planning functions on industrial and business sites (albeit under the general supervision of the planning department) and the planners were required to consult the officers responsible for economic development in preparing their own plans for such sites. The planners were most concerned about losing functions when the industrial development office was directly attached to the town development planning *Amt*.

In England planning departments have often been responsible for initiating economic policies and structure plans have been important for this at county level. In most cases, however, whilst planners were seen to be capable of providing a useful overview of problems and an initial assessment of priorities, planning was not felt to be particularly useful by other officers and by many councillors in correcting those problems. Both leading officers and councillors want to see action take place and this means that local authorities are more committed to specific measures than to pursuing some kind of coherent development plan. This orientation encourages the more pragmatic industrial development officers rather than the planners who are concerned with longer term trends.

On the other hand several county planning departments in England have seen the responsibility for economic development as a means of overcoming the weaknesses associated with strategic planning. Some district planners have become involved for similar reasons, since an interest in economic development offers the possibility of access to resources which are usually left to service departments. Industrial development officers can survive relatively easily within county planning departments, partly because their work often bears little relation to planning policies and there are few conflicts over development control, but at district level the need to operate such control directly is always likely to cause frustration for them.

Whilst there is always some potential for conflict with the aims of planning and with planning officers, there is little to show that this seriously inhibits economic development and those officers responsible for it. Since planning departments have been increasingly reluctant to restrict industrial development in recent years, any conflict of aims has tended to be resolved to the advantage of the industrial development officers.

In both countries industrial development officers also complained about the lack of financial resources even though in most cases the funds allocated to economic development were rising. But in few of the English cases was this blamed on any reluctance by the Treasurer's department to allocate resources to them and difficulties were instead blamed on the restrictions imposed by central government financial policies. In one English authority the Treasurer's department has itself become involved in the economic policy area, providing advice and preparing proposals for possible subsidies to private industry. In Germany, however, the attitudes of Treasurer's departments were seen by most industrial development officers to be more serious constraints. Treasurers in Germany tended to see the operation of economic development policies as a major cost to the authority, despite the expectation of future income from business taxes, because of the levels of subsidy involved in land sales, whilst in England economic development was viewed more sympathetically because it was expected to bring a reasonable financial return or at least break even, some of it being supported by income from previous development. In Germany, to a greater extent even than in England, Treasurer's departments perform a bookkeeping function and are more concerned with short-term balance sheets.

In both countries examples of conflicts with estates departments or with that section of the authority concerned with estates could be identified in a few cases, but in others economic development and the estates department were closely connected. Limited conflicts arose in some German authorities as estates officers were concerned to charge commercial rates for land whilst economic development officers hoped to attract or encourage development by offering land at lower rates. Similar conflicts between the goals of efficiently managing an authority's resources and attracting development also existed in some English cases, but to an even smaller extent, and both in the Federal Republic and Britain such conflict was minor.

In most German cases estates departments welcomed the development of economic activity since it increased their own importance as the authorities' agents in the land market. Similar attitudes existed within the English authorities, but in two cases there were conflicts stemming from the growth of a separate economic development function as a rival to the customary activity of estates officers in identifying and managing industrial land and premises. In both cases, too, these conflicts were reflections of wider ones, and resulted from attempts by the authorities' chief executives to reduce somewhat the role of the estates department or its parent department. The separate organisational identification of industrial development offered an opportunity to act in this sense.

POLITICAL ORGANISATION

Superficially the method of political decision-making shows considerable similarity in both countries. Specialist committees deal with particular subject areas advising the council and sometimes making their own decisions. But this apparent similarity in fact hides major differences. English committees (and sub-committees) are the most important decision-making bodies involving councillors and, although the full council generally has to endorse their decisions, they have large scope for making decisions which are implemented before the full council meets. The most important political figures in an English council are thus its committee chairmen. German committees have less political importance, as do their chairmen, and it is not unusual for German committees (including the economic committee in one of our cases) to be chaired by members of the opposition or minority party. This is partly because of the rather greater importance of the full council in Germany and partly because of the greater political involvement of leading officers of the council. The committees of German authorities are not intended to carry out the same detailed policy-making and executive tasks as are those in England.

In the economic development area this difference finds a confused expression, however. The committee responsibility is more clearly identified in Germany, usually involving principally some form of estates committee (because of the importance of land) and often a specialist economic committee. In England by contrast only one of the authorities we visited had a specialist committee (in this case a sub-committee of the policy committee) and the responsibility is usually that of a main committee (estates, planning or policy and resources) as one task among many. Despite the differences outlined above, therefore, and the possibility of creating sub-committees to deal with small areas of policy which is unknown in Germany, the German structure would appear more appropriate for the role which committees are expected to perform. The range of committees concerned with economic development is set out in Table 7.3 for authorities in both countries.

The committee system in both countries tends to follow the allocation of departmental responsibilities, and the general lack of specialist economic committees or sub-committees in England reflects the absence

Table 7.3   *Committee responsibility*

COUNTIES

South Yorkshire			Policy
	Land & Buildings		Employment, Development
	Sub-Committee		& Publicity Sub-Committee[a]
Nottinghamshire[b]	Environment[a]		Land & Buildings
Cambridgeshire	Planning		

DISTRICTS/STÄDTE

Essen	*Wirtschafts- und Grundstücksausschuss (Economic & Estates Committee)*		
Sheffield	Corporate Estates[a]	City Promotion Industrial Development Advisory	Policy & Resources Employment Advisory
Bielefeld	Wirtschaftsausschuss (Economic Committee)	Liegenschaftsausschuss (Estates Committee)	
Gelsenkirchen	Stadtentwicklungsausschuss Town Development Committee)	Liegenschaftsausschuss	
Nottingham	Policy & Resources[a]	Land	
Recklinghausen	Wirtschaftsausschuss	Bau- und Grundstück- ausschuss (Building & Estates Committee)	
Peterborough		Policy & Resources Finance & Property Sub-Committee	
Gütersloh	Gründstucks- ausschuss	Planungsausschuss (Planning Committee)	Haupt- und Finanzausschuss (Main & Finance Committee)
Fenland	Planning & Development[a]	Policy & Resources	

[a] Main responsible committee
[b] Since our visit to Nottinghamshire an economic promotion sub-committee of Policy and Resources Committee has been set up.

of separate economic departments and as a consequence acceptance by councillors and officers that little detailed control or policy-making is possible in this area. Councillors are unlikely to develop a specialist knowledge of the issues involved, seeing them rather as only a part – often a small part – of wider committee responsibilities.

The different roles played by policy and resources committees and *Hauptausschüsse* in the two countries are well illustrated in the economic policy area. It is common for economic development to be the responsibility of English policy and resources committees and still more common for them to have an overall brief which includes the local economic situation. In Germany it is unusual for the *Hauptausschuss* to be given responsibility for economic policy except in the rare cases where there is no economic or related functional committee. English policy and resources committees often, at least in principle, lay down or attempt to lay down policy guidelines for the authority as a whole. Some of the policy activity developed by policy and resources committees in England is more clearly the responsibility of the *Oberstadtdirektor* and the political leadership in Germany. In England it is becoming increasingly common to set up one-party sub-committees of the policy and resources committees to emphasise this leadership role.

In some cases the acceptance of economic development as a direct responsibility of the policy and resources committee is an indication of the importance attached to it by the political leadership (for example, in South Yorkshire). But this should not be taken to imply that the allocation of responsibility to a policy and resources committee always has the same significance. In some smaller authorities the policy and resources committee retains the responsibility principally because there is no other obvious home or because it arises out of the existing functions of the committee or its sub-committees. In an authority such as Sheffield, with strong departmental traditions, the activity will be more likely to be given greater priority if it is attached to an existing strong departmental committee such as the corporate estates committee.

The influence of political parties which in England is felt through the control of committees, is extended into the administrative structure in North Rhine-Westphalia. The *Oberstadtdirektor* and other leading officers are usually elected for twelve years by the council as party nominees, although it is not unusual for some positions to be given to members of the opposition parties. This ensures a very close relationship between party leaders in the council and leading officers, particularly the *Oberstadtdirektor*. This is underlined by the fact that there have been few changes in party control of German city councils since the early 1950s, so that there has been a greater degree of stability for political appointments than would have been likely had similar conventions applied in England. Chief officers also have a higher degree of independence than in England, having their own defined legal competences and a degree of political legitimacy instead of simply being appointees chosen on the basis of specified skills to serve the council.[10] It means that a great deal of political supervision is operated outside the formal council structure and that the role of officers in policy-making is not simply advisory. They are clearly and openly involved in policy discussions, although the council (*Rat*) retains final decision-making powers. In the field of economic development the leading officers are usually members of the majority political party, which is particularly important as so many decisions have to be taken in the absence of any clearly specified guidelines.

Despite the formal differences, which have important practical implications, there is nevertheless an interdependence of councillors and officers in Britain's more bifurcated system. The formal and informal links between leading officers and councillors are vitally important, although the practice of political neutrality is generally carefully maintained. It has become widely accepted, for example, that officers may make reports to political party groups within the councils, although usually without directly putting forward any proposals and chief officers frequently meet leading politicians and committee chairmen outside formal committee or council meetings. At county council level it was common for informal groups of officers and leading councillors to hold regular meetings to discuss structure plan proposals before their presentation to committee meetings. These relationships are, of course, not equivalent to those in Germany, but they do indicate that a sharp division between the administrative and political leadership is hard to maintain.

Within the more active authorities in both countries there is a wide level of agreement, even consensus, on economic development issues between the major political parties. This may hide minor political differences in England, but in Germany the disagreements are only over who would best manage the activity. Some Conservative-controlled authorities in England are more convinced by arguments which would orientate development towards growth points, whilst some Labour-controlled authorities are more sympathetic to the policy of aiding economically weak areas. But such differences are not easy to pinpoint and are almost always overlaid by local issues. Among our cases, for example, Labour-controlled South Yorkshire Metropolitan County Council supports aid for certain Job Priority Areas, but within the same county Labour-controlled Sheffield City Council supports a policy of concentrating growth at growth points of which Sheffield is one.

In Germany the organisation of party 'fractions' or groups has been a long-standing element of council structure, and this has also been true of the more urbanised English authorities, particularly those which used to be county boroughs. In neither country (except on some planning issues) have party groups played a major part in the direction of economic policy, although statements in party election manifestos have sometimes been important in initiating interest. Changes in party organisation also seem to have made some difference in those English authorities which until 1974 had a significant membership, and sometimes a majority, of Independent councillors. There is some evidence that the existence of stronger Conservative Party groups in those councils has made it easier to embark on wider policy discussions (including economic policy) than had previously been the case. Officers and leading councillors found it difficult to prepare policy when no predictions could be made about its acceptability to the council meeting.

DECISION-MAKING IN THE ECONOMIC DEVELOPMENT FIELD

As we have implied above, despite the formal role of committees in England and of the *Rat* in Germany council officers play a major part in most of the decisions taken or endorsed by councillors. There is ample evidence in both countries that the preparation and presentation of information to unpaid and non-specialist councillors strengthens the position of the officers. The economic policy area does not differ significantly from this overall model – indeed, the fact that many decisions (particularly in Germany) have to be made without reference to council committees (the so-called 'urgency procedure') increases the importance of the officers. In Germany such is the political importance of case by case negotiations on land prices that decisions on major developments normally involve the *Oberstadtdirektor* and council leaders. It is one of the tasks of an economic development officer to assess when matters must be referred upwards in this way. In England such decisions are more decentralised, largely because there is usually less scope for price variation, but also as a result of the stronger position of committee chairmen who can often make decisions subject to later confirmation by the relevant committee. It is also more common for powers of decision-making on land and premises to be delegated to the responsible officer.

The *ad hoc* individual decisions which have to be made in the economic development field fit uneasily with an effective role for council committees or full council meetings. Even in Germany where committees tend to meet far more frequently than the monthly cycle common in England it is difficult for them to discuss the detailed process of attracting one particular firm. In Germany too, the need for negotiations on land prices to be confidential strengthens the position of the officers by reducing the public agenda of much committee business, whilst the election of chief officers, as we have seen, gives them their own political legitimacy.

Councillors in both countries may react to a report from officers or introduce a new element into an existing policy, often in response to some current or newly perceived problem, for example youth unemployment or difficulties faced by a particular employer. But in general they perform a facilitating function, allowing or encouraging their officers to carry on with some generally agreed task.

CONCLUSIONS

This study has been concerned chiefly with describing what kinds of economic activity local authorities undertake, for what purposes and under what institutional constraints and possibilities. Underlying the descriptive material is the question whether differing institutional conditions in the two countries can be said to contribute significantly to different outcomes in terms of policies and concrete forms of activity. If they do not, then this is likely to be a reflection of the fact that in this policy area it is the very nature of what is being attempted and the external conditions affecting local authority attempts to encourage economic development which explain the many similarities in activity already set out.

An important institutional difference between the two countries seems to lie in the fact that the formal position of English local authorities is weak, whereas in the Federal Republic they enjoy local autonomy (*Kommunale Selbstverwaltung*) and are recognised as basic units of government with rights guaranteed in the constitution. This contrast, however, cannot be drawn too sharply because it exaggerates the effective autonomy of local authorities in Germany and underestimates the discretion which can be claimed by English authorities. In Germany, for example, the *Land* exercises a general right of supervision over the activities of local authorities (through the *Regierungspräsident*) which does not exist in England. It could therefore even be argued that the formal system of control is tighter in Germany, since in England spending can be challenged only by the action of the District Auditor or by an aggrieved ratepayer through the courts. More important, whatever the legal position, English local authorities do not see themselves merely as the agents of central government, nor do they act as if they were. They see themselves as having a responsibility to respond to local problems and often do this on the basis of an imaginative interpretation and adaptation of existing legislation and functions.

The economic field provides a good example of such a response. Nowhere in any general legislation are British local authorities given strictly economic powers but, for example, Housing Acts give powers to provide industrial estates, Planning Acts allow activity designed to help the proper planning of the area and s. 137 of the Local Government Act allows limited spending for the benefit of the area or its inhabitants. Advertising is also explicitly allowed, the management of council-owned land is expected to be efficient, and local authorities are able to lend money to firms which are operating on land owned by or sold by a council.[11]

Whether adapting existing powers or acting in virtue of a general competence local authorities must operate within the wider framework of national and regional policy and the constraints this establishes. This fact, however, often does no more than set limits rather than exert a direct influence on the actual use of its discretion by a local authority. National governments and, in the Federal Republic, the *Land* governments too, are primarily concerned with treating problems on a wider scale than can be encompassed by the territorial area of a particular local authority. This tends to leave the local authorities free to focus on their own areas and on filling what they perceive as gaps in the national structure of economic support.

There is obviously a close relationship between the intensity of the economic problems affecting an authority and the degree of commitment to positive measures of support for economic development. This study confirms the findings of other recent reports[12] which show that local authorities in the assisted areas tend to have a greater organisational commitment and undertake a wider range of activities than other authorities. Similar results were apparent in Germany. The interesting thing about this situation is that it means that the bulk of local authority economic activity can be seen as supporting national government policies rather than as conflicting with them. The extension of activity by authorities with less acute problems since the early 1970s reflects a shift away from an emphasis solely on regional economic problems and a recognition (especially in England) that development is now welcomed in most parts of the country.

We have already discussed the control exercised by higher levels of government through their planning powers and general supervisory functions and it is clear that some constraints stem from this, at least formally and particularly in Germany. There supervision is carried out by the *Land* and its agencies whereas in England the main supervisory function is carried out by a local authority – the county – and its role is far weaker than that of the *Land*, because it relates principally to the certification of local plans which themselves rarely contain detailed conditions for development. At no stage is there any requirement that the Department of the Environment or the county councils endorse planning applications before development can take place, although the requirement that all applications for industrial development outside the Development Areas had to be accompanied by an industrial development certificate issued by the Department of Industry has in the past been seen by some authorities as a major constraint on development. District planning authorities, therefore, rarely see higher levels of government as sources of direct restriction in the planning sector, except as a result of the time taken by the consultation process and the fear that county planning departments will try to define areas of decision as county matters by extending the scope of structure plans.

The danger of assuming that formal relationships of subordination or supervision must seriously hamper local authorities can be illustrated from German experience. In principle the *Regierungspräsidenten* in Germany should see that local authorities discharge in full their planning obligations. But in practice they often allow planning departments to follow a flexible policy by 'turning a blind eye' to the fact that building plans have been prepared only when a development is actually being proposed. The regular interaction between the lowest state levels[13] and local authorities is vital to this since personal relationships between the officers involved make it possible to extend the local authorities' scope for action. A formal source of constraint can, therefore, be identified in so far as local authority officers often have to negotiate with officers of the *Land* before some actions can be taken. But such a constraint rarely results in serious impediments being put in the way of the local authority determined to act as it sees fit. The conflicts between county and district levels of government in England are more extensive than those between the *Regierungspräsidenten* and the local authorities over whom they preside.

The ability of local authorities to identify with a narrowly local situation has disadvantages as well as advantages. It makes it difficult for authorities in either country to co-operate with each other, because each sees a gain for another as a loss to itself.

In Germany, price competition between authorities is rather greater than in England partly as a result of the need to maintain local income from the business tax, and this itself places significant constraints on successful policy implementation. One result of such competition is that the price of land is often manipulated to very low levels in the hope that large firms will not go elsewhere. This competitive bidding for industry, coupled with an existing adequate supply of suitable land, means that a buyers' market has been created, so that local authorities find it increasingly difficult significantly to influence potential developers. As we have seen, English authorities also compete among themselves, but the emphasis is less on price and more on the preparation and supply of sites. This distinction is important, first because it indicates a different degree of competition, and secondly because it reflects a slightly different decision-making process. The German system emphasises the importance of case by case decision-making as prices are negotiated with individual firms, but this is slightly less important in England since the quality of individual sites or advance factories can only be varied within narrow limits. An indication of growing competition between English authorities can, however, be seen in the decision of one council to withdraw from its regional development association so that it could use the funds saved in subscriptions for its own economic development activities.

The form of competition outlined above can best be described as horizontal – in other words, there is competition between the same type of authority (*Gemeinde* and *Gemeinde*, district council and district council, county council and county council). Such competition can also be seen as competition between different areas for limited resources and limited employment opportunities. But a second and potentially more important vertical division between English authorities lies in the split between the district and county levels, which only has a minor reflection in Germany at *Kreis* level. There is little competition with that level in Germany because the *Kreis* with its elected council has few powers of direct control over the municipalities within its area; its role is supervisory and complementary. Most large cities are *'kreisfreie Städte'* and, therefore, have little or no contact with the *Kreis* and where there are large *'kreisangehörige Städte'*[14] the *Kreis* authorities tend to leave economic development to them. Only where the local authorities making up a *Kreis* are small and relatively weak is the *Kreis* itself likely to take an active part in economic development.[15]

In England economic development is a policy area or problem which can be taken up by both county and district levels and metropolitan counties have been particularly keen to become involved as they have few major spending responsibilities under the Local Government Act 1972. The larger districts (both metropolitan and non-metropolitan), however, have been reluctant to work with the county councils on economic development since they fear that the counties will take responsibilities away from them. This has been particularly noticeable among authorities which were county boroughs before 1974 and have already lost some powers to the counties. Some of these have not only opposed county policies which they felt to be against their interests but have rejected assistance to emphasise their own independence.

The specifically local context of organisations and pressure groups with an interest in economic conditions and prospects does not appear to affect local authorities substantially in their own economic role. Despite a network of regular formal and informal contacts with organisations representing employers and trade unions, such bodies are not generally seen to be important at the local level. Chambers of Commerce in both countries, for example, are consulted and their ideas considered, but they do not usually significantly influence the regular work of planning and economic development. Nor does there seem to be a great deal of competition between local authorities and Chambers of Commerce, although some of the advice and promotional work is duplicated.

Nevertheless, the perception of problems held by many officers and councillors is heavily influenced in an indirect way by sectional groups. In Sheffield, for example, the decline of the cutlery industry has called forth a larger response from both the county and the city councils than might have been expected, at least partly because of the influence of the local based Cutlery and Silverware Association and the ceremonial role of the Master Cutler. In Recklinghausen the concerns of the coal industry tend to play a disproportionate part in the council's deliberations because its employees are well represented in the council groups of both major parties.

English authorities are more concerned to set up formal channels to involve representatives of local business and industrial interests than is the case in Germany. In three of the English cases special committees have now been set up with this aim in mind. Such committees are not usually considered necessary in Germany, largely because the informal relationships with industry have traditionally been better and the status of local government has been higher. In Germany the *Oberstadt-direktor* will usually play a more important role in local society than his English counterpart,[16] and this brings him into regular social contact with leading local businessmen.

German authorities have always seen themselves as having the dual functions of regulatory control and the provision of assistance to industry. In England the division between government and industry has gone much deeper and local authorities have been subject to regular criticism for their alleged lack of sympathy for industry. English local authorities have, therefore, looked for formal organisational contacts both to emphasise their new attitudes and to assist in making the informal links which have previously been lacking.

All of the authorities studied in both countries emphasised the extent to which the success of their activity depended on the decisions of others, the state of the national economy and its expression at local level. Although the bigger city authorities with larger budgets and greater resources believed that they were influencing the local situation to a small extent at least (often on the basis of impressionistic estimates of job creation), even they accepted that their activities were likely to be of only very limited importance. It was fully recognised that authorities depend on a response from actual or potential entrepreneurs: without such a response the incentives provided and offers made remain ineffective.

The increased attention paid by local authorities in both countries, but especially in England, to small firms is an expression of this problem, since authorities feel less able to influence the large national and multi-national concerns which usually provide the highest levels of employment. Whilst the extent to which industrial development officers can increase the economic activity of small firms and thus offset part of the loss of employment caused by contraction of larger employers is limited, it is understandable that local officials and councillors believe that their best hopes of actually persuading firms to invest lie in the small firm sector.

This is also congruent with the central opportunistic strategy adopted by local authorities in both countries, even if it is not openly stated in council documents. Industrial development officers attempt to gain *any* potential developments and are not keen on differentiating between them. They rarely feel able to be selective and attempt instead to tailor their own responses to the needs of individual firms. Naturally this renders the preparation of anything like an overall economic programme almost impossible.

It is clear that in the attempt to develop economic support policies local authorities are involved chiefly in putting land, services and, in England in some cases, premises on offer in the hope that there will be takers with whom serious negotiations can take place. The external governmental system places no serious obstacles in the way of local authorities who develop a policy of this kind, regarding it as politically acceptable and unlikely to come often into serious conflict with the aims of more broadly based state economic policies. But neither do the levels of government above the local authorities give the latter a great deal of active encouragement to take employment-creating initiatives: there seems to be a general readiness to leave the matter very much to the local authority as the best judge of what it is expedient to do in and on behalf of its own area.

The internal institutional conditions also appear to have little importance in explaining in either country the growth of economic activity on the part of local authorities, or such differences in scale and method as have been discussed. In Britain the growth of corporate systems of management, the more active role of chief executives and in some cases the strengthening of party leadership may have assisted towards the identification of an economic role within what is basically still a compartmentalised administrative system. Yet in fact it seems probable that it was the combination of a wider view of the land use planning function with rising unemployment which has had most influence in encouraging the growth and acceptance of local authority efforts to attract industrial investment and jobs.

There are many signs pointing to a somewhat similar pattern of events in the Federal Republic. Whilst the political and administrative organisation of local authorities does help in the maintenance of a broader conception of the local authority's overall policy role than has been usual in Britain, there too it is a clearer perception of economic difficulties that has chiefly shaped the type and scale of the current economic development policies at the local level. In the Federal Republic there has also been in the past ten years a shift towards a more integrated view of land use planning and development, and this in turn has encouraged a closer local concern with economic problems. On the other hand the German planning system remains in important respects more formalised and more detailed in its terms than the British, and thus in order to accommodate more emphasis on economic development it has been necessary to operate this system with rather more flexibility than it seems to allow.

Neither do the political differences to be found at work in the two systems of local government appear to result in major differences in what is done and how. There is little basic disagreement between parties about what kind of measures it is appropriate for a local authority to take in encouraging economic development in its area, and there is a general recognition – though rarely expressed decisively in public statements – that the positive action taken by local authorities in this policy sector can have only a limited effect on the economic conditions in any particular local authority area. Whilst it is true that there is usually in German local authorities a more tightly integrated structure of executive leadership than in their English counterparts, characterised by closer party political ties between elected representatives and leading officials and by more open recognition of the policy-making role of the administration, it cannot be said that this results in significant differences in the policy outcomes in this field. This is because of the inherent limits affecting what a local authority can actually hope to achieve by seeking to maintain and attract sources of employment and income, and because the methods which must actually be used in the pursuit of this objective put the matter back into the hands of relatively specialised units within the local authority's administration. As has been shown, there are various ways of organising such units and it is impossible to assert on the basis of the available evidence that any single organisational solution allows the economic promotion function to be carried out more successfully than all others. What is apparent in both countries, however, is recognition of the need to distinguish this function in some way from the other local authority functions out of which it may grow and to which it has to be related. There is at present a clearer organisational reflection of this tendency in the Federal Republic than in Britain. But it may be that in the years to come there will in Britain be a continuing reappraisal of what is understood by 'planning' and that this will eventually result in a much clearer recognition of the economic promotion function described here as a major element within the wider field of land use planning.

NOTES

1 'Verwaltungsorganisation der Gemeinden', Part 1 (Cologne: KGSt, 1967).
2 The local authority association for the simplification of administration. This is a local authority sponsored body: see Chapter 5, note 1.
3 *The New Local Authorities: Management and Structure* (London: HMSO, 1972).
4 The closest English equivalent is the Chief Executive.
5 The *Verwaltungskonferenz* is a legal requirement in North Rhine-Westphalia, but the management team is a voluntarily adopted instrument of management in England.
6 South Yorkshire Metropolitan Council, for example, has a Programme Area Team covering this policy area. See Table 7.1.
7 B. Wrobel, 'Aufgabenfeld und Organisation kommunaler Wirtschaftsförderungsdienststellen' (draft) (Cologne: Deutsche Institut für Urbanistik, 1978), p. 17.
8 *Beamten* in local government are essentially professional administrators with their own examinations and career structure. The closest English equivalent would be to imagine local government officers to be higher-grade civil servants.
9 Over 30 per cent of local government IDOs were formerly planning officers according to N. Falk, *Local Authorities and Industrial Development: Results of a Survey* (London: Urbed, 1978).

10   This should not be taken to mean that they are not also highly qualified. German chief officers are at least as well qualified as their English counterparts and their status and pay are significantly higher. See D. Eversley, 'Britain and Germany: local government in perspective', in R. Rose (ed.), *The Management of Urban Change in Britain and Germany* (London and Beverly Hills: Sage, 1974), pp. 243–8.

11   Local Authority (Land) Act 1963. The Inner Urban Areas Act 1978 has extended this power to all land in designated inner areas, and the limits of the mortgages have also been raised for these areas.

12   M. M. Camina, *Local Authorities and the Attraction of Industry* (Oxford: Pergamon, 1974), and Falk, op. cit.

13   These include *Oberkreisdirektoren* (chief executives of the *Kreise*) and *Bezirks-planungsbehörde* (district planning authorities covering several local authority areas), both of which have some responsibility to local authorities but are also intended to carry out policies of the *Land* as its lowest governmental agencies.

14   These are similar to the former municipal boroughs or urban district councils in England.

15   For a further discussion of the role of *Kreise* in *Wirtschaftsförderung* see C. Schumacher, 'Zwischenergebnisse der Diplomarbeit: Kooperation zwischen kreis-angehorigen Kommunen und dem Kreis – Eine Fallstudie zur Problemlosungsfähig-keit verflochtener Entscheidungssysteme in der kommunalen Wirtschaftsförder-ungspolitik', Institut für angewandte Sozialforschung (Cologne 1979).

16   He is 'the acknowledged, known, and respected civic leader': Eversley, op. cit., p. 246.

Appendix

THE ENGLISH CASE STUDIES:
RESEARCH METHODS AND SELECTION

(a) THE PHASES OF RESEARCH

Most of the research on which this study is based was carried out by means of case studies of individual local councils. This was supplemented by consideration of documents supplied by the local authorities examined as well as by information gained from other bodies. This approach was intended to facilitate a detailed study of the processes of policy-making and implementation in a few authorities. It was deliberately preferred to the broader but shallower coverage which might have been achieved by carrying out a wide-ranging survey of many or all local authorities by written questionnaire.

The research was carried out in four logically, but not always chronologically distinct stages. These were as follows:

(i)   The choice of cases after the consideration of a range of institutional, demographic and economic factors whose operation might be expected to influence an authority's actions or its system of policy-making.

(ii) Preliminary consultations with representatives of the selected councils to enable decisions to be made on the key officers, councillors and other persons to be interviewed in the course of the case studies. Similar discussions were conducted with the local authority associations and officials of central government (from the Departments of the Environment and Industry).

(iii) Case study interviews in each selected local authority were carried out between November 1977 and August 1978. Between eight and eighteen interviews with relevant officers and councillors were completed in each of the seven cases, usually over a period of two weeks during which a wide variety of documents were also consulted (for example, Council and committee minutes, officers' reports to committees, internal officers' reports, corporate plans, local and structure plans). In each local authority the development of 2–3 decisions was followed through from inception to implementation in so far as this was practicable. Where appropriate representatives of Chambers of Commerce and Trades Councils were also interviewed.

The interviews were conducted on the basis of questionnaires prepared in advance. These concentrated on a number of issues of interest in all of the cases, but were supplemented by additional questions appropriate to the particular case being examined. When relevant matters not covered in detail by the questionnaire arose in the course of interviews, these were followed through and no attempt was made to restrict discussion to matters dealt with in the questionnaire.

(iv) Interviews with representatives of national and regional bodies were also used. The most important of these were with regional offices of the Departments of Industry, Environment and Transport, representatives of the regional Economic Planning Councils, specialist sections of the Department of the Environment (on planning and local government finance) and the main local authority associations (including the Society of Local Authority Chief Executives). Some additional interviews arose from the cases themselves and the Development Commission, the Cambridgeshire Organiser of the Council for Small Industries in Rural Areas, the Peterborough Development Corporation, and the Yorkshire and Humberside Development Association were visited.

(b) THE CHOICE OF CASES

It was important to look at a range of authorities exemplifying the main institutional variations in England showing the influence of differing economic and demographic conditions. Furthermore the sample selected had to bear some similarity in respect of the range of economic conditions encountered in it and the size of local authorities to the group of local authorities chosen for the German case studies. It was decided to limit the institutional variations between cases by restricting the choice to English local authorities outside the Greater London Council area.

At least two sets of authorities had to be chosen – one metropolitan and one non-metropolitan – because of the different distribution of responsibilities and powers between the tiers in each type. Clearly such institutional variations are likely to have some impact on how functions are carried out. Since there are very many more non-metropolitan than metropolitan authorities and they differ greatly in economic structure and size, it was decided to take a third set of non-metropolitan authorities.

Pairs of authorities had to be chosen in each county: in two of the sets it was decided to visit the county and its 'dominant' district council, [1] and in the third (where there was to be no 'dominant' district) it was decided to visit two districts in addition to the county.

The initial choice of authorities was at the county level, primarily because the relevant statistics are more easily available in relation to counties. But, of course, in practice the selection of districts was closely linked with the choice of counties, and if a county did not contain a suitable district it could not be chosen for a case study.

Rough indicators were used to help make the choice and information was gathered under the following heads:

population size and density (as a measure of urbanisation);
unemployment rate (as a measure of the prevailing economic condition of the area);
proportion of employees in production industry, the service sector and agriculture (as a guide to industrial structure);
average rateable value of domestic property (despite its weaknesses, as a guide to personal wealth).

These variables were chosen because they might be expected to influence the economic activity and policy-making of local authorities and the counties were ranked in order of magnitude for all the indicators listed above.[2] Additional information was gathered on the area of counties, the level of average male earnings, the extent of population change between 1974 and 1975, the proportion of the population over the age of 75 and the political composition of the councils, and this was used later to help confirm the final choices.

The counties were divided into Classes I (population over 1m.), II (population 0·6m. – 1m.) and III (population less than 0·6m.) and into similar bands (e.g. High, Middle, Low) for each of the other indicators. This was intended to permit the cases to be chosen in a manner offering a spread across the three bands in each category. This was broadly possible because each population class tended to be associated with a different combination of economic and demographic variables. Although the application of such indicators did not of itself show decisively which authorities should be chosen it did effectively narrow the field of choice. The choice from Class I, for example, was likely to be in a poor economic situation with a low average rateable value and high proportion of employment in production industry, although such a case could also have been found in Class II. Conversely the choice from Class III was likely to be in a good economic situation, although an authority could be found in this class whose economic situation was poor.

Some authorities were excluded because they exhibit characteristics of an unusual kind which might be expected significantly to distort their local economic situation. While it is impossible to find a 'typical' local authority, it was thought to be reasonable to eliminate the most obviously 'untypical' from consideration. The factors taken into

Table A.1 *Counties selected*

	Population		Unemployment %		Average RV		Employees in production industry		Districts chosen and population
	Rank	*Class*	*Rank*	*Band*	*Rank*	*Band*	*Rank*	*Band*	
South Yorkshire	9	I	11	High	42	Low	4	High	Sheffield 0·5m.
Nottinghamshire	13	II	27	Middle	32	Middle–low	8	High	Nottingham 0·2m.
Cambridgeshire	31	III	38	Low		Middle–High	34	Middle– Low	Peterborough 0·1m. Fenland less than 0·1m.

account at this stage included: the extent to which employment in neighbouring authorities dominated journey to work patterns; an unusually high or low level of unemployment; the extremes of county size; the extent of domination by seasonal (tourist) trade; and the size of the retired population.

A limited number of potential cases was, therefore, left in each Class. These were then considered individually. Available information on aspects of county policy, politics and organisation, and on the local district councils was also taken into account. The counties finally selected were South Yorkshire Metropolitan County Council, Nottinghamshire County Council and Cambridgeshire County Council. These fitted the balance of the criteria well and contained suitable district councils for the size categories agreed for the German side of the project.[3] There was a slight bias towards counties with a high proportion of employees in production industry, but this corresponds to a similar bias in the German cases which are concentrated in the Ruhr area. For characteristics of counties selected see Table A.1.

Once the counties had been chosen two districts, Sheffield and Nottingham, were automatic choices on account of the need to have district authorities within that size range to match German cases. In the case of Cambridgeshire, however, no final decision was made on the districts to be studied until exploratory discussions with the county had been completed. These confirmed the choice of two further cases: Peterborough provided the example of a small city with the additional element of new development in partnership with its Development Corporation and the county council, whilst Fenland offered the chance of looking at a small council (population 66,000) in a mainly agricultural area yet with some commitment to economic development activity.

NOTES

1   Defined as an authority with a population which is 25 per cent or more than that of the county total.
2   In the case of industrial structure, according to the proportion of employment in production industries.
3   One district with a population of over 0·5m., one between 0·2m. and 0·5m., and one below 0·2m. In fact two in England in this third category were chosen.

INDEX

administrative organisation of economic activities 68–72, 75–7, 111, 112, 113, 114, 120, 148, 149, 156, 157, 158, 159, 150–3 (Table 7.1)

advance factories 30, 46, 47, 48, 54, 138

Association of Metropolitan Authorities 58

Basic law 97, 99

Bielefield 104, 105, 106, 107, 109, 112, 113, 114, 115, 120, 143, 150–3 (Table 7.1), 164 (Table 7.3)

Cambridgeshire C. C. 38–45, 50–1, 60, 61, 63, 69, 74, 81, 85, 87, 91, 149, 150–3 (Table 7.1), 164 (Table 7.3), 179, 180

capital expenditure by local authorities 26–8, 57, 127

central government control 6, 9, 10, 25–31, 88, 89–91, 125, 126, 169, 173

Chambers of Commerce 93, 117, 160, 171, 176

Chief Executive, role of 23, 72–6, 113, 156–7, 165, 172

committees of councils 76, 80–3, 85, 101, 115, 163–5

Community Land Act 1975 18, 45, 46, 47, 78, 79, 90, 138

corporate planning 23, 44, 45, 68, 72–5, 145, 173

council employment 57, 137

COSIRA (Council for small industries in rural areas) 46, 50, 61, 86, 91, 177

councillors and officials, relations between 82, 84, 85, 114, 115, 131, 132, 166, 167

Development Associations 86, 90, 177

Development Commission 61, 86, 177

Economic Planning Councils 85, 89, 91, 177

educational services 19, 59

Employment Promotion Unit (SYMCC) 70–2, 73, 81

Environment, Department of 14, 15–16, 20, 25, 27–9, 31, 43, 59, 61, 62, 79, 88–91, 144, 146, 169, 176, 177

Essen 104, 105, 106, 107, 109, 110, 112, 113, 115, 117. Table 7.1, Table 7.3

Fenland D. C. 38–41, 43, 44, 46, 50, 53, 55, 58, 61, 63, 65, 69, 79, 81, 82, 84, 86, 91, 94, 149, 150–3 (Table 7.1), 164 (Table 7.3), 180

financial incentives to industry 53, 54, 55, 56, 109, 110, 139–40

Gelsenkirchen 104, 105, 107, 109, 111–15, 117, 149, 150–3 (Table 7.1), 164 (Table 7.3)

Gütersloh 104–9, 112, 114, 116, 119, 120, 150–3 (Table 7.1), 164 (Table 7.3)

Horizon Midlands 58, 84

Housing Act 1957 18

housing provision 19, 59, 111

Industrial Development Officers 44, 48, 49, 50, 51, 69, 72, 77, 79, 80, 82, 94, 159, 160, 161, 162

industrial mortgages 55, 56, 140

industrial policy 99, 128, 129

Industry Act 1972 29, 30

Industry, Department of 6, 17, 29, 30, 50, 52, 53, 85, 89, 90, 91, 129, 169, 176, 177

information services 51–3, 141, 142

infrastructure spending 110, 143, 144

Inner Urban Areas Act 1978 14, 18, 55, 61

inter-departmental conflict 77–80, 122, 160, 161, 162

KGSt (*Kommunale Gemeinschaftsstelle für Verwaltungsvereinfachung*) 97, 148

Kreis 119, 171

Land prices, variation of 109, 110, 138, 139, 170

land, provision of 18, 45, 46, 70, 108, 109, 110, 121, 137, 138

land use planning 4, 14, 15, 16, 17, 62–5, 69, 71, 85, 86, 87, 90, 116, 144–6, 160, 161, 169, 173, 174

Local Authorities (Land) Act 1963 17, 18

local authority expenditure 13, 57, 78, 79, 127

For Product Safety Concerns and Information please contact our EU
representative GPSR@taylorandfrancis.com Taylor & Francis Verlag GmbH,
Kaufingerstraße 24, 80331 München, Germany

Printed and bound by CPI Group (UK) Ltd, Croydon, CR0 4YY
11/04/2025
01844012-0014